THREE PLAYS

FRANCIS POLLINI

THREE PLAYS

FRANCIS POLLINI

ALL MINE
THE ROW
THE PARTNERS

NEVILLE SPEARMAN

CONTENTS

FOR DON

ALL MINE

CHARACTERS

STAN: a young man.
DAN: another young man.
FRAN: a young woman.

ALL MINE

SCENE: *A room. Not many furnishings. Two beds, simple type.*
A chair or two, a table, very simple type. The beds are occupied
by two men. They are under the covers. They are either asleep
or dead. The tops of their heads are toward the audience. The
beds are on either side of the room. The aforementioned other
furnishings are between them. The men do not stir. They may
well be dead. Presently, one of them makes strange noises. It
starts as a grunt and works its way to a moan. It subsides.
Silence. It appears to be morning. Or mid-morning. Or after-
noon. It could be afternoon. A bell tolls, far off. Traffic. A
crashing sound, terrific. Whistles. Bells, ambulance maybe. A
while, then, silence. Neither man makes a move . . . Finally—

STAN [*In bed to the Right. Slowly. American*]: What time
is it?

DAN [*In bed to the Left. Very slowly. American*]: What?

STAN: What's the time? What time is it? The time?
[*Silence. No movement. Then, a sort of mumbling, mutter-*
ing, cursing, not audible, from Dan's side.]

STAN: What?

DAN [*Breaking the surface*]: I don't know! What would I know?
[*mumbling, cursing, inaudible again*] Would I know?
[*Finally*]
[*Silence. Complete. Utterly.*]

STAN [*softly*]: What's the date? [*louder*] What the hell's the
date, man, anyhow?
[*Silence. A few mutterings from Dan, only.*]

STAN [*Finally*]: We shouldn't have thrown away that calendar,
man. Remember that calendar? We had it stuck up on the
wall there. *Right there.* I remember it. [*pause*] Goddamn it,
you could see it from the other end of the block, man. The
other end! If a guy wore glasses he could take them off and
see it *from there*, man. That's a fact, what a fact that is, man.
Remember it? *Mother-fugger*, yellow bellied draft dodging
hands-off-Vietnam commie prick of an un-American American
you! *Sonuvabitch!* Do you remember it? What do you
remember of it? You tacked it up, you were the one who

11

tacked it up, you ought to remember it! Why did you tack it up. Were you hot stuff? Did you think you were hot stuff, tacking it up? Did you think about it? Did she know you were thinking about it? Who are you? Who the hell are you? How old are you? Will you grow up? You ever going to grow up? It's about time you grew up!

[*Silence. Complete*]

STAN [*quietly*]: Who threw it away anyhow? [*pause*] I used to like looking at it. I could lay here all day long looking at it. That was a treat waking up every day with those knockers smiling at you. Spilling out, smothering you! *April*. What a pair. Jesus Christ that was a pair! Was that a pair? I'll say that was a pair! The guy who drew those outclassed Renoir anyday. Right, pal? Didn't you always tell me that was right, old pal? Pal! What about the January one? Remember that one? Was that a gal? Special deluxe, A-1, plus plus. What A Pair! That was a pair! Who could handle those? *Gargantua*? Oh Man! *What happened to it?* I woke up one morning—*it wasn't there.*

DAN [*mumblings, muttering, cursing, none comprehensible*]: . . . *there* [*finally*]

STAN: What?

DAN [*as before*]: . . . *to be there* . . . [*finally*]

STAN: Are you still asleep? Are you talking in your sleep?

DAN: . . . *Goddam it* . . .

STAN: Hanging out! Keerist, Swinging out! In my face, right there like punching bags, *don't ask where*! There!

DAN: *GOD*damn you—

STAN: *Man!* [*pause*] You cursed. You promised you wouldn't curse. Think of her. You promised, *in front of her!*

DAN: [*mumbling only*]

STAN: What?

DAN: Ain't she good enough for ya?

STAN: Oh, *yeh!* Yeh!

DAN: Well then—?

STAN: I didn't mean *that!* Don't get me wrong. You get me wrong! How come you always get me wrong? I didn't mean that *at all*, man! I wouldn't trade her in for anyone, *anyone else in the world*, Man!

DAN: Jesus Christ, if there ain't enough there for ya—

STAN: I didn't say that! What kind of a nut would want to say *that*?

DAN: What did you say?

[*Silence. A while*]

STAN [*finally*]: I said . . . I only said . . . [*trails off*]

[*Silence*]

DAN [*muttering*]: Calendars.

STAN: I only meant . . . I meant . . .

[*Silence again*]

[*Suddenly,* STAN *starts to cry. He starts quite spontaneously and it is a genuinely heartbreaking crying. Not very loud. But crying*]

DAN [*moaning, moving, raises his head slightly. He looks over at Stan for a while.*] Shut up. [*finally*]

[STAN *cries louder*]

DAN: *Shut up, Man!*

STAN [*through his sobbing*]: Yeh it's alright for you, isn't it? You're alright, aren't you? You get that nice fat check each month, *you* have no worries! Not a *goddam* worry! Do you?

DAN: What are your worries? I take care of you! Jesus Christ, don't I take good care of you? What the hell are your worries? If I wasn't around, alright, then you'd have worries. What worries? I take care of you like your own mother! Don't I, buddy? You have to be a prize mother-fug of the highest relative order to deny that, old buddy!

STAN: Buddy! Is that what I want from a buddy? I used to walk around on my own two feet once—look at me now, *Buddy!* I worked—I used to work—Who would ever think that now? Could anyone take a look at me and say: *He* used to work—? Who? Name the name! *You corrupting bastard you—*

DAN: *Wo!* Just *Wo! Keeerist!* Buddy! Who the hell's stopping you from working? I've spent 90 percent of my time since I had the misfortune to bump into you trying to get you to work, you mother-fug you! The equipment—Jesus Christ— the goddam studio you talked me into fixing up for you— Remember all those months you rode my ass about that, buddy? 'There's no room here, I'm going nuts trying to work here, I need room, a room of my own, *a studio*, man . . .' Oh yeh—remember that crap? You buried me in that crap! I got you the studio, didn't I, man? I got you equipment, the finest in the land—*Yeh! Man!* Well what the hell have you done with it? Soon as it was all set up you started laying on your ass—if it wasn't for Fran you'd never make a goddam move off your ass—

STAN: *What about you,* Buddy?

DAN: We're talking about *you,* old Buddy!

STAN: DON'T GIVE ME THAT SHIT!

DAN: You're the shit! What a pile of shit! You landed on me!

STAN: Wait till Fran shows up again!

DAN: Just wait! I can't wait! *Buddy!*

STAN: Don't think she comes to see you—

DAN: She doesn't give a fug about you—

STAN: She doesn't give *one fuggen* fug for a commie sonuvabitch of a draft dodging Vietcong depraved degenerate parasite scum of an un-American fluoridated prick like *you,* man!

[*Silence.* STAN *has stopped crying. They stare at one another. Soon,* DAN *settles back into supine position again. Utter silence*]

DAN [*finally, muttering, barely audible*]: . . . *what a prick* . . . [*Silence*]

STAN [*finally*]: Maybe I ought to move it back in here. [*pause. A groan from* DAN] Yeh, maybe I just ought to throw out all the fancy equipment and move my own original stuff all back in here. [*pause*] Maybe that would be it, moving it back in here . . . [*pause*] The trouble all started when you loaded me down with that fancy equipment. [*Another groan from* DAN] It was alright when I had my own stuff. A couple of brushes. A board. Second hand strips of canvas. [*pause*] IT WAS THAT CRAPPY FANCY STUFF! [*long pause*] [*now, very quietly*] Don't think I didn't appreciate it though. I appreciated it, Dan, Bo. Don't get the wrong idea. I appreciate it even now. I do. You know that, don't you, Bo? [*pause*] That was a fine move, one hell of a noble move, on top of everything else, on your part, ol bo. I want you to know. Now you know. [*pause*] It's just that —I sort of feel that—having it in *there*— [*pause*] that— terrific stuff—[*pause*] all that stuff—[*pause*] *What stuff*— [*longer pause*] Well—face it, man—Have I done a stroke of

14

work since? [*pause*] What was the last thing I did?

DAN [*barely*]: Why not do Fran?

STAN [*dumbstruck*]: Fran?

DAN: Yeh. Fran.

STAN: Are you—Are you kidding me around—man?

DAN: Oh man!

STAN: That's not anything—that's one thing you don't want to kid me around about—man—

DAN: I'm not kidding you, man.

STAN: What the hell are you doing, then?

DAN: I mean it, man.

STAN: *You're a dirty sonuvabitch, man!*

DAN: Aw, crawl! Go take a crawl, Man!

STAN: *Just how perverted can your goddamn ideas get,* man?

DAN: What the hell's perverted about that? *What?* What, man? You're the goddamn painter, not me, remember that, man! Who the hell in the world would be a better subject than Fran? Who the hell have you ever painted, man? It's about time you painted a real, decent, human being, man. She's great! She's a saint! She's Fran! She might just get you off your ass. Who the hell paints laying on his ass? Are you Michelangelo? He's the only guy I know ever painted flat on his ass!

STAN: *It's on account of you I'm flat on my ass!*

DAN: DON'T HAND ME THAT CRAP!

[*Silence. Absolute*]

STAN [*finally*]: Is she coming today? [*quietly*]

DAN [*barely audible*]: She's all mine—

STAN: Is that dream, that honey of a gal, that gorgeous gal—is she coming today?

DAN [*barely audible*]: And she's all mine . . .

STAN: When did she last come? [*pause*] It seems a long time. One hell of a long time. I ought to know. [*pause*] I ought to write these things down. I used to write everything down. I kept track of things. I knew everything. [*pause*] When I met you—[*pause*] It was when I met you—[*pause*] What the hell did you throw away that calendar for? I could have kept track of it there. It was you who threw the calendar away! [*pause*] A long time . . .

DAN [*still hardly audible*]: Mine . . .

STAN: She walked in that door. I can see her, walking in that door. That doll! That hon! In that door! [*pause*] She just walks in the door . . .

DAN: What a door . . .

STAN: Who knows? How long ago was it, bo?

DAN: She knows . . .

STAN: She knows! She knows everything, Bo!

DAN: And mo . . .

STAN: What good does it do me, though? I like to know the score! How things stand! Where I am! I like to know where I am! [*pause*] I don't. How come I don't? How come I lay here, day in, day out, night and day, all night, all day, all the day, every day. Every Goddamn Day! What for? What the hell for? Who knows the score?

DAN: What's the score?

STAN: I ought to know the score!

DAN: *What a score* . . .

STAN: Has she lost our address?

DAN: What's our address?

STAN: You're cocksure! You're sure! You don't give a damn!

DAN: *She knows the score* . . .

STAN: Do you know the score?

DAN: Fug the score . . .

STAN: Yeh! Sure! A depraved, lost, hopeless sonuvabitch like you can say that. What about me? Ever think about me? That's who I think about—ME!

DAN: Better get another fuggin fugged-up fuggin calendar in here, bo . . .

STAN: DON'T THINK I'M NOT TELLING HER ABOUT ALL THIS CURSING, MAN!

[*Silence. Complete*]

STAN [*finally, quietly*]: Whose turn is it?

DAN [*moaning only*]

STAN: That's just another little thing I'd like to know. That theatrical-literary crowd you used to hang around with in those days—When were those days? A thousand years ago? Were those the days? You *told* me about those days!—they'e the ones who put the finishing touches on you, man. Don't hand me any crap about that at all, man. You may have been a worthless hunk of Yankee crap when you got here already, man, but by the time they got through with you, boy, you were nothing. But Nothing At All there, Man! That's when you lost all touch with time, wasn't it, *Dan*? I'll bet those little hot little twats sure liked calling you *Dan!* Remember how many you rammed? Well, you told me! Wang! Bang! Bang! Bang! *Dan Bang!* They had a special corner on their bulletin boards: *Hours of Operation—Dan the Bang . . .* Man! Well, here you are—Where are your theatrical-literary friends?

DAN [*as above*]: . . . fug . . . friends . . . [*trails off*]

STAN: Fran! What she sees in you! Man!

DAN [*as above*]: . . . little sleep . . . shutup . . . man . . .

STAN: A saint! That gal's a saint! That's all! Man!

DAN [*as above*]: . . . fuggin . . . sleep . . . oh man . . .

STAN [*very quietly*]: If I only knew. [*pause*] I wish I knew. [*pause*] When she turns up, you'd think I'd know. [*pause*] You'd think I had a record of that someplace. [*pause*] Any-place. [*pause*] Wouldn't need a calendar at all for that. [*pause. Louder*] You'd think I had a record someplace. I don't know at all. And it's all the same to you. It doesn't matter at all to you. Right? Buddy? Is that right? Ol Buddy? [*pause*] That's how things are. I don't have the slightest idea. Not a clue! Not one goddamn clue! Except you. *You!* Buddy! Great, huh? Pretty goddamn great, huh? *Don't you think that's great?* Huh?

DAN [*as above*]: . . . great . . . uh . . .

STAN: She knows! Oh yeh, she sure knows! What doesn't she know? She knows everything, man! And that's the way you like it, you wouldn't want it any other way, you don't give one damn, right? Right, man? Damn right! I know, oh yeh, don't worry, I know you like a *book*—A Book—old buddy! Well I don't like it that way! I'm not that kind of a guy! I never fugged around with flocks of theatrical-literary lays! How do I know you did? You only *say* you did! You're a lying sonuvabitch on top of everything else—How Do I Know You Did? Look at me—look what you did! You know what I used to be! You dragged me down so low

I can't even stand. What I used to be! *An artist,* Buddy!
Even you know that. You're laughing like hell there, knowing
that. Don't kid me! I was so good they sent me over here on
a scholarship. When was that? Jesus Christ—ten, twenty—
it could be—How Many Years Ago Was That? Was the
Korean War on then? What about Vietnam? You'll never
get near Vietnam! You yellow bellied son of a draft-dodging
Bitch! You Bitch! You're a Bitch! How many years ago was
that? Does she know *that?* How come she never answers
when I ask her that? I'll ask her again, first thing, next time
she shows up. See If I Don't Get An Answer To That! You
try and stop me asking her that! [*He turns in his bed, on
his side. He mumbles and mutters for a few moments, in-
audibly*] Talent! Jesus Christ I was Loaded with talent!
They all said, '*The Talent!*' They said. *And I Met You.*
That damn day. That party. THAT STUPID PARTY! [*pause*]
MOTHER FUG OF A STUPID FUGGIN PARTY!

[*Silence. Absolute*]

DAN [*barely*]: She's a saint . . .

STAN: What the hell, was I jinxed? Born under the wrong
comet or something? How come I met *you?* Poisonous You!
Of all the million and one guys in this town—YOU!

[*Silence.* DAN *raises his head slowly, painfully, peers over
at him*]

DAN: Ain't you ever gonna sleep? [*The head sinks*]

STAN: *What the hell do I care about that?*

DAN [*muffled. Barely there*]: She'll come. She's gonna come.
Don't worry. Bud . . .

STAN [*suddenly, violently*]: I don't care if she *never* comes!
That pig! The goddamn pig! What a pig! Never! Comes!
Understand that? *Buddy?*

DAN [*as above*]: . . . oh buddy . . .

STAN: If she changes her ways, if she stops fuggin around with
you, if she does that, I'll care if she comes! How The Hell
Come She Fugs Around You?

DAN [*as above*]: . . . New Brutalism . . .

STAN: What?

DAN [*only inaudible mumblings*] . . .

STAN: ONLY A PIG WOULD FUG AROUND YOU!

[*Silence*]

STAN [*finally, quietly*]: A man of talent. [*pause*] I'm a man of extraordinary talent. [*pause*] It's a crime. [*pause*] It's criminal. [*pause*] How long have I lain on my ass? [*pause*] Would I even know how to hold a brush? [*pause*] I'm not blaming you. [*pause*] I'm not even blaming the—studio. [*pause*] That snatsy studio. [*pause*] You fixed up for me. [*long pause*] Ever since she started coming . . . [*pause*] When did she start coming? [*pause*] It started then. [*pause*] I started stopping then . . . [*pause. Somewhat louder*] I haven't worked . . . I haven't done one stroke of work— [*pause. Louder still now*] You don't know what I went through in Korea, boy! A yellow draft-dodging crumb like you wouldn't know a fug about that, boy! I was face to face with the commies, I saw their eyeballs, joy boy! That's what the hell that last painting was about, the very last one, yeh, it's in there, it's in that crappy fancy studio of yours, *my boy*! You sure fixed me up good! *You and that pig* —REAL GOOD, BOY!

[*Silence*]

DAN [*finally, barely*]: Some way . . . [*pause*] What a way . . . [*pause*] Paint her . . . [*pause*] I'm tellin' you . . . [*pause*] *The honey* . . .

STAN: WHEN SHE'S GIVING IT TO YOU?

DAN [*as above*]: . . . toodle oo . . .

STAN: The painting of the year! We could hang it from the ceiling, in front of your nose—How about that? You prick, *you'd like that!*

DAN [*as above*]: . . . I'm out flat . . .

STAN: I don't give a damn!

DAN: . . . move your crap back in here . . . wreck the studio . . .

STAN: What good would that do?

DAN: Try it . . . bud . . .

STAN: It won't do any good at all—it won't help—won't matter —because—I've become just like you! I lay on my ass—that's all I can do—all I ever do—Just Like You!

DAN: I get up, don't I?

STAN: *Yeh! To go to that headshrinker!*

DAN: Can I help that? I can't help that, can I? Want me to lose my allowance? Where would we be then? You know that's the *prima facie* condition of my allowance . . . Where would we be then? Think of that, man . . . Picture it! Just try and picture *that*, Stan man!

STAN: Might be the best thing that's ever happened to you—

DAN: Ha Ha!

STAN: I might even get back to work—*Back On The Ball,*—I might work! Buddy!

DAN: *Who's stopping you?*

[*Silence*]

STAN [*finally, quietly*] : Goddamn allowance . . . Always rubbing my nose in that allowance . . . [*trails off, muttering*] Crazy sonuvabitch of an old man . . . *He* ought to be seeing a head-shrinker . . . [*pause*] Both of them, together . . . [*pause*] Side by side . . . [*pause*] At the headshrinker's . . .

DAN [*barely*] : . . . Am I stopping you? . . .

[*Silence*] [*A bell tolls, far off. A jet liner passes, not far off*]

STAN [*quietly*] : Is she coming?

[*No answer*]

STAN: Maybe she's stopped coming.

[*No answer*]

STAN: She could have stopped coming. [*pause*] Did she have a contract? [*pause*] She has *no* contract! [*pause*] She might have gone back. [*pause*] Got married. [*pause*] Gals get married [*pause*] She's sick of it! [*pause*] Yeh! Goddamn sick of it! Why shouldn't she be sick of it? A pig like you—*a looney prick of a pig like you*—She's Not Taking Your Shit The Rest of Her Life, Buddy! A life of her own—She has a right to a life of her own, Old Buddy! Is she your slave, Buddy? Think she's like me, Buddy? You haven't got *her* pinned to the floor, my buddy! She'll throw you for a loop any old time, old buddy! That gal's got life! She's life! She's full of life, Buddy!

[*Silence*]

DAN [*finally, barely*] : She's coming . . .

STAN [*quietly*] : That's when I started going to hell. It had nothing to do with that—studio. [*pause*] It started [*pause*] Exactly when she started coming . . . [*pause*] Buddy . . .

DAN [*as above*] : She offered to pose for you . . .

STAN: *Buddy!*

DAN: Didn't she offer to pose for you?

STAN: HO BUDDY!

DAN: She goddamn well did, buddy . . .

STAN: *What a buddy!*

DAN: That saint . . . posing for you . . . just for you . . . that hon . . .

STAN: I don't want to talk anymore! Go to Hell! Take a flying trip to Hell! With her! I'm sick of her! Go to Hell with Her! I hope she gets hit by a goddam truck or something on her way over here—If She Is On Her Way Over Here! That's all I hope—Buddy!

DAN: Masterpiece . . . Would have been a masterpiece . . . Put you on your feet . . . Would have . . . Buddy . . . You said no. You got the shakes. The goddamn room shook with your shakes . . . What shakes . . . [*pause*] They were shakes [*long pause*] She doesn't hold it against you though. She's not that kind, bo . . . She'd do it even now, for you. I can ask her . . . for you. [*pause*] Want me to?

STAN: NO!

DAN: Always no . . .

STAN: She's ruined my life! Look what I'm reduced to!

DAN: You've got no Go . . .

STAN: *You oughta know!*

DAN: Where's your Go?

STAN: GET TO YOUR HEADSHRINKER!

[*Silence. Screeching brakes. Horns blowing. Silence*]

STAN: You had a letter today.

DAN: Yeh.

[*Silence*]

STAN: The old man?

DAN: Yeh.

[*Silence*]

STAN: What does he say?

[*Silence*]

DAN: You wanta know?

STAN: Yeh!

DAN: Yeh?

STAN: Quit screwing around! *Yeh!*

DAN: It's a good one.

STAN: Send the check?

DAN: Oh, yeh. The check.

STAN [*relieved*]: Well then?

DAN: What a good one.

STAN: *What The Hell's He Say?*

DAN: Quit hollering at me that way!

[*Long pause*]

DAN: He says—*Get a job.*

[*Silence. Utter*]

STAN: A job?

DAN: Yeh.

STAN: You?

DAN: Yeh!

STAN: He means you?

DAN: Yeh!

STAN: That's A Good One!

DAN: What a good one!

STAN: Does he mean it?

DAN: I dunno.

STAN: He must be kidding around. You know what a great one
he is for kidding around.

DAN: I wouldn't know—

STAN: *What the hell would you do with a job?* When have you
ever had a job? Because you're such a draft-dodging prick you
haven't even been in the Army! I know you fugged around
in the Air Force for five years—I know all about that, Buddy!
A job!

DAN: I went to school—

STAN: Ho!

DAN: I got good grades in school—

STAN: YO HO!

DAN: College—

STAN: HO HO!

DAN: I got my B.A. from college—

STAN: *Holy Crow!*

DAN: Damn good college—

STAN: What a college!

DAN: That was a college—*The coeds at that college*—

STAN: Don't start handing me all that dirty no-class stuff about you and the coeds at that college! I AIN'T INTERESTED IN THAT FILTH! THAT FILTHY COLLEGE!

DAN: I hit the Air Force—

STAN: You snuk your way in when the Army started eyeing you—You mother-fug, you tore down to that Recruiting Center soon as you heard they had their eye on you—like a bat out of Hell, *you beat all records*—

DAN: I'd finished college—

STAN: Stumbled out of it—

DAN: I'd just finished college—

STAN: *What About The Courses You Took At That College?* [*Silence*]

DAN [*finally*]: I was five years in the Air Force.

STAN: How'd you last so long?

DAN: It's a hell of a process getting kicked out. It takes a hell of a time. *Five* years! *Man.* They even had me down for Pilot Training—

STAN: Wo Ho!

DAN: They tried like hell to get me into Pilot Training—I was scheduled to go! [*pause*] Yeh, one hell of a process. [*pause*] What a process. [*pause*] Especially a Lieutenant—

STAN: *You were a Lieutenant?*

DAN: First Lieutenant.

STAN: You never told me that! Buddy!

DAN: Didn't I?

STAN: I never heard a goddamn word about that!

DAN: Didn't I?

STAN: I thought—I always thought you were in the ranks—an enlisted man—one of the ranks—That's what I always thought!

DAN: The hell with it.

STAN: Holy *Christ*!

DAN: I said the hell with it.

STAN: How'd you do it? I gotta hear this! How'd you ever do it?

DAN: *I* didn't do it. They needed Lieutenants. They screened the Squadron records. They made me a Lieutenant.

STAN: And all the time I was getting my ass shot off in Korea!

DAN: I didn't send you there!

STAN: And you were fuggin around some fat fuggin Air Force Base a sweet little Lieutenant!

DAN: Trying hard to get out, Man!

STAN: You motherfug! You draft-dodging yellow bellied degenerate sonuvabitch of a motherfug! Know how many commies I killed?

DAN: You could have been a Lieutenant—

STAN: I can tell you about Lieutenants—

DAN: The Painting Lieutenant!

STAN: Don't push it—*Don't Push It Too Far*—It wouldn't take me *two seconds*!

[*Silence. Complete*]

STAN [*quietly*] [*finally*]: I'll paint again some day. [*pause*] You'll see. [*pause*] See if you see [*pause*] Throw out that fancy equipment. [*pause*] All that crap. [*pause*] That equipment . . . [*pause*] That lousy . . . [*pause*] *Corrupting* equipment . . .

DAN: Nothing's ever like the original . . .

[*Silence*] [*A while*]

STAN [*Suddenly, explosively*]: IT'S YOUR TURN!

DAN: Huh?

STAN: *It's goddamn well your turn!* You know it's your turn! Don't kid me around anymore! You said you didn't know but I know damn well you know! Don't fug me around anymore! Don't jazz around! It's about time you stopped jazzing me around! Who the hell are you? Just who the hell are you? Your old man's got dough—Piles of dough—What Does That Make You? What's it ever done for you? I got rights! I used my GI Rights! I studied! I learned! I got a scholarship over here! Who shipped *me* over here? *My* old man never had dough to fork all around! You can't lay on your ass there night and day and jazz me around! STOP JAZZING ME AROUND!

DAN [*raising his head, they have both raised their heads, they face one another, across the way*]: What's up with you? What in hell's got into you? What the hell are you screaming about? What's all the screaming about? Trying to get us kicked out of here? That what you're trying to do? Ungrateful bastard you are! If you have to flip, get your ass outside and

do it! When were you last outside? Don't flip in here! I like it here! Understand? Think you can understand that? *Buddy?*
[*Silence. Their heads go down again, after a while*]
STAN [*quietly*]: What else does he say?
DAN: Nothing.
STAN: Nothing, about the allowance? Nothing?
DAN: Nothing.
STAN: Think he'll stop it?
DAN: I don't know if he'll stop it.
STAN: *He might stop it!* Ever give that a think? He just might stop it! You're a big boy now—*How The Hell Old Are You Now?*—He just might turn around and stop it! That would be a first class jabbero! How about that? What the hell's got into him—What's hit him? All of a sudden this job jag hits him! What's your personal view? This could be a premier kick in the crew—What's your view? Going to maintain your detached view? When you going to join up with yourself? Ever think it's happening to *you*? I mean YOU! *What's your view?*
[*Silence*]
DAN [*finally*]: He mentions the headshrinker's latest report—
STAN: Yeh?
DAN: Yeh.
[*Silence*]
DAN: I'm making progress. [*pause*] He says I'm making real progress.
[*Silence*] [*Complete*]
DAN [*finally, with some force*]: *I don't write the friggen reports!*
STAN: I could write a report!
DAN: That's what's hit him I guess—I'll do more than guess!
STAN: Kick the guy in the ass! Take the letter next time you go—shove it down his throat! A left, a right—Put Out The Lights!
DAN: What kind of a fuggin half-ass is he? I always thought he was alright!
STAN: Who's alright? Your mulla's alright! Jesus, that's sweet alright!
DAN: What a hell of a thing to say!

STAN: That's the way!

DAN: You'd think I didn't pay!

STAN: You pay and pay!

DAN: I oughta have value for dough!

STAN: Your old man's dough!

DAN: He worked hard for it! He broke his ass for it! He sucked ass for it! He's at the top! Up there! That slippery pole! You try making it up there!

STAN: I'd get nowhere!

DAN: I might have to take steps—

STAN: Think of the next report!

DAN: Goddamn him! The hell with him! I'm good for ten more years!

STAN: Maybe he's sick of you—What if the guy's getting sick of you? Five times a week—*ten years*—Face it, man! *He might be getting sick of you!*
[*Silence*]

DAN [*finally, quietly*] : He loves me.
[*Silence*]

DAN: I know that guy loves me—
[*Silence*]

DAN: *You think he doesn't love me?*

STAN: Your old man's *dough* he loves! *Buddy!* How much you dished out so far? Any idea? Give me a rough idea! Oh Buddy!

DAN: Don't frig me around, man! *He loves me! Loves Me!*

STAN: Enough to rebuild a palace! A friggen palace! Thousands, thousands and thousands! Ho Buddy!

DAN: Think the old man wants me back home? Think he wants that? He ain't a barn door! He shipped my ass over—It's the price he's gotta pay! I ain't worried about *that!*

STAN: Yeh but the friggen reports! *Think of that next report!*

DAN: I'LL JUST HAVE TO TAKE STEPS!
[*Silence*]

STAN [QUIETLY] : It'll end one day. [*pause*] It's got to end one day. [*pause*] The biggest ride of all time. [*pause*] What progress have you made? [*pause*] You just sucked me in and dragged me down with you. [*pause*] You sonuvabitch. [*pause*] Down, down, down and down . . . [*pause*] With you . . .

26

DAN [*very quietly*]: I drag my ass there five times a week. [*pause*] He loves me.

STAN: Didn't I pledge allegiance to the flag? [*pause*] Each morning, every morning, for twelve years, I was a kid of six—*six*—I started at six . . . [*pause*] 'I pledge allegiance to the flag . . . and to the Republic for which it stands . . .' [*pause*] *Every morning*, man . . . [*pause*] *What the hell am I doing here?* This goddamn mother fug of a place! This foreign place! This stinking place! What a place! For a guy like *you* —Just The Place! Did you pledge to the Flag? How the hell'd you make it through school? What kind of a school? Did your old man own the school? *I Loved That Flag!* I'll bet you didn't even know the words! You just stood up, mumbled any old fuggin words! Remember that trip to the Embassy here —*how* many years ago? What a fug of a farce that was! What did the guy say? That vice-consul there, what did he say?

DAN: Raise your right hand—

STAN: Right! That's right! That's what he said! And where was your other hand?

DAN: In my pocket—

STAN: And he said?

DAN: Take your hand out of your pocket—Please—

STAN: He said 'Please'?

D'AN: Please—

STAN: To a mother-fug—a fug—a friggen fug of a fug—a crumb —a crumb of a bum—YOU?

DAN: Me.

STAN: And you said—?

DAN: 'What for'?

STAN: 'What for'! Right! That's what you said! *And what else?* There, right there, in the Embassy of the United States, before a fully qualified, notarized, certified, bona fide, first class, genuine, positively patriotic, sober and earnest Embassy Official there!

DAN: He was a creep—

STAN: What?

DAN: A stinking creep—

STAN: *What?*

DAN: They're all creeps—

27

STAN: What a farce! A goddamn farce! Good thing I didn't know you then!

DAN: When did your passport expire?

STAN: YOU DRAGGED ME DOWN!

[*Silence*] [*Complete*]

STAN: It was slow. [*pause*] So slow. [*pause*] It happened so slow. [*pause*] You took hold. [*pause*] What a hold. [*pause*] More. And more. All over me. [*pause*] You floored me!

DAN: He won't kick me out . . .

STAN: Here I am—floored by you!

DAN: That next report . . .

STAN: You're on your way out! The handwriting's on the wall! You're out! *Out!* He's laid the groundwork. The preliminary bombardment. *Wait and see!*

DAN: We'll see—

STAN: He's no dope! He won't be floored!

DAN: Fran—

STAN: What?

DAN: Fran'll talk to him—

STAN: You'd Use Her In That Way! You creep! You frig! You would, wouldn't you? I got *news* for you!

DAN: I'll take steps—

STAN: It's been a long time since you took steps!

DAN: I know what to do—

STAN: HE'S SICK OF YOU!

[SILENCE]

DAN [*finally, quietly*]: I don't like you.

[*Silence*]

DAN: I've never liked you.

[*Silence*]

DAN: Rude. Crude. [*pause*] You're rude and crude. [*pause*] You're crude.

[*Silence*]

DAN: I've never known a guy so crude . . .

STAN: They'll kick you out of the country! Those nice Home Office chaps—you know—*The Chaps!* Out on your ass! The old heave-ho! You'll see who's crude!

DAN: They don't know I exist . . .

STAN: I'll let them know you exist!

DAN: *And what about you?*

STAN: *Do you give a fug about me?*

DAN: What the hell do you mean? Since I first picked you up off the street, since I saw what a jerk, a shnook, a deadbeat you were, a stoogats, a nobody, a shmuk from a no-class town you were—

STAN: *An Ex-GI, Buddy!*

DAN: WHO THE HELL'S BEEN TAKING CARE OF YOU?

STAN: You've been over here too long! You're a disgrace to the USA! Did you *ever* pledge to the flag? What about the *Star Spangled Banner?* Do you know one-half of half of the first line even? What do you know? Where are you from? Where are you now? You're un-American, anti-American—*you're practically a goddam Limey! Bo!*

DAN: *Get The Hell Out!*

STAN: *No!*

DAN: *Hit The Road!*

STAN: *You Go!*

DAN: This is *my* goddamn place!

STAN: *What A Place!*

DAN: *I* run the show!

STAN: FUG YOUR SHOW!

[*Silence*]

STAN [*finally, very quietly*]: She'll take care of us . . .

DAN: Don't worry about a thing. Not a thing. She'll take good care of us . . .

STAN: What about dough?

DAN: Don't worry about dough . . .

STAN: No?

DAN: What's dough . . .

[*Silence. Then, activity from* DAN'S *bunk. His hand grabs something*]

STAN: What's that? [*pause*] What the hell is that?

DAN: This little bug crawling over my sheet—

STAN: Over your sheet?

DAN: I got the creep—

STAN: Off your sheet?

DAN: Look—take a look—is it a flea? You're always telling me about those Korean fleas!

[*Holds it out.* STAN *leans out, looks at it*] [*Looks and looks at it*]

STAN: Nawwww. [*pause*] Uh uh. [*pause*] No. [*pause*] Hell no. [*pause*] It's got wings. [*pause*] Can't you see? [*pause*] It's some kind of a fly. [*pause*] A goddamn fly. [*pause*] It's no flea.

DAN: Sure?

STAN: Sure. [*pause*] A flea's hard. They jump around. Was that thing jumping around—?

DAN: It walked. [*pause*] It was walking. [*pause*] I'm pretty sure it was walking. [*pause*] I saw it walking. [*pause*] *Right across the goddam sheet*—

STAN: Alright!

DAN: What's alright?

STAN: It's no flea!

DAN: It could have gone in my mouth! I worry about them going in my mouth [*pause*] Think it could? Think one of them could? [*pause*] When I sleep—sometimes I open my mouth—

STAN: *They ain't interested in your mouth.*

[SILENCE] [*A while*]

DAN: How'd it get in here, anyhow?

STAN: The wind blew it in, probably. Most likely. The wind carries those little things along, all over the place, everyplace. It blew in through a window.

DAN: We don't have any windows open!

STAN: It probably blew in yesterday. Or day before. Sometime when we had a window open!

DAN: When the hell do we have a window open? [*pause*] You been frigging around? [*pause*] When I go out—When I go to my session—Do You Frig Around?

STAN: When Fran comes she opens the windows! [*pause*] Right?

DAN [*after a pause*]: Right.

STAN: *Alright!*

[*Silence*]

DAN: That's—some time ago . . . [*pause*] A—hell of a time ago . . . [*pause*] What's it been doing here? [*pause*] What the hell's it been up to here? [*pause*] What would it want in here? [*pause*] *How the hell could it survive in here?*

STAN: I don't know.

DAN: You seen it?

STAN: I didn't see it.

DAN: It was around though! Don't kid yourself about that, Bo!

STAN: Not necessarily.

[*Silence*]

DAN: What do you mean—*Bo?*

STAN: It could have blown in through a crack.

DAN: A *crack?*

STAN: It's pretty damn small. It could have easy come through a crack. [*pause*] Any crack.

DAN: I'll check those windows next time! I want to check out those cracks! That's the only place there'd be cracks!

STAN: It doesn't worry me, man.

DAN: No! Hell no! No! It wouldn't worry you! Would it, man? You just lay on your ass and worry about your own little world! Nothing else matters at all. You're an island—you think everything else is for the birds! *Frig it all! Fug on it all!* That's all! That's the way your goddam mind works! Let them blow up Vietnam! Burn the goddamn place off the map! Right off the map! Who the frig are they? Those rice-eating slant-eyed stupid frigged-up shrimps! Burn it right off! The runts! The shrimps! Don't they know the score? Korean hero you! You blew that goddamn fruggen place up—you showed them there, didn't you, Bo! You can't even count how many commies you fried to hell there, right, Mobo? Ho Mobo! Stand up, Bo! Attention, Bo! About face, right face, turn, turn you mother-fug there Bo! Fire! Fire away! Don't stop firing once you mother-fuggin you fug Bo! You'll show them! You showed them! Blow them all to Hell! That's the kind of mind you have! *Talent*—YO! *Artistic talent*—HO! That flea's got more goddamn talent than you! You ain't got the talent of a flea! Hell, he's survived—That takes real goddamn talent in here, Bo! How long's he been here? *You don't know a fly from a flea!* Korean fleas—You ain't ever seen a flea! *That's a flea!* Who the hell ever told you those things in Korea were fleas? I'll bet the goddamn place'll soon be crawling with fleas! What you gonna do about that, man? Burn the goddamn place down? Put a match to my bed—for a start? Wait for Fran to clear them out? Scholarship! Who

31

the hell ever gave you that Scholarship? The Ku Klux Klan?
You don't like nigs, you don't like Jews, you can't stand
Chinks, Japs, Gooks, Vietnamese, Indians, Russians, too—the
Limeys stink—*these poor fugged-up skirts around their asses
ever-loving fuggin Limeys stink*! What the hell kind of an
Artistic Mind is that? You should have been Adolf's Chief
Artist, man! There's Your Man! You narrow prick! You
stupid prick! You Prick! Drag your ass into that studio, you
talented bastard you, slap something together on that canvas,
that first-class canvas, pal, see if that makes you feel good!
Yeh! You'd have no worries at all but not at all then, right,
old pal? Pal! You'd be happy, that's all it would take to make
you happy—And Frig The World! Especially if they started
coming down and taking pictures of you for the Press—The
Press! You'd love that, pal! A goddamn brush or two stuck
between your toes, or up your asshole, you'd probably stick
one up there! You'd show them something new! You'd start
a new school! They'd write you up in LIFE! Your stupid face
crapping out at me from LIFE! That's all! *Your Little World!*
Well, let me tell you, man, put it to you pretty goddamn
straight there, man—You're living in an *interdependent
world!* It's about time you woke ass up and realized that!
You better come to terms with that! Open up! YOU GOTTA
REALIZE THAT! You ever gonna come to terms with that?
You're not an island, man! You oughta start worrying, man!
The crunch'll come! Your sweet ass in the crunch! Every
little thing's important, man! They oughta worry you like
Hell, man! STAY THE HELL AWAY FROM ME, MAN—WHEN THE
CRUNCH COMES!

[*Silence*] [*Complete*] [*Long*] [*No movement*]

STAN [*finally, quietly*]: You're good for another ten years, man.

DAN: It's alright with me, boy!

STAN: I'm gettin' out while I got the chance, boy. You're not
dragging me any lower, boy. You'd like to, wouldn't you, boy?
You'd like to keep me here until there was nothing left except
enough to fit into a little jug. A Jug! You'd sure like that,
wouldn't you, boy? *My Boy!* That's the whole goddamn object
of the game! I just caught on! I got it now! *That's your
game!*

32

DAN: Go. You can go. Anytime. Drop me a line. Fran'll read it to me. You know the address. Let me know how you're making out. A hotshot like you—*all that talent*—you ought to make out!

STAN: I'll make out!

DAN: Get the hell out!

STAN: I hate it here! I can't stand it here! I *hate* the Limeys! The dirty, lazy, perverted, degenerate, corrupt, corrupting Limeys! What about those short skirts they're wearin? Up to their assholes—*you told me*—They're Wearing Them! The filthy Limeys! Where's my home town? I come from a decent home town? My friends? All my friends? I had lots of friends! That nice little home town—that town—

DAN: That crappy home town!

STAN: My town—

DAN: What a crap-pile of a town!

STAN: What am I doing here? How'd I get here? *I'm Getting Out Of Here!*

DAN: *You Got A Passport?*

STAN: What?

DAN: A VALID PASSPORT?

[*Silence*]

DAN [*very quietly now*]: I know just the place for you, man, if you have a passport. [*pause*] A valid passport [*pause*] I'm not kiddin, boy . . . [*pause*] Perfect.

[*Silence*] [STAN *has turned, in his bed, and is staring at him*]

DAN: South Africa! [*pause*] There's the perfect place for you, my boy. [*pause*] You'd see eye to eye there—with all of them. There'd be the world's best mutual champion understanding between you. You ought to go there. She whatsis, the guy in charge there, see all of them. They'll take good care of you. Recognize your talent, bo. Know you at once as a genuine man of talent. You'll be the head of a new school—*New Brutalism*—Top Dog—Prima Donna—the cat's meoww! You, Bud! Whaddaya think of that, old bud? Just stand back, grab a handful of paint, pitch it at the canvas—You Can't Miss! You'll be in! Like Flynn! What you waiting for? Drag your ass out of that bed—all you have to do is drag it out of that bed! And what the hell, just what the hell, if you get

tired of it down there, why take a flit to Spain! *Portugal!*
You'd *love* that place! What about Germany? Give them a
few more years yet—They'll Be O.K.! They're up and coming
yet . . . You'll be *O.K.!* All O.K.! [*pause*] You got that passport? [*pause*] Up to date? [*pause*] How is your passport?
[*pause*] O.K.?

STAN: I've got—

DAN: Up to date? Everything stamped alright? Fees paid? Sig-
natures? All that?

STAN: I—

DAN: *Expired!* Holy Shmo! Oh Bo! I should have known! *I
knew it!* Boy I knew it! [*pause*] Wait till those Embassy
jerks hear of it. [*pause*] You think you can fox them? [*pause*]
Pull the wool over on them? [*pause*] *You're Illegal,* man!
What the hell you going to say to them? [*pause*] One of
those upstanding, solid, Vice-Consuls there! Any of them!
[*pause*] They'll hang you! You'll be swinging from that
eagle, man!

STAN: I—

DAN: *The Home Office!* What about the Home Office? Boy!
Buddy Boy! You can't *move!* [*pause*] A canoe! [*pause*] The
only way out of this place for you is by *canoe!*

[*Silence*]

DAN: You're in the soup.

[*Silence*]

DAN: Christ!

[*Silence*]

DAN: What soup.

[*Silence*]

STAN [*finally, very quietly*]: How'd it happen, Bo?

DAN: Laying there on your ass, you shmo! You stupid shmo!
What flag you gonna pledge allegiance to now? *Bo!* Even a
goddamn frig of a fuggin Ex-GI's gotta be *Legal!* Know? Even
an ex-ace-frig of a Korean commie-killer who doesn't know a
friggen fly from a flea! *Oh Bo!* You got a Congressman,
Shmo?

STAN: She'll Take Care Of It!

DAN: You friggen shmo!

34

STAN: She knows the ropes, she's a smart girl—she's taken care of everything else—

DAN: She can't work miracles, Shmo! Not even that saint of a honey gal can do that, pal! You're stuck! You can't get out of here!

STAN: *She'll Get Me Out Of Here!*

DAN: I wish she would! Jesus Christ! If she only could!

STAN: She could!

DAN: She'd be mine! At last! *All Mine!* At long last!

[*Silence*]

DAN [*barely*]: No more . . . pain in the ass . . .

[*Silence*]

STAN [*quietly*] [*hesitantly*]: As soon as she comes—I'll tell her . . . [*pause*] I'll tell her. [*pause*] Watch her—spring into action . . . then. [*pause*] She'll take the right action . . . then. [*pause*] Wheels will turn . . . [*pause*] She'll take care—of everything . . . [*pause*] Then.

[*Silence*]

DAN [*suddenly*] [*explosively*]: WHAT A SHMO!

[*Silence*] [*Long*]

DAN [*quietly, strangely*]: When you introduce acid into a situation you give a person who isn't real a certain position, which is an advantage.

[*Silence*] [*Complete*]

STAN [*finally*]: What?

[*Silence*]

STAN: What was that?

[*Silence*]

STAN: What did you mean by that?

[*Silence*]

DAN [*finally, quietly*]: She'll be here.

STAN: *Who isn't real?*

DAN: My god she's real . . .

STAN: Did you say it in your sleep? Is that it? Were you asleep? Half the time I don't know when you're asleep!

DAN: Are you asleep?

STAN: You're flipping, man! You're screwing me around, man! What the hell's up, man?

DAN [*barely*]: . . . here . . .

35

STAN: You were asleep. You must have shot that out in your sleep. Don't jazz me around! You make me creep!
[*Silence*]

STAN: *Who the Hell Isn't Real—Around Here?*
[*Silence*]

FADEOUT. SLOW

SCENE: *It is dark. We hear a moaning. Groaning. Then, a figure crawling about. There is a scratching sound. A flicker of light, a match has been lit. It is* STAN, *on the floor, warily crawling, searching. He is in an obviously disturbed state. Searching. He crawls about, painfully. The match goes out. More scratching. He lights another one. He finds, finally, what he is looking for, on the floor, in a corner: A phone. He has to clear away various objects to get his hands on it. By the light of another match he manages to dial a number. He glances furtively over at* DAN's *bed. He appears to be sound asleep. The match goes out. All is darkness . . .*

STAN [*in a subdued voice*]: Embassy? Is that the Embassy? [*pause*] The *American* Embassy! [*pause*] Oh? Yeh? Good. Let me speak to the Ambassador. [*pause*] What? [*pause*] I can't help that! This is the only time I can call. The only possible time I'm free to call. [*pause*] What? [*pause*] I'm a citizen! [*pause*] An artist! [*pause*] I'm here on an Artist Scholarship! [*pause*] Listen—[*pause*] I have a problem—no, no one else can possibly help me with my problem! [*pause*] Get him! You've got to get him! [*pause*] What are you talking about? What? What was that? [*pause*] *A man of talent!* Do you know who you're talking to? You can't talk to me like that! I was sent over on a Scholarship! What's your name? Grade? The Ambassador knows all about me! He's actually *responsible* for me! It's a Government Scholarship! [*pause*] Wake him! I don't give a frig—[*pause*] I just don't give a frig! He must have a line—you must have a way of plugging him in—wherever he is! [*pause*] Don't frig with me! [*pause*] Plug me in! [*pause*] Don't kid me [*pause*] He's the only one who can possibly help me! What? Of course he knows! He certainly knows! He gave a reception for *all* of

us—[*pause*] Once—[*pause*] He knows! [*pause*] What? *Holy*
What? Nine to Five? What are you talking about? *Office
hours?* What in hell are you talking about? It's an *Emergency*
—Yeh—An *Emergency*—can't you tell? Can't you get that
through your head? Plug me in! I must speak to *him*! I'm a
citizen—*an ex-GI*—Ever hear of *Korea*, Bo? Where the hell
were *you?* A man of talent! I must explain everything to him
—*everything*—The thing's too big—You've got no rules there
to cover *this*! Listen—he'll understand—He'll send someone
—Maybe *he'll* even come! Get me out of here—on my way—
[*pause*] What? [*pause*] On My Way! [*pause*] What was that?
[*pause*] Don't talk to me that way! You can't talk to me that
way! You can't get away treating me like that! Wait! *Just
Wait!* I've been in this hole for years! The best part of my
life is frittering away—My Creative Years! Dribbling away!
Plug me in! You jerk! You frig! You insensitive frig! You
mere mindless extension of that mechanical thing you're
holding—*The Ambassador!* YOU CREEP!
[*A click. A dial tone. He plays with the phone. He replaces
the receiver finally. We hear him mumbling, groaning. He
starts to crawl toward his bed again. A scratching. A match is
lit. By* DAN. *He is half-sitting up, the match extended by him,
between him and* STAN. *They are illuminated by the flickering
light of the match.* STAN *looks up at him.*]

DAN [*finally*] : What a nit. [*pause*] You twit. [*pause*] Have you
flipped? [*pause*] *You shnit!* [*pause*] Look at you! [*pause*]
Want a mirror? [*pause*] Shall I get one? [*pause*] You ought
to see, not to be missed—*I'll get one*—

STAN: You're awake?

DAN: I'm awake! Discovery of the decade! Hooray!

STAN: You heard?

DAN: I'd be dead if I hadn't heard!

STAN: I didn't think you heard—

DAN: Man of Talent! Great Man of Talent! Scholarship! The
Ambassador! What more?

STAN: I could have sworn—

DAN: Whaddaya want—a medal or something? You sure gave
him the works on that Korean stuff!

STAN: You looked dead asleep—

DAN: I wake up at the slightest noise. How come you don't know that? After all this time—the time—What the hell's the time? What's the idea? What's up? I thought you were gone! [DAN's *match goes out and* STAN *lights one. This alternating match lighting effort goes on throughout the scene. It is the only light.*]

STAN: I'm not gone.

DAN: I heard everything! I haven't heard such a ridiculous and embarrassing performance like that for one hell of a long time! How long? Sweet holy Jesus, oh Jesus, I don't know!

STAN: Who cares?

DAN: What?

STAN: I don't care.

DAN: Where'd you find the phone? Where the hell was it?

STAN: You're not ruining me, pal! I've got my rights! You've come pretty close, pretty damn close—but—*That's All!*

DAN: You nut!

STAN: Just stick around—

DAN: The wrong guy's been going to that headshrinker! That's all! What a ride. Can they trace the call? We'll switch. We'll make a switch! Tomorrow, buddy, when that phone rings— when he gives me the old signal to get up and go—*You Go!* Yeh! Right! *Go!*

STAN: Not me! I'm on my way out of here—you heard me on the phone—Didn't you?

DAN: Boy! Did I!

STAN: Alright!

DAN: Yeh! Fine! Alright! Ha Ha Ha! Ha! Right!

STAN: Go ahead—laugh—have your last laugh at that!

DAN: Tomorrow—You Start!

STAN: Not me—No, Buddy!

DAN: I had a feeling all along something was wrong. The wrong guy! All along! Sonuvabitch—what a ride—Ten years! The wrong guy!

STAN: Am I a dumbo? Who the hell you think you're dealing with—some dumbo? Do I look like a dumbo? I've got years, years behind me, good solid chunks of years and experiences behind me—think this is all I've ever known? *Talent* behind me! *In me.* That's it, old buddy pal. This is *finis*, my buddy pal. I'm breaking out of this jail!

[*In the darkness,* STAN *has crawled back into his bed. Now only* DAN *strikes the matches.*]

DAN: Yeh, boy?

STAN: *And You Can Have Her All To Yourself!*

D'AN: That right, boy?

STAN: See if I'm here tomorrow! Let me know! When you come back from your trip—Ha Ha!—Your Little Trip—take a look around—Let me know!

[*Silence*]

D'AN [*finally*] [*quietly*]: *You're* taking that trip. [*pause*] I'm through wasting the old man's dough. [*pause*] You're the man. [*pause*] Not me. [*pause*] Not anymore . . .

[*Silence*] [*Darkness*] [*A while*]

[*Moans in the darkness. Turning and stirring in one of the beds*—STAN's *bed*]

STAN: *NO!*

FADEOUT

SCENE: *The following morning. Probably. They are still in bed.*
DAN *stirs. Looks around. Sits up.*

DAN: Christ!

[*He gets out of bed, staggers out of the room*]

DAN: Holy Christ!

[STAN *wakes*]

STAN: What?

DAN [*outside*]: Sweet Christ!

STAN: It's morning!

DAN: Another morning—

STAN: What a nice morning! It's nice to see another morning! I have hope, I feel life, I'm alive again! It's always been the same—ever since I was a little kid, I can remember all the way back—I'd wake up in that town—I'd see the trees, the sun—I'd feel so good! Even now I feel good! I'm lifted out of the dungeon you stuck me in—right out! I hear violins— a great orchestra surging—I want to sing! I feel so good I want to sing! Have you ever sung? I'll bet you've never once sung—not once in your life—You wouldn't know how to sing!

You're a creature of darkness—the deepest darkness—You'll
never sing!

DAN: Sing.

STAN: Right! You bet! I'll sing! Today's my day—what a day
—I'll sing!

DAN: Let's sing.

STAN: Don't hand me that—you're *grotesque*! In the mornings
I know that for sure. Don't kid me! I have crystal clear vision
in the mornings. Don't try kidding me!

DAN: What'll we sing?

STAN: *I'll* sing! You think I can't sing? Buddy, this is a red-
letter day and I'm gonna sing! You think I'm handing you a
lot of bull. A fool, handing out bull. Like hell I am! What are
you doing in there? Stringing yourself up in there? That's
something you oughta consider doing, Bo! When she comes
she could find you strung up—There. Listen— [*Hums a starting note*] You listening, you creep? [*Hums one more note then
launches into a unique rendition of 'Oh What A Beautiful
Morning!' He sings with gusto. Next he launches into 'Battle
Hymn of the Republic'—He has climbed out of his bed. He
is standing on his bed, singing.* DAN *enters, slowly, barely dragging himself. He has on khaki trousers, a T-shirt, and is
carrying a cup of something. He stands and gazes at* STAN,
*who stops singing soon, under the gaze. They face one another.
Silence.*]

DAN [*quietly*]: What's your background?

STAN: What?

DAN: Just what's your background, man?

STAN: Go to Hell! Have your last fling! Today's the last you
see of me!

DAN: I ought to know that. All about that. You've been here
all this time—[*pause*] What a hell of a time—[*pause*] What
do I know about it? That Scholarship. Korea. A lot of crap
about some crappy home town. [*pause*] That town—[*pause*]
What the hell do I really know? I oughta know. Don't you
think I oughta know? I have a right to know. I should know.
Was your father white? Where's your mother from? Is she
alright? What about your sisters, Bo? What about compulsive
production with a built-in trend toward obsolescence, Bo?

What are your theories on it? Are the Chinese really a menace today or will they just turn out to be a joke—a croak? Are you a joke? What kind of a joke do you think you can get away with here? Do you hope to be President one day? Ever have clap? What about Vietnam? Why the hell aren't you in Vietnam? Aren't you on the Reserves? In them? Can't you volunteer? Why did your Passport expire? What are you doing in this country illegally, incognito, unknown, and foresworn? Who do you think you are? Just what kind of crappy friggen crap do you think you're pulling off? Why do you make strange phone calls in the night? How did you find that phone? It rings, every day it rings, sure, but I've never found that goddamn phone. I've never looked for it! What the hell are you, a sleuth? A private eye? Do you write thrillers on the side? Who smuggles them out of here? What kind of an accent have you got? What is that crappy accent you've got? Are you southern? Ku Klux Klan? Southern shit? Are you southern shit, man? Southwest? Are you southwest trash? *What the frig is the right end of the twig? And you're starting therapy today!* You phoney creep! You shit! You frig! You never told me that!

[SILENCE] [*Complete*] [STAN *does not move.* DAN *wanders to his bed, sits on it, takes a sip from the cup*]

DAN [*finally*]: Southwest trash. [*pause*] The Ozarks. [*pause*] I'll lay it ten to one. [*pause*] You rotten frig, you bastard—you came here under false pretences! I'm not so sure he'll take you! Why should he take you?

STAN [*finally, weakly*]: I'm from Pennsylvania, man.

DAN: *That* friggen Yankee State! Keerist! That crappy State! That explains a lot, my boy. What a hell of a lot you been keeping under your jockstrap, boy! What else? Christ! Just what else is there to spring on me? A Pennsylvania boy! Ahoy! I'll just be frigged! Polaks, Wops, Lithuanians, Russians, Irish—all that shit! How long you been here, sponging off me? Stealing from me? You crook! You typical Pennsy crook! Did you go to Penn State? U of P? Duquesne? What about Duquesne? They wouldn't take you at Duquesne! What about your old man? Is he a nig? A friggen nig? Are you half-nig? Is that why you joined the Ku Klux

Klan? What kind of a warped sonuvabitch are you anyway, man? I oughta have a social history to turn over to the boy before you go today, don't you think? It'll save a hell of a lot of time, man! It might cut it down to nine and three-quarters years, something like that, ever stop to think of that, man? [*pause*] C'mon, what the hell else are you keeping from me? Make a clean breast of it! Are you Catholic? Have you lapsed? I thought you were a Nice American Boy! What you doing frigging around with the friggen Catholics, boy? That outfit's run by a goddamn bunch of frig-eaten Wops, din't you know that, my boy? What's your story? Did you go to juke joints? Jive around a lot in juke joints? Press yourself against those nice soft knockers of those snatsy warm high school girls? Those friggen red-hot Polak gals? Those little gals? I want to hear it. All of it! It's time, the time has come, it's about goddamn friggen mother-fug time, boy! You've taken me for a ride just long enough there, boy! Ol Dan's got a kind heart, Jesus Christ, you oughta know that, the world's kindest—but—oh yeh—BUT—Stop frigging me around! Show some gratitude for all this time! Look what I've had to put up with all this time! What's the score? Did you finish high school? Put any of those gals against the wall—in that juke joint? What about the high school? Play football? Were you on the team? A yellow bastard like you—On The Team? You never went out for the team! I'll bet you drove those teachers mad. *Mad.* With a technique like yours—Jesus Christ—a mother fug of a master technique like yours—Oh Man! Crazy phone calls to the Ambassador at night! A dialogue by match-light! Who the hell are you? Get Lost! Living off me all this time! On your ass—All This Time! To top it all—Throwing me off my headshrinker's couch—*Like That*—What next? Just what in hell is next. What kind of Pennsylvania crap is *next*? There's no limit in your crappy Pennsy mind, is there, man? Let's hear the rest. All the rest. Start from far back. All the way back— *Don't Skip A Thing*!

[*Silence*] [STAN *sinks slowly to his bed. He looks very dejected. He finally crawls into bed.* DAN, *after a while, having apparently finished whatever was in the cup, does likewise. They are both in bed.*]

42

STAN [*finally, quietly*]: I've never seen such legs . . .

DAN [*also quietly*]: She's got the finest legs . . .

STAN: What flanks . . .

DAN: The shanks . . .

STAN: The greatest shanks . . .

DAN: Man . . .

STAN: What hips . . .

DAN: Those hips . . .

STAN: My hands on those flanks . . .

DAN: The shanks . . .

STAN: Gliding over those shanks . . .

DAN: What shanks . . .

STAN: I love those flanks . . .

DAN: What shanks . . .

STAN: Her hips . . .

DAN: Christ what hips . . .

STAN: Did I know they made such hips?

DAN: What hips . . .

STAN: A gal . . .

DAN: What a gal . . .

STAN: A saint . . .

DAN: She's a saint . . .

STAN: Her waist . . .

DAN: That waist . . .

STAN: What a waist . . .

DAN: Who's got such a waist?

STAN: That waist . . .

DAN: The rest . . .

STAN: Oh Christ!

DAN: All the rest . . .

STAN: Holy Christ!

DAN: My hands on the rest . . .

STAN: Your hands . . .

DAN: That face . . .

STAN: Your dirty hands . . .

DAN: What a face. Those lips. Those luscious lips. The eyes. What a pair of eyes. Her nose. Her perfect nose. The shape of her nose. Man, what a nose! Her hair—You ever seen such hair?

STAN: What hair . . .

DAN: What a gal! There never was such a gal! I dream, I dream and dream—I'll always dream—About That Gal!

STAN: My gal . . .

DAN: Oh My Gal!

STAN [*in absolute reverie*]: What a set. The world's loveliest set. Divine set. She let me have that set. I'll never forget the first time she gave me that set. I was on my last legs. I was out, on my last breath. It wouldn't have been much longer, you didn't give a damn, and there she was, that gem, that dream, that golden hon of a dream, she turned up, lucky for me, I thought it was a dream, she turned up, just in time, she gave them to me, *she saved me* . . .

DAN: Treasure Gal!

STAN [*violently*]: You pig! What a pig! You make me sick! Your dirty mind makes me sick! Your depraved mind on that gal, your sonuvabitch of a yellow, dirty mind drooling over that gal! Your hands on that gal! Your Filthy Hands All Over That Saint of a Hon Of a Gal! Taking advantage of that golden heart, that angel, that Golden Gal! What the hell do you want with that gal? Ain't you spread enough corruption in this world? Try the next world!

DAN: Those lips . . .

STAN: DON'T TALK ABOUT THOSE LIPS! She oughta spit on you with those lips! YOU FILTHY PIG! You lay there awake half the night thinking about her—I know what goes on there, don't think I don't know all the perverted corrupt filthy dirty depraved mother fuggin lousy low stuff that goes on in that bed, Thinking Of Her! What the hell do you think, you can Kid Me, Bud? I *know*, you sonuvabitch! I ain't no queer of a camp counsellor, Kid! I know all about you, Pig! Since when do you think you can get away with that stuff around here? You think this is one of those snatsy schools your old man owned that you went to, Kid? Who the hell are you? This is the age of democracy, kid. What have you done to defend Democracy, old kid? Don't blind me with those five half-ass years in the Air Force, Kid! *Those* fuggen years, Kid! You're a sonuvabitch of a draft-dodger if there ever was one! One of the sneakiest of ones! You filthy kid! You ain't fit to breathe out her name! Don't say her name! I'll hammer you into the floor if you mention her name! Do you think she's one of those Limey whores? Those theatrical literary whores? Those whores? She doesn't wear those swinging-round-the-asshole skirts! Her dresses are o.k. All o.k.! She's got dignity. She's a gal who's loaded with dignity. What the hell do you know about that? Does a pig like you ever come across a concept like that?

DAN: That's Enough Of That Crap!

STAN: *Crap?* You're the crap! Filthy Crap!

DAN: That Phone's Gonna Ring Pretty Soon!

STAN: Don't Hand Me That Crap!

DAN: You know the way? You better let me draw you a map. When were you last in the street? You'll be dazzled at first. Watch out for the cars. Don't get knocked on your ass first thing by a car. I'll draw you a map. It'll be crystal clear. Get off your ass, go into your studio and get me something I can draw you a map with. I'll give you a note. I won't mince words, I won't say a hell of a lot on the note, I don't believe in that crap. 'He's taking my place.' That's all I'll say. Get your ass in the studio! It must be filthy as hell in that studio! Dust, cobwebs, crap—all over the studio! I couldn't bear to see it like that! How much did it all set me back! *That's a Studio!*

STAN: I worked! I'll work! I could do tons of work! My middle name is Work! I could fill up this whole goddamn crap of a crappy so-called place with work! My Work! You'd have to sleep standing up! Lay on your ass standing up! You couldn't move, or turn around, you'd be hemmed in—

DAN: Don't holler like a goddamn nut in my place, buddy! Show some respect! You can holler all you want when you go to the boy—he's got a soundproof room there, boy! Don't fling that southwestern shit around here—

STAN: I'M FROM PENNSYLVANIA, BOY!

[*They look as if they will murder one another this time, and just at this point, the apex, as it were, of this fierce exchange, the door at Center swings open and there stands* FRAN. *She is a well-developed, healthy looking young lady, perhaps past her mid-twenties. She is most appealing, And she looks like*

45

she can take care of herself. She wears a skirt (slightly above knees) and blouse. A sweater, half done up, over the blouse. Her hair is light brown. She stands in the doorway. Her entrance has silenced them. In fact, they are paralyzed. They stare, frozen like statues, from their beds. She looks from one, to the other. Her face is loving, tender, understanding. And— a bit, just a bit, apprehensive. She smiles . . .]

DAN [*finally*] : *Fran!*

STAN: *Fran!*

DAN & STAN: *It's Fran!*

FRAN: My men! [*American accent*] [*She flings her arms out*] [*pause*]

DAN: We're not up yet—

STAN: You caught us under—

DAN: How you been, Fran?

STAN: You o.k., Fran?

DAN: Just getting up, Fran—

STAN: What's the word, Fran?

FRAN: How are you?

STAN: What's new, Fran?

DAN: Any news, Fran?

STAN: How short are they?

DAN: Yours is perfect—

STAN: Perfect—

DAN: What's new in the world, Fran?

STAN: Has Wall Street crashed, Fran?

DAN: Is it over?

STAN: Are the boys back, Fran?

DAN: Movies?

STAN: Seen any good movies?

DAN: How's the job, Fran?

STAN: How's Mom?

DAN: Dad?

STAN: Heard from home, Fran?

DAN: What's new, Fran?

STAN: Anything happening, Fran?

DAN: We're not up yet—

STAN: We were just getting up, Fran—

DAN: It's been a hell of a long time, Fran—

STAN: *How long's it been,* Fran?

[*Silence. They remain in their beds. In fact, they creep slowly further into their beds.* FRAN *starts walking towards them. She is radiant, smiling. They sink further under the covers . . .*]

FRAN: How are you? [*pause*] It's nice to see you. [*pause*] Real nice to see you! [*pause*] My favorite Yanks! [*pause*] You really make me feel back home—[*pause*] How are you? [*pause*] And just how are you? [*pause*] Now now— [*pause*] There there—[*pause*] Don't Disappear!

[*They have both now almost disappeared from view under the covers. There is a stirring under* STAN'S *blanket.* DAN *moves slightly. One of them, perhaps both of them, mumble something. Inaudible*]

FRAN: What? [*pause*] What was that, Lover? [*pause*] Oh, come on now, I want to see your face! Your faces! Come on, don't play hide-and-seek! Don't be cruel to Fran! Let me see your faces—I want to see your nice American faces—[*pause*] Think of me! [*pause*] Lovers! Me! [*pause*] All day long I see only Limey faces! All around me, everywhere, those funny Limey faces! [*pause*] What was that? [*pause*] What did you say?

STAN [*muffled*]: We're not up yet . . .

FRAN [*good humored*]: You're never up yet!

DAN [*muffled*]: I was up yet . . .

FRAN: Have I come here once and found you up yet? Have I? Now, think about that a little bit—just a teeny little bit— Have I?

DAN: You come early—

STAN: You always come so early—

DAN: It's been a long time—

FRAN: Any idea what time of the day it is? Hmmmm? Care to guess? Care to make the Big Guess?

[*She is near their beds. She peers, trying to see under the covers*]

FRAN: Now who are you? [*moves to other bed*] And which one are you? [*pause*] Shall I guess? [*pause*] Want Franny to guess?

DAN: Dan—

STAN: Stan—

FRAN: Dan and Stan! I'm Fran! Now what are you doing under those covers? And just what do you think you're up to under those covers? Telling Fran? Will my big boys tell Fran?

DAN: I'm tired, Fran—

STAN: I'm really tired, Fran—

FRAN: Do you know something? That's exactly what you said the last time I was here! Do you know when I was last here? Do my boys mean to say they haven't moved from their beds —since I was here?

DAN: When were you last here?

STAN: Give us a clue—

DAN: Been back home, Fran?

STAN: He threw the calendar away, Fran—

ERAN [*looking around*]: You threw the calendar away, Dan? Did you, Dan? That absolutely gorgeous calendar? Did you do that, Dan? Danny Dan?

[*Silence*]

FRAN: I'll have to get you a new one. I'll get you one of those thrilling Pan-American ones!

STAN: I know the ones!

DAN: Terrific ones!

FRAN: I wish I'd known—I'll have to bring it next time, I guess —I'll have to, I'm afraid—

DAN: Don't forget!

STAN: You won't forget?

FRAN: How could I forget! Do I ever forget? Where are my two naughty boys? Hmmm? Deep, deep, snuggled away? And how far away? Do you know the time of day? Listen—I've got a basketful of surprises for you, just outside the door . . .

DAN: Yeh, Fran?

STAN: No kidding, hot dog, that right, Fran?

FRAN: Have I ever kidded you, Stan? Would Fran kid Stanny Stan?

STAN: No, Fran.

DAN: She wouldn't kid you, man—

FRAN: I'll bring it in a little later, shall I? Shall I wait till a little later? And what are you doing there?

[*She is beside* STAN's *bed, she is playing with the covers, she*

48

is trying to pull them away, gently. STAN *holds on tight to them*]

FRAN: Oh what's the matter! Whatever's the matter? *It's Time!* [*And with this she rips away the covers.* STAN *is exposed on the bed, all curled and cuddled up, in his shorts and T-shirt of course*]

STAN [*weakly*]: Is it time?

[*Now she turns to* DAN's *bed. He hangs on to the covers for dear life*]

FRAN: And what about you now, my Danny Dan? My, aren't you strong! You're really strong! Don't you think it's *Time?* [*She rips off his blankets*] [*He is similarly exposed*]

DAN [*very weakly*]: It's time—

FRAN [*standing, looking from one to the other*]: Now! There you are! There you *just* are! And how you are. Here we all are!

STAN: Fran—

FRAN: Yes, Stan?

DAN: Fran—

FRAN: Yes, Dan?

STAN: C'mere, Fran—

DAN: Come over here, Fran—

STAN: Here, Fran—

DAN: Don't go there, Fran—

FRAN: Now now, bow wow, shall I wag my tail now?

STAN: Bow—

DAN: Wow—

STAN: Bow Wow—

FRAN: One at a time—

STAN: Fran—

FRAN: Let's start with you. Stan?

STAN: Give me a break, Fran. I can't get up. I can't move. I'm stuck. I'm stuck to the bed, Fran.

FRAN: Poor Stan—

DAN: I'm here, Fran—

FRAN: Hush, now. You be still, now.

STAN: C'mon, Fran. Give me some life, Fran. I don't know when I last moved, Fran. *Geez*—I'm sorry, Fran—you came just in time, you been away a long, long time, Fran—

49

FRAN: No more than usual, Stan—

DAN: Don't forget I'm here, Fran—

FRAN: Be *quiet*, Dan—

STAN: Help me out, Fran—

FRAN: There, Stan—[*pause*] There, my Stan—[*pause*] And how's Stan?

[*She is sitting on the edge of his bed now. She is caressing his face, as a mother would, she murmurs to him, tenderly, gently . . .*]

FRAN: Did I come just in time?

STAN: In time . . .

FRAN: Sweet Stan. Sweety sweet Stan. Stanny. Stan.

STAN: Fran . . .

[*He raises himself with an effort. His head is in her lap.* DAN *looks on at all this.* FRAN *holds* STAN *like a baby. She continues murmuring, caressing him*]

FRAN: My Stan—

STAN: Take care of me, Fran—

FRAN: There's my Stan—

STAN: Give me, Fran—

FRAN: There, there Stan—

[*She unbuttons her blouse. Her breast emerges and* STAN *takes it in his mouth*] [*Note: For prudish audiences, directors, actresses, as and if the case may be, the actress can have her back to the audience during this scene*]

STAN: Ahhhhh—

[*He is in bliss. He sucks hungrily at the breast.* FRAN *murmurs to him, holds him, like a baby*]

STAN: Ahhhhh [*pause*] Ahhhhh Ahhh . . .

FRAN: Is that nice? Is that what you want? Is it alright?

DAN: Not too much, Fran—

FRAN: Hush—you hush—now—Dan—

STAN: Ahhhhhhh . . . [*pause*] Fran . . .

DAN: *Don't give him too much, Fran*—

FRAN: Will you hush? Just hush? Dan—

STAN: Fran . . .

FRAN: How's that? How is that? Did you like that?

STAN: Fran . . .

FRAN: Shall we save some for Dan?

STAN: Little more . . .

FRAN: Just a little more? Stan?

STAN: Little more . . . Fran . . .

DAN: That guy was in Korea, Fran—

FRAN: Stop it, Dan—

STAN: Fran . . .

FRAN: And shall we try the other one? Just a teeny bit from the other one? Hmmm? Stan?

DAN: *Don't give him the other one!*

STAN: Fran . . .

FRAN: Well, what do you think? Shall we save the other one? Shall we give Dan the other one? Shall we see what he does with the other one?

STAN: Give him the other one . . .

FRAN: There's my Stan.

DAN: *Don't let him touch the other one!*

FRAN: Oh you're in a pet. What a pet. Isn't Danny Dan in a pet?

STAN: What a pet . . .

FRAN: Danny Dan, my Dan, don't fret—

DAN: Is it wet?

FRAN: You pet—

DAN: Did he make it wet?

FRAN: Isn't he a pet—

DAN: He slobbers—how can you stand the way the guy slobbers—?

FRAN: You're next—

[*Gently, after a few final caresses, she eases* STAN'S *head onto his pillow. He is smiling, warm, truly in bliss. She bends over, kisses him on the lips.* DAN *stares. She rises*]

STAN: What a kiss . . .

DAN: How come you gave him that kiss?

FRAN: Don't I give you a kiss?

STAN: That's a kiss . . .

[*Now she is near* DAN'S *bed. She gazes down at him, smiling. She touches his face with her hand. She sits on the bed*]

DAN: Fran . . .

FRAN: How's my boy Dan? Danny boy Dan—Is Dan a man?

DAN: Give me a hand . . .

FRAN: How've you been? How's my big boy been?

DAN: *Please give me a hand . . .*

[*She smiles, she opens her blouse,* DAN *places himself in her arms, she gives him her breast, he relaxes, taking her breast . . .*]

FRAN: How's that? And how's that? Aren't you strong. Aren't you big and strong—

DAN [*murmuring in bliss*]: I'm strong . . .

FRAN: So strong . . .

STAN: Don't hurt her, man—

FRAN: You're strong—

STAN: Don't bite her there, man . . .

DAN: Fran . . .

STAN: I'm feeling better, Fran—

FRAN: My Dan—

STAN: I feel alive. I've come back to life. I've got life, Fran . . .

FRAN: There, Dan—

STAN: You always come—you come—just in time—Fran . . . I'd die here. I'd just die here. Nobody'd give a damn. Not a damn. Fran . . .

FRAN: Is that nice? Is it? Dan?

STAN: Where's that basket of surprises, Fran? Say it was just outside the door? Did you say that, honey, Fran? Fran honey? Is he hurting you, Fran? I knew you'd be here. I knew this was the day you'd be here. Don't go away. Why do you always have to go away? Is he hurting you, Fran?

DAN: Fran . . .

FRAN: More? Danny wants more? Does my Dan Danny boy want a bit more?

DAN: Little more . . .

FRAN: There's more—

DAN: I want more . . .

STAN: Is he hurting you, Fran? Is he being greedy, Fran? Don't give him too much, Fran. You don't want to go and give him too much, honey, Fran . . . [*pause*] Did I tell you my plan? I've got a plan. Fran, I'll tell you my plan. [*pause*] Gosh I feel great. Don't I feel great. [*pause*] I'm getting out of here, Fran. I'm going on my own, I'm going to start work again. What do you think about that? Fran? Did you hear what I said? Fran, you're lovely, Fran. You look lovely.

Even over there, next to him, near him . . . taking care of him . . . [*pause*] There's no one lovelier anywhere, my Fran. [*pause*] Couldn't you come with me? We could go back home, back to the States, anywhere in the States, if you liked, Fran. We wouldn't have to stay here. [*pause*] Here. [*pause*] Over here . . .

FRAN: Is it nice?

D'AN: So nice . . .

STAN: I feel it back in me, Fran. Like it used to be, once. I can feel it, Fran. It's all back in me. Now. I could do anything, Fran. Ideas are pouring into my head, good ideas, Fran . . .

FRAN: Enough?

DAN: That's enough . . .

[*He sighs, goes limp, in bliss. She places his head on the pillow. Does herself up*]

DAN: The kiss . . .

FRAN: Here's a kiss—

[*She kisses him on the lips*]

STAN: Did he bite? Did he hurt? Are you alright? Fran—say you're alright—

FRAN: I'm alright—

DAN: That kiss was alright—

FR'AN: You see?

DAN: You bet I see—

STAN: Why couldn't you see?

DAN: Oh man . . . Fran . . .

STAN: Where did they make you, Fran? What do you think of my plan? You can tell me, Fran. Think it over. Tell me anything, Fran.

DAN: Man . . .

FRAN: Now—

[*She gets up on her feet, after caressing him a bit more*]

FRAN: Let's have a little air!

STAN: Opening the windows, Fran?

D'AN: Open up a few windows, Fran—

STAN: Open them all, Fran—

DAN: Not too many—Fran—

STAN: I don't mind how many you open, Fran—

FRAN: It's an awfully nice day. Spring's in the air!

[*Silence*] [*She goes around the room, opens windows. She leaves the room. She is elsewhere, opening windows*]

FRAN: Don't you just *love* the air!

[*Silence. They are still in bed, half-raised on their elbows, listening to her opening windows*]

FRAN: Just *marvellous* air!

[*She re-enters, finally, she is carrying a basket full of things. DAN & STAN perk up*]

FRAN: And look what I've got here!

STAN: You've got it there!

DAN: What'uv you got there?

FRAN: Ah! It's all here!

DAN & STAN: Show us what's there!

FRAN: Well, first of all—a little present for Dan—[*She pulls out a box*] And Stan—[*another box*] Two presents—one each—[*she holds them out*] Dan—Stan—[*she stands there, holding them out*]

DAN & STAN: Oh Boy, Fran! [*They dive for them. They take them back to their beds.*] [*They start unwrapping them*]

DAN: I wonder what it is—

STAN: I'll soon know what it is—

[*FRAN watches them. The wrapping papers fly*]

DAN: You sure wrap presents, Fran—

STAN: You know how to wrap them, Fran—

DAN: Hey—what's this?

STAN: Look at this?

[*Their presents emerge, finally. Each holds a clock. A Noddy alarm clock. They are rather large. A Walt Disney figure, possibly Donald Duck, is on the face of each clock*]

FRAN: Like your clocks?

DAN: Look at that clock!

STAN: That's a clock!

DAN: Ha ha! Fran!

STAN: That's really a clock!

FRAN: Try the alarm—

[*They wind up the backs, set the hands. They ring—a very comical ringing, loud, clattering*]

DAN: Listen to that alarm!

STAN: Ha ha! Wow! Fran! What an alarm!

[*They are utterly delighted with their presents*]

FRAN: I thought you'd like those clocks—

STAN: You're great! Nothing better you could have got!

DAN: Where'd you ever find these clocks?

FRAN: You can keep them beside your beds—

DAN: That's a great place!

STAN: You're right—hey—look—isn't it great?

[*They put them beside their beds. They laugh and play with them beside their beds*]

STAN: Fran, they're great!

DAN: You're a gal and a half—what a gal—Just Great!

STAN [*finally*]: What else you have in there, Fran?

DAN: Dig it out, Fran—break it out—Don't keep things hidden in there! Fran!

FRAN: I'll tell you, shall I?

DAN & STAN: Tell us, Fran!

FRAN: I have a nice—tablecloth—[*she pulls it out*] [*They whoop*] and a very very nice selection of—Groceries! [*They really whoop*]

DAN: You're going to cook!

STAN: We'll have a feast!

DAN: Oh man, Fran, you honey Fran—

STAN: What a Feast!

FRAN: And I've got—[*she pulls more things out*] I've got some soap—[*Silence*] And some towels—[*Silence*] Scrubbing brushes—[*Silence*] Sponges—[*Great silence*] Because—guess what? Can my big boys guess what? [*Silence*] It's Bath Time! [*Silence, They remain perfectly still, DAN and STAN, then begin to retreat back to their beds, slowly, under the covers*] Uh Uh Uh Uh! It's time to get up! Up Up! Don't my boys want to get up? You must get up! Fran can't give you a bath *there*! Now—can she?

STAN [*weakly*]: Have a heart, Fran—

DAN: Can't hack it, Fran—

FRAN: Up! My boys must get up!

STAN: Can't you let it go till next time—Fran—?

DAN: How about that, Fran—

FRAN: Don't you want me to cook the feast?

DAN & STAN: Fran!

FRAN: That's how it is—I'll just have to put everything back in the basket—I'm awfully sorry about this—

DAN & STAN [*springing out of their beds*]: Look, we're up!

FRAN: Now for a bath!

DAN & STAN: A great little bath!

FRAN: A marvellous bath—

STAN: And then the feast—

DAN: We'll have the feast—

FRAN: All in time—

DAN: There's plenty of time!

STAN: Going anywhere, Fran?

DAN: You sure look great, Fran—

STAN: Give us a terrific bath, Fran—

FRAN: Here we go—

DAN: Take a look—are we up?

STAN: We're up!

DAN: What's the feast?

STAN: Could we take a peek?

FRAN: The bath—

DAN: Let's have that bath!

STAN: Is the water warm? What's the water like these days?

DAN: Last time it was warm—

STAN: Some bath!

DAN: That was a bath!

STAN: Who's for a bath?

DAN: What else you got in the basket, Fran?

STAN: What's in there, Fran?

DAN: Did I tell you he's taking my place, Fran?

STAN: What are you talking about, man?

FRAN: Fresh clothes.

DAN & STAN: Terrific!

FRAN: Fresh bed linen.

DAN & STAN: But terrific!

FRAN: The bath—

DAN & STAN: Let's have that bath!

FRAN: Here we go—

DAN & STAN: Let's Go!

[*They whoop and romp noisily, they start to peel off their clothes as they pile out of the room, shepherded by* FRAN. *We hear them offstage, whooping, romping. Now they are in the bathroom. The wild romping and whooping continues. Water splashing.* FRAN *admonishing them*]

DAN: Everything alright Fran?

STAN: Right down the line—?

FRAN: Where are your clean towels? Did you forget to bring in your clean towels?

DAN: Aw, get them for us, Fran—

STAN: Go on, Fran—

FRAN: Now you know you should have brought your clean towels!

STAN: Fran!

D'AN: Getum for us, Fran!

[*Much giggling, whooping, laughing, splashing*]

FRAN: This is the last time! Mind!

[*She re-enters the room, looks about, rather annoyed. Finds the towels. Exits. More whoops and splashing*]

FRAN: Now then—now now then—*Stan*! Will you keep still? For heaven's sake! *Dan*! Naughty, *naughty* Dan!

[*Much splashing, whooping, etc. . . .* FRAN *admonishing . . .*]

DAN: Look out! Don't fall in!

STAN: *Fran*!

FADEOUT

SCENE: *The same. But things have been spruced up. The beds are made, the pure white collars of the clean sheets peer out at us. There is a divan. The windows are open. There is a dinner table, and it is obvious a hearty meal has been enjoyed. Empty plates. Bottles. Glasses. On the divan,* DAN *lies with his head in* FRAN's *lap. She is caressing him.* STAN *sits across the room, luxuriously relaxed, smoking a large cigar. From time to time he glances in their direction.* DAN *and* STAN *both wear fresh khaki trousers and T-shirts. They are well-shaved. There is music. Soft, romantic music.*

DAN: Ahhh . . . MMMM . . . ah ahhhhhh . . .

STAN: Aha . . .

FRAN: Enjoy your feast?

DAN: Was that a feast . . .

STAN: Who can cook like that in the world? Tell me if you know anyone who can.

DAN: I don't know anyone who can . . .

FRAN: You seem lots better. You both look *much* better.

DAN: Did we look bad?

STAN: Were we bad?

FRAN: I won't stay away so long. I'm awfully sorry I stayed away so long.

STAN: How long was it?

DAN: It was long . . .

STAN: Was it long? How long? Fran?

FRAN: I'll get you that calendar—

STAN: Where did you get these cigars?

FRAN: Like them?

STAN: They're Cuban.

DAN: Terrific cigars.

FRAN: You can get them here, Stanny Stan.

DAN: Didn't you know that?

STAN: Last time you brought Dutch cigars.

DAN: What kind will you bring next time?

FRAN: Korean.

[DAN *laughs. It is a great joke.* STAN *is silent*]

FRAN: The studio was quite a mess. You haven't been anywhere near it, have you?

STAN: Uh uh, Fran—

FRAN: Want to go in and look at it?

DAN: She did a terrific job on it, man.

STAN: Uh uh, Fran. Not just now. Not now, Fran.

FRAN: You're such a talented fellow, Stan. [*pause*] My Stan.

DAN: I didn't hear that phone ring today.

STAN: I didn't either.

DAN: There's still time. It could ring anytime. Today.

FRAN: There's an unfinished painting on the easel, Stan. Did you know that?

DAN: What soft hands, Fran. You've got hands like the princess of my dreams, when I was a kid, I dreamed all the time about her, Fran.

STAN: I knew that . . .

FRAN: You like them, do you? Your face is nice and smooth now.

58

DAN: You're getting me warm, Fran . . .

STAN: I know it's still on there.

FRAN: Do you remember anything about it, Stan?

DAN: Where'd you ever get such hands? Those are pure princess hands . . .

STAN: I can see it all now, it could be in front of me.

FRAN: Will you ever finish it, Stan?

DAN: The temp's going way up, Fran . . .

STAN: You know what to do when that phone rings—

DAN: I gave you the note, the directions . . .

FRAN: I'd love to see it when it's finished—

DAN: What about a little dance, Fran? This one's terrific.

[*'Moonlight Serenade', Glen Miller, is playing*]

FRAN: Alright then.

[*They rise and begin to dance. They are clasped in a tight embrace. DAN dances smoothly, sensuously, dipping with her, far back, from time to time. STAN watches them*]

STAN [*quietly, almost to himself*]: He doesn't know anything at all about painting, Fran. Nothing. He's ignorant. He's one of the most ignorant guys I've ever run across in my whole life, Fran. Low, crude, ignorant. How ignorant. Insensitive. He has the sensitivity of a beanpole, Fran. He's dragged me down under. When I first came here I was an artist. I was on my way to supreme achievements in the sphere of artistic activity. Fran, he dragged me under. He has a way about him, he is a guy who can poison anything. Anything. You're terrific, Fran. You're the greatest, Fran. Why do you dance with him? Why, when you come, do you bother with him? How come you monkey around with him? He's a nut. He's nuts. His family don't want him. His old man threw him over here. He'd be in the streets, in the klink, without his old man behind him. He's been driving some poor headshrinker nuts for ten years. Ten years, Fran. You heard about that farce at the Embassy. You know all about what went on that day he went down to the Embassy. The American Embassy. Our Embassy. That's the country you and I love, Fran. He doesn't love it. He doesn't give one frig about it. I'm sorry I used that word, Fran. I never used words like that before I met him, Fran. And I was in Korea. You should have heard what they used in Korea. How come you dance with him? Why do you let him hold you like that, Fran? I danced in the juke joint. In my home town. My town. My—crappy—town—See what I mean, Fran. He's infiltrated me so much I talk just like him sometimes. I come from a great town. You know all about those towns. You're from one yourself. You told me. What does he know? He's from no town. He's a no thing, from no town. I danced in the juke joint. I—wish—you—could have been—there—that—juke joint. Holding you. Close. Warm. Soft. That jerk. You dance like you mean it, Fran. With that jerk. They'd have kicked him out in the street. He wouldn't have been allowed in the place. No girl would look at him. Who would want to look at him? Are these cigars really from Cuba, Fran? That country's on the list, Fran. You think I oughta be smoking these commie cigars, Fran? I shot more commies than you could count in a day, Fran. That guy shot nothing. A lot of bull. Nothing. He doesn't even know the Pledge of Allegiance, Fran. Are you a schoolteacher? Did you ever teach school, Fran? I knew terrific teachers who you remind me of a lot, one hell of a lot. Fran. I could just see you. Teaching. What a teacher . . . Is it his turn, Fran? Is he first, Fran? How do you remember? You sure he wasn't first last time? When you bring the calendar I'll keep track for sure, Fran. It's a hell of a thing, it's lousy, sitting here, not being sure. Even after that meal. Some meal. Fran, that was a meal. What did you say the name of it was? What a meal. It was delicious. Succulent. Tender and succulent. The flavor. That was the thing, the flavor. You gave it the flavor. What are you doing there with him, Fran? He sure is rubbing up against you, Fran. How can you stand that, Fran? The dessert. That was a prize, that dessert. The fruit. The cream. The smooth cream. The rest of it. All—the rest of it. Fran, what a treat. That topped it all off. Supreme treat. Who but you could make such a treat? What a cigar, Fran. I know you didn't mean anything by buying these commie cigars, Fran. I know they sell them all over the place over here. I know about that, Fran. Here. Over here . . . You remind me a lot of my mother, Fran. My mom. I was in Korea. She died. Mom died. The smells that came out of her kitchen. Fran, you'd have loved them. Appreciated them. When I came home from school, after a hard day at school . . . [DAN *and* FRAN *kiss. They begin this long, passionate kiss. It goes on and on*] [STAN'S *voice increases a bit in volume*] What are you doing, Fran? What kind of a kiss is he giving you, Fran? Is his tongue in place? In the right place? You're not letting his tongue go all over the place—? It's not—it's not penetrating your lips—*it's not* —Is It, Fran? You're not letting him kiss you *like that?* Is he giving you a clean kiss, Fran? Why are you kissing him, Fran? That guy was in Frisco for a couple of years, did you know that, Fran? His old man shipped him out there for a while, that was the first headshrinker he tried. You know what happened, Fran? Did he ever breathe a word to you about what happened, Fran? That was the first one, Fran. There were a few more. Have him tell you about those few more. *I heard all about them.* He landed up over here. His old man was smart, sharp, that's why he made it to the top, he's at the top, he got him out of the country, shipped his ass over here. Fast. Sharp. Pardon me, Fran. I don't mean to use obscene profanities like that in front of you, Fran. I never used to talk like that, never, Fran. I respected Mom. No matter where I was: Supreme respect for Mom. Until—until —*He's a psychopath, Fran.* That's the correct word, if you want to know the full truth of the matter and no mincing words about the matter there, Fran. *A psychopathic personality*, that's what he has, Fran. Did you hear about the college days? The filth, that would fill two books, of those college days. He got a B.A., Fran. Know the courses he took getting it, Fran? Want to hear about them? What a list, Fran! There's a list if there ever was one, I'm not kidding around, Fran. They gave him that B.A. in Liberal Arts finally, Fran. That guy is a Liberal Artist, Fran! He went to church when he was a kid, how's that for a laugh, Fran. He sat in the middle row and played with it. Or was it the back row? Was it in the back there, capocatz, that you played with it? While the service was going on. He had it out of his pants, Fran! In church, in the middle of the service, Fran! He grew up with his hands in his pockets, Fran! What were they doing there? At the Embassy, he was friggen around, right there,

before the vice-consul, taking the Oath, Fran! The Oath of
Allegiance, Fran! That's the kind of a frig you're kissing,
Fran! Listen, you don't know the half of what the hell you're
kissing like that, Fran! He's no person! Nothing! He's got
no passport, Fran! He's in this country illegally, unknown,
to sundry and all, ALL, Fran! Does he give a frig, Fran? One
teeny friggen frig of a frig, Fran? No! Hell No! It's all the
same! There's no laws! He gives a frig for the Law! That
illegal mother-fug of a fuggin psychopathic mind of his! Does
he pay income tax, Fran? On that fat allowance his shit of an
old man ships him each month—does he pay one penny of
income tax on it? Know something, Fran? He even frigged the
Government out of the income tax they knocked off that
goofin-off time he put in the Air Force, Fran. He got it all
back! Every penny of it back! 'Medical Expenses'—Fran!
Yeh! That's right! I'm not kidding you, Fran! That guy's
never paid one friggen penny in income tax! How much does
he owe the *Limey* Government, Fran? Ten years! Who can
figure that one out, Fran!? That tax-evader, illegal, draft-
dodging, psychopath of a dirty French-kissing sonuvabitch,
Fran! That prick, Fran! What does he know about the
dignity of woman, Fran!? Did you know he was in the Boy
Scouts, Fran? Ever hear about his *Boy Scout* days? That Guy
Was A Boy Scout, Fran! What the hell are you doing, Fran?
What the hell are you letting him do to you, Fran? [*pause*]
[*ever louder now*] Frig! [*pause*] *Fran*! [*pause*] Frig, Fran!
[*pause*] *FRAN*!
[*He is in quite a state now, on his feet, as* DAN & FRAN *continue
the long, long kiss,* DAN's *hands now straying all over her
back and downwards, and hers all over him. The phone rings.
It doesn't phase* DAN & FRAN. *It rings and rings.* STAN *doesn't
say a word. He is frozen. It continues to ring. Sowly, woodenly
he heads for the door. Somehow, he makes it out of the door.*
DAN & FRAN *are near the bed. With passionate moans, they
fall onto the bed, kissing, tightly embraced. The ringing stops.*]
[*A crashing noise, as if someone has fallen down a long flight
of stairs. It doesn't phase them . . .*]

FADEOUT

SCENE: *The same. Some time later.* DAN & FRAN *are still on the bed. She is in a slip. They are cuddled up, laughing lightly, giving little nips and kisses to each other. Post-love-play.*

FRAN: There—

DAN: Where?

FRAN: There there—

DAN: I'll never know where—

FRAN: Alright?

DAN: That's right—

FRAN: Everything's alright—

DAN: You're right—

FRAN: Ummmm

DAN: Don't bite!

FRAN: Would I bite?

DAN: Ummm hmmmm

FRAN: Hmmmmmmm

DAN: You're alright—

FRAN: A bit of alright—

DAN: Any night—

FRAN: Tonight's the night—

DAN: The big flight?

FRAN: *What* a tyke!

DAN: Kite—

FRAN: You flew a kite?

DAN: Right—

FRAN: It's alright—

[*They go on for a little while. Then, the door opens and* STAN *enters. He wears a white bandage around his head. Generally, he looks the worse for wear. They don't seem aware of him. He looks at them. He crosses and sits on the edge of his bed, across from them. He stares at them.*]

STAN [*finally*]: Then there was that theatrical-literary crowd—

FRAN [*suddenly aware of him*]: Stan!

DAN: You're back.

STAN: Ever hear about that, Fran?

DAN [*sitting up*]: Old buddy, boy, man, you got back!

FRAN: How are you, Stan?

DAN: What's that around your head, man?

FRAN: Whatever's *happened* to you, Stan?

[*She sits up. She gets up. She goes over to him. Examines him.*]

DAN: Somebody roll you, man? Don't tell me one of these Limey bastards rolled you, man!

FRAN: It's a lovely bandage, Stan.

STAN: The hospital did it, Fran.

DAN: You were in a *hospital,* man?

FRAN [*tenderly, stroking him now*]: And what happened, Stan? Tell Fran—

STAN: I fell down the stairs, Fran.

DAN: What stairs, man?

STAN: Just outside here. I forgot there were stairs here.

DAN: When?

STAN: When I left.

DAN: Holy man!

FRAN: Ah what a shame. What a shame. Stan. [*She strokes him.*]

DAN: All the way down? Down all those stairs? Man?

STAN: You're not dressed, Fran.

DAN: Put on your dress, Fran!

FRAN: There, there—

STAN: Did he take your dress off, Fran?

FRAN: Now there—

STAN: What soft hands, Fran—

DAN: Those are hands, huh, man?

FRAN: Dan—

DAN: Yeh, Fran?

FRAN: It's time now—

STAN: It's about time now—

DAN: Aw, man—

FRAN: Bye Byes now—

STAN: Under the covers now—

DAN: I'm not tired, Fran—

FRAN: You must be very tired, Dan—

STAN: How the hell could you stand on your feet, man? You'd fall down if you tried getting up on your feet.

DAN: You sure look funny, man—

FRAN: Does it hurt, Stan?

STAN: It did. It doesn't—now. Not too much. When you touch

me—it doesn't hurt—much at all—*Fran*—

DAN: Put your clothes on, Fran—

STAN: Is there—do you have—what do you have on under the slip, Fran?

FRAN: Now Stan—

DAN: How was the hospital, man?

STAN: They found me at the bottom of the stairs.

FRAN: Stan—

DAN: They load you in a meat cart, man?

FRAN: Dan—

STAN: Under the covers, man—

FRAN: Hushabyes—bye byes—Danny Dan—

DAN: So—How was it? How did things go? Make it on time?

STAN: I didn't get there—

DAN: *What? Man? You didn't even get there?*

FRAN: Where?

DAN: Whaddya mean? What are you talking about? What's going on? You trying to kid me? Pull one over on me?

STAN: I got lost.

DAN: Whaddya mean you got lost? What are you pulling on me? I wrote all the directions down. I couldn't have done a better job of writing them down. How could anyone get lost?

FRAN: Did you go out, Stan?

STAN: Yeh, Fran.

FRAN: You should have told Fran—

STAN: I should have, Fran—

[*She is stroking him*]

DAN: Christ!

FRAN: *Dan*—

STAN: What a dirty mouth, Fran—

DAN: It was *all down*! I even had it down to the *last step*! *What happened*, man?

STAN: I had to start from the hospital. Remember, man.

DAN: Oh Man!

FRAN: When were you last out, Stan?

DAN: What in hell's gonna happen NOW, man?

FRAN: What always happens now, Dan—

DAN: You don't know what I'm talkin' about, Fran!

FRAN: Tell Fran—

STAN: The headshrinker, Fran—

FRAN: Mustn't be late, Dan—

DAN: I probably won't have that chance again now, Fran! This guy's really taken care of everything—*real nice*—Man!

FRAN: Hush—bye byes—Dan—

STAN: I don't think you have anything under it, Fran—

DAN: Put your clothes on, Fran!

STAN: Any chance of that phone ringing again today, man?

DAN: I don't think it'll *ever* ring again, man! Oh Man! He gets hot, he hits the roof, the ceiling, he lets fly, he really gets *mad*! Remember that time I missed the 28? Jesus! That was the time I started taking off a half-hour earlier even, I mean, after that time, man! He warned me! He put it to me! If ever again! And he meant just *late*! You never ̆showed! You didn't *turn up*! You didn't even *show up*! Now What The Hell Next?

FRAN: Dan—

STAN: Little shuteye, man—

DAN: SCREWED!

STAN: Cut it out, man—

DAN: That next report! Oh Jesus! Christ! Jesus! Sweet Holy Christ! My Christ! Man!

FRAN: Really—Dan—

STAN: I'll write him a note. I'll phone him up. I'll explain every-thing—man—

DAN: That guy doesn't take explanations, man!

STAN: A hell of a note—

FRAN [*very cooingly*]: Did Danny want you to take his place at the headshrinker's? *Hmmm? Stan?*

STAN: Right. That was the idea, Fran—

FRAN: Now what would Danny want Stanny to do that for? Now then—what for? Hmmm?

STAN: How was he, Fran—?

FRAN: What a man—

STAN: Better than Stan?

FRAN: You're a man—

STAN: I'll say, Fran—

FRAN: Stanny man—

STAN: Man—

DAN: Ain't you gonna put your clothes on, Fran?

STAN: He won't go to sleep, Fran—

FRAN: Now Dan—

DAN: You sure frigged everything up, man!

FRAN: *Dan—*

DAN: Fran! I don't give a damn! If you only knew what this guy did, Fran! The works! Everything, man! Can't a guy ever depend on you for anything, man? You realize what the hell the consequences of this little frigup are going to be, *my man?* You won't ever hear that phone ringing again now, man! Somebody else is gonna jump into the slot, like a shot, just like a shot, man! And what the hell's he gonna tell the old man? Where we gonna be then—Man? I'd like to hear your answer to that, what kind of an answer you gonna dream up to that? Man! *What's the answer to that?* Don't hand me any crap! I'm sick of your crap! Take off that bandage—I'll lay you two to one it's a fake—a put-up job—a sham—you took it on the lam! There's not a goddamn thing under that bandage! You threw something down the stairs—you didn't fall down those stairs—*I Never Heard Anything Fall Down Those Stairs!* This is about the crappiest piece of crap you ever pulled off, man! How'd you get back from the 'hospital'? C'mon, give us the answer to that? How would a creep like you ever find his way back from the 'hospital'? What hospital? What the hell was the name of the 'hospital'? Huh? Man? *Stan the Man?* You never moved from those stairs! You stood out there, all this time, crapping around, trying to figure a way out! Don't kid me, pal! Who gave you the bandage? Was there one in Fran's basket? You pull one out of the ever-lovin' kid's basket? That kid? Her basket? Fran, any bandages missing from your basket?

[*Silence*] [FRAN *gazes on him disapprovingly, sadly.*]

STAN [*finally*]: I took a taxi.

DAN: A taxi! Ha! Ho! You! Yo! You in a taxi?! Ho ho! Oh Ho! What do you know about taxis? Fran! Yo! This guy in a taxi! And what did you pay him with, the Limey driving the taxi, just what the hell did you pay him off with? *Talent?* Your goddamn talent? That talent? *Don't shit me around anymore*, Buddy!

67

FRAN [*really cross now*]: Dan! [*pause*] Really, Dan. [*pause*] Now that's enough, Dan. [*pause*] That's entirely enough of that, my Dan. [*pause*] It's just about time you went bye byes, my Dan. [*pause*] [*tenderly now*] Waiting for Fran to come and tuck you all in? [*pause*] I know—Fran knows all about Danny Dan. [*pause*] I'm going to tuck you in. [*pause*] I'm going to sing you a little song, a story, a story-song. [*pause*] That's what you really want, isn't it, *Dan*? [*pause*] Tell Fran. [*Silence*]

DAN [*finally*]: Yeh, Fran.

FRAN: Alright then.

[*She rises and goes over to his bed. Sits on the edge of it, after tucking him in.*]

DAN: The story, Fran—

FRAN: Just a *minute*, Dan.

STAN: It's the story of his life, Fran—

DAN: Then put some clothes on, Fran—

STAN: Mind your own damn business, man.

DAN: Don't run around here in just that slip. Not with him around. Not him. Please, Fran.

STAN: He sure needs a long sleep, Fran—

D'AN: He's an alleycat. He's hot. Hot as a tomcat. That's the way they are, from that State he comes from. He's a *Pennsylvania Tomcat*. Know what he did in Korea? Tell you that? *Fran*. Please, Fran—

STAN: Shut your goddamn mouth, man—

FRAN: Stan!

DAN: See what I mean, Fran?

STAN: It's him, Fran—

[*Silence*] [*She looks from one to the other, reprovingly*] [*She turns finally to face* DAN]

FRAN: Once upon a time—

DAN [*relaxing*]: Fran—

FRAN: There was a big Big boy called Dan—

STAN: Dan—

FRAN: He would always talk, and talk, and talk—

DAN: What a voice—Fran—

FRAN: And one day—

DAN: What a day—

FRAN: He was in the kitchen while his mother was baking a great big lovely lovely lovely—

DAN: Delicious—

FRAN: Apple pie—

[*Silence*]

STAN: What a pie—

[*Silence*]

DAN: Man—

FRAN: And, naturally, standing around, chattering and chattering away—[*pause*] There was Dan!

DAN [*getting drowsy*]: Now sing it, Fran—

FRAN [*singing*]: Dan, Dan, Dan—There Was Dan—There in the kitchen was Danny Dan Dan—he talked and he talked—his mother baked—a delicious apple pie—

DAN [*very drowsy*]: My favorite pie—

[*Now* FRAN *hums to him*]

DAN [*falling away*]: What a pie . . .

[*Silence. He is asleep.* FRAN *hovers over him, kisses him very lightly, turns, faces* STAN.]

STAN: Hello, Fran—

FRAN: Stan—

STAN: It's been a long long time, Fran—

FRAN: And how's Stan?

STAN: He didn't hurt you, did he, Fran?

FRAN: How's my man?

STAN: You look great. Great. Christ you're great.

FRAN: Does it seem a long time?

STAN: You came just in time—

FRAN: I came, didn't I—

STAN: He's sleeping like a baby, Fran—

FRAN: He's very contented, Stan—

STAN: Come over here, Fran—

FRAN: Shall we dance?

STAN: Kiss me, Fran—

[*She rises, slowly, drifts to him. He remains seated on the bed. She stands before him. He looks up at her, then buries his head in her belly. His arms are about her. He rises, slowly. His head slides upward, slowly. He reaches her lips, they kiss, passionately*]

69

STAN [*finally*] : Is that a kiss?

FRAN: You kiss marvellously—

STAN: What do you think of that kiss?

FRAN: I've never been kissed so marvellously—

STAN: How are you?

FRAN: I'm fine. Just fine. Stan—

STAN: That sure was some feast, Fran—

FRAN: Like it?

STAN: Almost as much as I like you, Fran—

FRAN: Ummmmm. Stan—

STAN: Let's dance, Fran—

FRAN: Love to, Stan . . .

[*They dance to same tune as we heard before, 'Moonlight Serenade'*]

FRAN: Ummmmm.

STAN: Hmmmmm.

FRAN: What a Stan . . .

STAN: My Fran . . .

FRAN: Did you really fall down those stairs, my Stan?

STAN: All the way down, Fran—

FRAN: And they took you to the hospital, Stanny Stan—?

STAN: Stitches, I don't know how many, Fran—

FRAN: I didn't think you were fooling, Stan—

STAN: I don't fool around, Fran—

FRAN: How's your work? Have you tried to do any work, Stan?

STAN: How can I work around here, Fran? A guy like that, on my back, I gotta get out of here, Fran—

FRAN: You're very talented. You have a great deal of talent. I would just love to see you work again—

STAN: Once I get out of here—

FRAN: That's a wonderful thing on your easel in there. I dusted it off—you know, like I always do—

STAN: I'll bet it looks great in there—spic and span—sparkling in there—

FRAN: Want to see?

STAN: Not just now, Fran—

FRAN: You always say that, Stan—

STAN: I have to make a new start—a break—I can't go back to those things—they're—part of this place—[*pause*] Once I get out of here—[*pause*] A clean break—[*pause*] I've been dragged down so far— [*pause*] I'm down so far [*pause*] I'm under the floorboards . . .

FRAN: I'll bet a very few strokes would finish it—

STAN: I'd put my fist through it—

FRAN: Let's go in there—

STAN: I'd never make it in there—

FRAN: It's a few steps. Just a very few steps—did you know that?

STAN: You counted them last time—

FRAN: Not last time—

STAN: The time before last time—

FRAN: That time—

STAN: I'd fall over. I'd be dead. Kaput. The end of everything—

FRAN: Try it—

[*Silence*]

STAN: I'm not going to try it.

[*Silence*]

FRAN: He sleeps like a baby—

STAN: How long you staying?

FRAN: How long do you want me to?

STAN: Take me with you—

FRAN: You want to come with me?

STAN: Are you going back? Did you say that? Did I hear you say that, Fran?

FRAN: I didn't say that, Stan—

STAN: Let's do that. Take off. Hit the road. Let's take off, Fran. Get me out of here.

FRAN: Do you want to get out of here?

STAN: I've had enough. The show's over. It's all over now. He can't hold me down anymore. I've had enough of his holding me under the floor.

FRAN: What about him, Stan?

[*Silence*]

FRAN: He doesn't even have that—man to go to anymore. [*pause*] Does he? [*pause*] Stan?

STAN: Frig him, Fran—

FRAN: *Stan!*

STAN: I'm sorry, Fran. Geez I'm sorry, Fran. That's another reason I gotta get out of here. See how I talk, Fran? Even in

front of you, in your arms, here, dancing with honey you—
Fran—I'll learn to talk like a human being again—not—like
that guy's little friend—[*pause*] His friend—[*pause*] I don't
give a damn about him anymore, Fran—Look what he's
made of my life, turned me into—Who could see better than
you, Fran? [*long pause*] I'd love to go back to that little
town in Connecticut with you, Fran—[*pause*] That would
be great—[*pause*] That great little town—[*pause*] that town
—[*pause*] You—

FRAN [*after a pause*] : I'm from Massachusetts, Stan—

STAN: I meant that, Massachusetts, Fran—one of those great
little towns in that great—[*pause*] little State—[*pause*] one
of those great little New England States—[*pause*] Those
States—[*pause*] What a State—[*pause*] Don't you really
have anything on under the slip, Fran?

FRAN: No, Stan—

STAN: That's where History was made. It's the backbone of
American History up there, Fran, and you sure are lucky to
come from there. I'd be proud to go up there. You and me.
There. Bunker Hill. The Liberty Bell—

FRAN: That's in Philadelphia, Stan—

STAN: I come from the other end of the State—

FRAN: Pennsylvania's a wonderful State—

STAN: What a State. I grew up in that State. I was born and
brought up in that terrific State. High School. Did you really
teach school, Fran?

FRAN: Yes, Stan—

STAN: What a teacher you must have been, Fran. How are jobs
in Massachusetts, plenty of openings, Fran? If you want to,
you could teach for a while, till I make my name—I'm going
to turn out the work—What a load of work—I'll work and
work—If you want to you can—I don't mind. I won't stand
in your way. I'll bet the High Schools are terrific there—I can
smell that good smell of a school, Fran—I can smell the class-
rooms—I had some terrific teachers, Fran—I was in love with
quite a few—they were goddesses to me—

FRAN: You must have been fun to teach—

STAN: I did my best. I worshipped those teachers. I mean, those
I was in love with. I could never think of them—I never

thought of them—in—dirty ways. [*pause*] His ways [*pause*]
They were supreme things, super human beings. I couldn't
picture them having things—[*pause*] organs—[*pause*] Those
things—[*pause*] underneath their dresses, Fran—[*pause*]
That's right—[*pause*] I couldn't. [*pause*] They were above
that. [*pause*] All that—
[*Silence*] [*The music is now Harry James' version of 'You
Made Me Love You'*]

FRAN: Like that one, Stan?

STAN: I love it, Fran.

FRAN: It's a lovely one, Stan—

STAN: Since the first time I heard it, I loved it. In the juke joint
we danced to it. I was a real romantic kid, when I could get up
the nerve to ask one of those dreamboats to dance with me.
I danced and danced to it. What peaches went to our high
school. You must have been a real peach in your high school
—Fran—a real one—Were you a cheerleader?

FRAN: Yes I was, Stan—

STAN: I loved the cheerleaders. They inspired our team on to
victory. Victory after victory—

FRAN: Were you on the team, Stan?

STAN: I was in the band—

FRAN: You were?

STAN: You must have been some cheerleader—

FRAN: I didn't know you were a musician!

STAN: I played the cymbals—

FRAN: Oh how cute! The cymbals—

STAN: I bashed away at those cymbals—

FRAN: We had such fun with the band. We used to travel on the
same bus to the games, Stan.

STAN: What games I saw, Fran! We were State Champions.
Most of the boys on the team got Scholarships—Penn State,
Notre Dame, Michigan—the best, Fran—Nothing but the
best—for them—Fran—

FRAN: I loved the games—

STAN: I loved the ones most of all at night. The night games.
We played a few of those, Fran—

FRAN: I know what you mean, Stan—

STAN: Something—there was something—special about them, right, Fran?

FRAN: That's right, Stan—

STAN: The teams lined up—the kickoff—

FRAN: What a moment that was!

STAN: The kickoff—

[*Silence*]

STAN: I wanted to go out for the team. I couldn't get permission. It was Mom. She wouldn't give permission. [*pause*] She wouldn't let Pop give his permission—

FRAN: Ah, what a shame, Stan—

STAN: I would have been great. Terrific. I could bob and weave, fake, change pace, run like a rabbit.

FRAN: I would have loved cheering you!

STAN: I just played intermural—touch football. [*pause*] I played that, anyhow. [*pause*] They couldn't stop me from playing that, anyhow.

FRAN: Were you terrific?

STAN: Terrific. Coach Ludnik—the football coach—used to spot me—we played our games on the field next to where the team was practising—anyway, he would have heard about me— [*pause*] All about me—[*pause*] He'd come up to me, he'd talk to me—

[*Silence*]

FRAN: What did he say, Stan?

STAN: What a half-back you'd make, Stan.

FRAN: You'd have made a great one, Stan.

STAN: I tried talking to your old man, Stan—

FRAN: Did he try your Mom, Stan?

[*Silence*]

STAN: They'd just—[*pause*] They would have just—[*pause*] Had to shake me loose—

FRAN: I can see you, Stan—

STAN: It was the speed—and the fantastic—change of pace—

FRAN: I'd have turned cartwheels—the cheering would have been heard miles away—

STAN: Away—

FRAN: That far away—

STAN: Fran—

FRAN: Oh my Stan—
[*He kisses her. A long kiss there. The record changes. Now it is. 'It's Been A Long Long Time', again Harry James.*]
STAN [*finally*]: That guy—he's never even—[*pause*] I don't think he's ever even—seen a football game.
FRAN: Really, Stan?
STAN: Hasn't he—doesn't he—[*pause*] What does he say to you, Fran?
FRAN: He doesn't really talk an awful lot, Stan—
[*Silence*]
STAN: Memorial Day—Fourth of July parades—[*pause*] the parades—[*pause*] Remember them, Fran?
FRAN: Do I, Stan—
STAN: Pop was the borough fire-truck driver—I rode on the truck with him—in the parades—when I was small—
FRAN: Did you, Stan?
STAN: What's greater than those small town parades?
FRAN: I loved them, Stan—
STAN: The bands—
FRAN: We walked right behind the majorettes, Stan—
STAN: The American Legion, the National Guard—all the local boys with the National Guard—The kids on their decorated up bikes—all the decorations—red—white—blue—everywhere—
FRAN: I loved those parades!
[*Silence*]
STAN: What a girl—you're a girl—I've never known such a girl—
FRAN: Stan—
[*They kiss. Another long one*]
STAN: What does he kiss like, Fran?
FRAN: You kiss divinely, Stan—
STAN: He doesn't kiss like that, does he, Fran?
FRAN: What a man . . .
[*Another kissing session*]
STAN: And I went to Korea. [*pause*] Fran.
FRAN: Stanny Stan—
STAN: It was there—That's where I learned—[*pause*] I found out I was an artist, Fran—

FRAN: You still are, Stan—

STAN: Up in those hills—around those hills—[*pause*] I started drawing—during the breaks—

FRAN: You always were good at drawing, weren't you, Stan—

STAN: I went to art school—when I came back—

FRAN: You turned a lot of those drawings into paintings, Stan—
[*Silence*]

STAN: The GI Bill paid my way—

FRAN: They recognized your talent, Stan—

STAN: I got this Scholarship—

FRAN: Travelling—

STAN: This Travelling Scholarship, Fran—
[*Silence*]

STAN: Here I am.

FRAN: Step into the studio with me—

STAN: Take me out of here, Fran—

FRAN: Do you want to go, Stan?

STAN: Massachusetts. You, me. *Fran.*
[*Silence*]

FRAN: I think you mean it, Stan.

STAN: If I ever meant anything in my life, Fran—

FRAN: You wouldn't consider—New Jersey—Stan?

STAN: You know New Jersey, Fran?

FRAN: I went to Rutgers for a while. I took my degree in Library Science there. Didn't I ever tell you that, my Stanny Stan?

STAN: It's a complete surprise, Fran—

FRAN: I'm a Librarian as well as a Teacher, my Stan—

STAN: What a surprise, honey Fran—

FRAN: New Jersey—

STAN: I was stationed there a while before—when I first went in—I took my basic at Dix—you know Fort Dix—

FRAN: Asbury Park—

STAN: You know Asbury Park? No kidding, Fran?

FRAN: I loved the place—

STAN: I spent a lot of time there!

FRAN: The ocean. [*dreamily*] The Jersey shore and the ocean. [*pause*] [*She clings, eyes closed, to* STAN, *as they dance, slowly*] I'm there, all over again. The dance hall—at the end of the jetty—jutting right out into the ocean—

76

STAN: I know that dance hall!

FRAN [*as above*]: Nothing all around but the ocean . . . The sounds of the ocean . . . The music . . .

STAN: Christ what music!

[*Silence*]

STAN [*very mildly*]: The music—

FRAN: I loved Ralph Marterie—

STAN: I heard him—!

FRAN: Looking out as you danced—all around—the night— and—the white caps of the sea—breaking—waves—far off—

STAN: Lights of a ship, far off—

FRAN: On the horizon—

STAN: Moving—

FRAN: I loved the place—

STAN: I love you—

FRAN: I love you, Stan—

STAN: Let's go, Fran—

FRAN: Jersey?

STAN: Anywhere, I don't care, *anywhere with you*—Jersey— sure—

FRAN: I'd get a job as a Teacher-Librarian—

STAN: One of those terrific high schools there—

FRAN: They have a wonderful high school system there, Stan—

STAN: Quite a few of my buddies in Korea were from there—

FRAN: Or would you rather I did Social Work?

[*Silence*]

STAN: You're a Social Worker too, Fran?

FRAN: I took my M.A. in Social Work from Washington U—St. Louis, Stan.

[*Silence*]

STAN: I passed through that Air Base there—what's the name of it—on my way back from Korea, Fran—

FRAN: Did you?

STAN: Scott Air Force Base—that was it, Fran—

FRAN: Oh yes—we did some field work once near there—what's the name of the town near there—?

STAN: Belleville, Fran?

FRAN: That was it—

STAN: Belleville—

77

FRAN: That's it, Stan—

STAN: I didn't know you were a Social Worker, Fran—
[*Silence*]

STAN: I see you more—as a Teacher, Fran—

FRAN: I'll do that—I don't mind, Stan—

STAN: Let's hit the road, Fran—

FRAN: Don't you really have a passport, my Stan?

STAN: Uh uh, Fran—

FRAN: We'll have to go to the Embassy. We'll explain everything to them, there at the Embassy. They're very nice.
They'd understand. Don't worry about that, Stan—

STAN: They wouldn't shaft an ex-GI—

FRAN: An Official Travelling Scholarship winner—

STAN: That's right—

FRAN: Let me explain everything to them—

STAN: You can do it, Fran—

FRAN: I'll see one of those nice Vice-Consuls there—
[*Silence*]

STAN: Right, Fran—
[*Silence*]

STAN: You'll explain—everything—?
[*She lifts her head a moment, away from him. Looks over at
the sleeping form of* DAN *a moment.*]

FRAN: I'll find him—a new man to go to.
[*Silence*]

FRAN: We can't go, really, till I've done that—my Stan—

STAN: Frig him, Fran—

FRAN: *Please* don't Stan—

STAN: We're not his guardian angels, hon—Fran—

FRAN: We can't walk off and leave him—like that—[*pause*] You
wouldn't really want to do that—[*pause*] Would you, Stan?

STAN: Yeh, Fran.

FRAN: He's been—awfully good to you, my Stan—

STAN: Fran! Don't kid me around, Fran—

FRAN: Ummm—my lover—love—Stanny Stan—

STAN: That guy's nothing but poison, Fran—He poisoned my
life—my whole life—I'd have been finished—kaput—if it
hadn't been for you—lucky thing you showed up—lucky *for*
me—Fran—

78

FRAN: Am I your first love, Stan?

STAN: Let's just—take off—

FRAN: It won't take me long—to find him a man—

STAN: You'd have to check it out with his old man—

FRAN: I'd do that—

STAN: We'd be here one hell of a time!

FRAN: Not all—that time—

STAN: I don't even know where he's from—

FRAN: He's mentioned several places—

STAN: Hawaii—Detroit—Louisiana even—

FRAN: He's from someplace—

STAN: Some place—

FRAN: *Oh Stan*—

STAN: *Fran*—

FRAN: *We'll go*—

STAN: *Oh Hon*—

FRAN: *Go*—

STAN: *Let's go*—

[*They are in the vicinity of* STAN's *bed. They start a long, passionate kiss. They are falling towards the bed. Just as they fall there is a sudden movement and a long, loud cry from* DAN. *The cry sounds like* WOOOOHOWWWWOHH! *The movement carries* DAN *off the bed and he lands on the floor with a thump. He is flat on his back, eyes closed, his arms spread apart.* STAN & FRAN *are not slightly affected by all this. They seem utterly unaware of it. They continue their long kiss, they are on the bed . . .*]

FADEOUT

SCENE: *The same, later.* DAN *is still on the floor.* STAN & FRAN *are on the bed, cooing, happy and satisfied, embraced.*

FRAN: What a man—

STAN: Was it ever like that in the Libraries—the High Schools—what about Rutgers, Fran?

FRAN: Never. Never never. *Stan.*

STAN: Where'd they ever make you, Fran?

FRAN: You're a woman's man—

STAN: Am I your only man?

FRAN: Always, Stan—

STAN: You're mine, Fran—

FRAN: Yes, Stan—

STAN: All mine—

FRAN: Stan—

[*They murmur and pet, she caresses his face, he kisses her hand*]

STAN: You'll love it in Pennsylvania, Fran—

FRAN: We're going to Jersey, my Stan—

STAN: There's a great State if there ever was one, Fran—

FRAN: You'll love it, Stan—

STAN: Are we hopping a plane back? Pan American? I hear the 707 is terrific—six or seven hours—isn't it?

FRAN: Are you in a hurry?

STAN: As long as I'm with you I'm not worried—

FRAN: We can go by boat.

STAN: Yeh? Boat?

FRAN: A nice, slow trip on the boat—

STAN: That sounds great—a great idea, Fran—

FRAN: The 'United States'—

STAN: What a boat—

FRAN: A snug little cabin—

STAN: For two—

FRAN: On the boat—

STAN: A stroll on the deck at night . . .

FRAN: Ummmm—

STAN: Hmmmm . . .

[*They continue this post-love-play. Then from* DAN, *barely audible, we hear one word: 'Fran . . .' It is more like a moan. She lifts her head and looks. She sees him, flat on his back, arms spread, eyes closed. He hasn't moved. He makes no move. She raises herself, rests on her elbow—*]

FRAN: Dan!

[*No response,* STAN *moves, raises himself, takes a look. He says nothing . . .*]

FRAN: You've fallen out of bed, Dan—

[*She rises, she is going over to him*]

STAN: Don't go near him, Fran—

FRAN [*near* DAN, *stooping to him*]: Are you alright, Dan?

[*pause*] How did you ever fall out of bed, my big man? [*She bends closer, puts her ear to his nostrils*] I can hear your breath—you're alright—

STAN: Don't touch him, Fran—

FRAN: Are you asleep? Still asleep? You've slept a long long time—[*She passes her hand over his face*]

STAN: What are you doing, Fran—

DAN: I can't see you, Fran—

FRAN: Open your eyes, my Dan—

DAN: They're sealed tight. I can't get them open, Fran—

FRAN: Try—just try—Dan—[*she passes her hand tenderly over his eyes*]

DAN: That's your hand, isn't it, Fran? Nobody's pulling anything over on me, are they, Fran? I'd know your hands from anybody's, anybody in the whole wide world, there's not a hand that feels like that to me in the world, Fran. Where would there be such a hand? Touch my hands—

FRAN: Can't you move your hands?

DAN: I can't move anything, Fran. Not one damn thing, what the hell's happened to me?

STAN: Get away from him, Fran—

DAN: What's that voice? I hear some other voice. What is that crappy Ozark voice? Is that some crappy Alabama voice? Is that creep here? That crappy creep—still here? What's he still doing here? Fran, I heard you say—was I dreaming or did I hear you say—you're going away with him? Back to the States, on a boat, a dreamboat of a boat—With Him? Christ, Fran. Touch my hands, Fran. Yeh. That's it. Yahhh, Fran. I was dreaming I was having one screwy screwed up dream of a dream there, wasn't I, Fran? You wouldn't step one foot outside the door with a capocatz like that, would you, Fran? A commie-killer, nigger-baiting Mississippi shnit like him, you wouldn't even dream of doing a friggen thing like that—That—don't kid me, Fran! Ever put your fist through a radio? TV set? How about newspapers? What do you think of the switched-on ever-jerking-off London newspapers then, Fran? How high will skirts go? You'll never walk in here flapping them two inches below your butt—that butt—don't take your hands away, Fran— Will you, Fran? Hon Fran!

Fran! You hon! My hon! Mine! Fran!

FRAN: Dan—

DAN: What the hell were you doing while I was sleeping, Fran? Was that pavement artist friggen around with you, Fran? What was he trying to do to you? You still have that slip on, Fran? Only the slip? Fran? Christ! If I could move! Fran! Did he pledge allegiance to the flag for you, Fran? He knows that by heart, it's printed on his red-white-and-blue heart there, Fran. It's the first thing they taught him, at that crappy school, that school . . . Fran. Know anything about those Pennsy schools? Did I hear you say you taught school? Fran —where was that school? You shoulduv seen the school I went to in Vermont! What a school! My school! Vermont! That's one of those crappy New England States. You wouldn't frig around in those states, any of those crappy states would you, Fran? Not a nice wholesome girl from Indiana like you! There's a State! The wide open plains! The plains! What a State! I knew right away the first time I laid eyes on you you were from that State! Back Home In Indiana! There's a place you can really go home to! Are there any nigs there? Many nigs there? Fran? Did you know his old man was one? Look at his nose, Fran. That's it. The nose, take a good look at that nig nose, Fran! What's your view on a multi-racial society, Fran? *Would you marry one?* That's the crucial question, the test, the heart of the matter, the acid test. That's What The Hell It's All About, Fran! That's the question you have to ask yourself, over and over again, Fran! What the hell's it got to do with economic opportunity, school integration, job equality, human rights—all that bullshit, Fran! Not one friggen thing! Hot air! For the birds! Crap! Pure crapulent crap! Fran! *Would you?*

FRAN: Dan—

DAN: I guess a pig like you might, though! It's the pigs just like you in this world that go in for that kind of thing, don't worry, I know, gal! And this sonuvabitch of a place is loaded with you! Thousands—millions—Just Like You! That's why this goddam government here is smart, sharp and smart, yeh man, they don't let too many of them in anymore! They know the score! Let them in and a couple dozen years—may-

be more—you'd have a nig on the throne! How'd you like
that? Wouldn't that just frig you flat? The Throne! It's guys
like that creep who keep them out though. That piece of nig-
ger-hating southern shit! You know! Know what they do to
niggers where he comes from, Fran? Know what kind of inhuman and barbarous crimes they get away with down there,
Fran? Ask him! He knows! He'll be glad to spill the beans,
tell you all about it, the works, he's proud as hell of it, all of it,
he'd tell the whole world about it—on *TV*, *yeh*, Fran! You
really think you can get a passport for him? No kidding,
Fran, is that what you're thinking you're gonna be able to
do? Gal! Pal! The only passport they'll hand him down
there is one back to the sidewalk! They know all about
him, Fran! He collected all the dough from that Travelling
Painting Whatever-the-frig-it-was-Scholarship and never did
one goddam piece of painting at all that anyone knows about,
Fran! He calls the Ambassador in the middle of the night—
Night after Night! You oughta hear one of those little gems,
Fran! Is he even *American*, Fran? What kind of an accent
is that anyhow, Fran? To me it sounds like a Frenchy-
German-Slovakian-Russian-Jewish accent to me, if you ask
me anything about it at all, Fran! Look at that nose! What
a nose! What would you say? Is that or is that not a typical
Jewish nose? Who is this schmoz? What's his act? What's
he pulling off? What's he take us all for? Goffs? Are we just
two goffs? Who's he work for? *The Nose!* Just Take A
Look At That Nose!

[*Silence*]

STAN [*quietly, yet urgently*]: Let's go, Fran—

D'AN: Where the hell you think you're going, man? How come
you're still hanging around? What the hell are you doing here,
man? This is your day, you told me that, you were singing
songs to me early this morning about it— Are You Still
Around? How much longer you gonna frig around? Did you
get there? How was it getting there? How did things look
out there? When were you last out there? See those short
skirts? Whaddaya think of those short skirts? Think I was
kidding around or something, man? Would I kid you? Name
one thing I ever kidded you around about, man! How was

the ride? Catch the 28? Did you get it out there, like I told
you to, like I drew it out on the map for you? Was I right?
Is the stop twenty-five yards from the light? Right? How was
the ride? Any nigs on the damn ride? Driver and conductor
nigs? There's a pile of them on that route! Did you get the
right change? Pull one over on you? You let a damn nig
pull one over on you? Did some sonuvabitch of a black
bastard nig pull one over on you? You still wearing that
bandage, man? Whud the boy do, kick you in the head?
What a way to start! Christ! Smart! Ain't you smart! How'd
it happen, man? Cross him right at the start? I told you,
didn't I tell you, don't you remember me telling you: play it
cool, Keerist, work your way in slow, easy, nice and cool—
don't let him have it all at once—at the start! He's got a hell
of a temper, Bart! Bart! How are things, Bart? Think you'll
ever make it back to sunny California there, Bart? Who the
hell are you kidding with that phoney bandage anyhow,
Clark? Take it off! Quit playing around! My boy wouldn't
kick anybody in the head—*nobody*—not even a nigger-loving
fart! His heart's gold! Pure gold! My old man's gold! Kindness! *There's* human kindness! Fran—where is he now?
Has he moved around? Is he on the bed? On a chair? Is he
on the floor, Fran? Get him off the floor, he's had one hell
of a kick in the head! How many stitches, man? The Limey
doctors sew you up o.k.? They've got this friggen socialized
medicine over here, you know— It's all free except our headshrinker—didn't you know that, man? You didn't let them
frig you out of a couple of dollars at that goddam hospital,
did you, man? *How dumb can you get?* Oh Man!

STAN: C'mon, Fran—

DAN [*quietly*]: Nothing's ever like the original, Fran. What you
were a minute ago is changed. What you'll be five years from
now—what a hell of a change. Change, Change. Grab the
moment while you can. Fixate on the moment, stay with it,
don't let it out of your hands. Fran. Fran . . . Only the
moment, Fran . . .

FRAN [*very tenderly*]: Shall we try getting you back on the
bed?

DAN: This is my bed. I like my bed. Where is he, Fran?

STAN: Here, man—

DAN: The All-American . . . lad . . .

FRAN: It would be much better—on the bed, my Dan—

DAN: Whatuv you got on, Fran?

FRAN: Nothing you couldn't take off, Dan—

DAN: I can't move at all, Fran—

STAN: What are you doing, Fran?

DAN: What's that crap voice, Fran?

FRAN: Dan, Dan—[*soothing him*]

DAN: Has he been handing you more crap about Korea, Fran? That little Police Action, Fran? Why the hell isn't he in Vietnam? He's in the Reserves, he could volunteer anytime, there's a few million Vietnamese to burn off the map! You want Indiana infiltrated by them? They'd hit California and work their way in from there. They're smart. Sharp. They'd spread all over the Ozarks, Fran. His home territory, while he sits on his ass! That's the kind of a Defender of Freedom he is! I don't think he was in Korea at all! This guy's a yellow lying bastard—that's all! Does he know one end of a Garand Special Springfield Adapted M-4 Quick Firing Shoulder Model Carbine Rifle from the other? What about Napalm? Has he seen companies of Chinese Commie Troops fried by it? What has he seen? This guy's crap! A phoney! Pure Crap! Living off me now for Christ knows how many years! I can't even count the years! Know what he told me one day? One of the first goddam things he ever told me Christ knows how long ago when I first had the unlucky experience of bumping into this creep at that party some of my friends were throwing, Fran? I used to have plenty of friends! He said he saw a sign outside a church—A Church, Fran!— he said the sign said, 'People are lonely because they build walls instead of bridges'. Wham! Before you knew it he was in. He had moved in. I felt sorry for the guy. This stupid half-assed church-sign-reading guy! He doesn't know a fly from a flea! He's let this place get infested with fleas! They crawl in my mouth—what a treat— He doesn't give a frig! Not one frig! He'd dance a jig! That's the way they are, down there where he comes from, that's what they are—Kentucky Jigs! The kid—Kid Jig! Know what he said to me one day, Fran?

It wasn't too long ago, he was laying on his ass in that bed, as usual, the friggen jig, he said to me, 'Know what Uncle Sam ought to do with all those troops in Vietnam?' Get this, Fran—'Send them down to South Africa, clean that place up.' The Commie Rat! The Rat! Where do they make such rats? He deserves the electric chair! Would I pull the switch! Me and LBJ, together, we'd take care of the rat! It ought to be public, the thing oughta be on TV, top-viewing hour! What a treat! Whose son is this jig? He'd have all those nice clean-cut South Africans co-mingling with his fellow jigs! Those goddam animals! Those pigs! They've solved the problem down there. We should take lessons from them. Look at the mess we're in! It's gonna get worse, wait and see! See if some jig isn't sitting in that White House some day! What a day! And all on account of the fact that his whore of an old lady married a jig! Fran, you're fooling around with a half-nig!

FRAN: Shall we get on the bed—?

DAN [*quietly*]: Who are you, Fran? Ever since I met you at that 28 bus stop I've been asking myself that. Are you a commie agent, Fran? Sent here to demoralize break and deprave two all-American lads? Who sent you, Fran? Was that an accident meeting like that? Who planted you there? What do you think of American Civilization, Fran? Is it contemptible? Beneath contempt? Is it near the end? Is it immutable and absolutely eternal, Fran? Is the proposition one designed to promote circular arguments otherwise doomed to obscure corners of dingy academic cloisters somewhere? Will the Adman triumph? What about cancer? Is it built-in, triggered off by our self-destructiveness? Is Man industrial? Where did you those shanks? The flanks? It's the flanks! Fran!

FRAN: Touch my flanks—

DAN [*remaining utterly still*] [*Quietly*]: I've never seen such flanks. Goddess flanks. What flanks. [*pause*] What about full production? [*pause*] How compatible—[*pause*] Does it relate—[*pause*] What is its relation—[*Silence*]

[*His eyes open. He sees* FRAN. *He stares at* FRAN.]

DAN: Did I hear you say you were a cheerleader, Fran? [*pause*]

86

One of those—sexy cheerleaders—Fran? What were—your colors? [*pause*] How good—is your apple pie? [*pause*] Last time—you made cherry pie— Did I hear you say—[*pause*] Did you say—[*pause*] Are you taking off with this guy?

FRAN: You have such lovely eyes—

DAN: Will you pose for the guy?

FRAN: Shall I kiss those eyes?

DAN: Bend down—give me a big kiss—Fran—

FRAN [*bending toward him*]: My Dan—

DAN: What a set— That set— When are you taking off with the guy?

FRAN: I— [*Her face very near his*]

DAN [*suddenly, violently*]: YOU PIG! THAT GUY! [*He comes to to life, grabs her around the neck with both hands, just as she is about to kiss him, he holds her in a throttling grip, she gasps, tries to free herself.* STAN *jumps up from the bed, lunges toward them*]

STAN: Let Go, Man!

DAN: *She's Mine, Man!*

STAN: *Get Your Goddamn Hands Off Her, Man!*

DAN: ALL MINE, MAN!

[*They struggle violently, but* STAN *does not seem able to break* DAN's *iron grip around* FRAN's *throat. They roll about the floor. Suddenly,* STAN *does not seem to be trying to break the grip. In fact, his hands are gradually replacing* DAN's *around her throat.*]

DAN: *What The Hell Are You Doing, Man?*

[STAN *is choking the last signs of life out of* FRAN]

DAN: *You Murdering Fug! You Fug! Mother-fug!*

[*At last, all is still,* STAN *relaxes his grip and* FRAN *falls back, lifeless, on the floor. They stare at her.*]

DAN: *What a fug.*

[*Silence. They continue staring at her. At last,* DAN *slowly rises, heads for his bed. He lies on it.*]

DAN [*very quietly, far away*]: That hon. [*pause*] That honey hon. [*pause*] Saint hon. [*pause*] That golden hon. [*pause*] What a hon. [*pause*] The set on that hon. [*pause*] Murdered. [*pause*] Hon. [*pause*] You murdered that hon . . . [*Silence*]

87

[STAN *finally moves. He is like a ghost. He stands up, some-how. He turns from* FRAN, *finally, slowly, somehow. He stares at* DAN. *His face contorts. His hands move, his fists clench. It looks like he will cry out. There may be another murder. A most piercing cry is about to come out. It doesn't. There is no murder. He goes limp again. He is a ghost, heading for his bed. He lies down on his bed. Finally.*]

DAN [*as above*]: That lovin—hon—[*pause*] My hon—[*pause*] *How could you murder that hon*—

    [*Silence*] [*It is growing dark*]

STAN: She was gonna bring a calendar—

DAN: Next time—

    [*Silence*]

STAN: It's getting cold—

DAN: All the windows are open—

STAN: I'm cold—

DAN: She left all the windows open—

    [*Silence*]

STAN: What are we going to do with her, man?

    [*Silence*]

DAN [*finally, very quietly*]: We'll put her in the studio, man.

    [*Silence*]

STAN: The studio?

DAN: In the morning, man . . .

    [*Silence*]

DAN: First thing in the morning . . . man . . .

    [*Silence*]

STAN: You asleep?

DAN: Little shuteye, man . . .

STAN: Can you sleep?

    [*Silence*]

STAN: Who was she, Dan?

DAN: She was always around.

STAN: Did she work for your old man?

DAN: The pig. Always around.

STAN: Was she from the Embassy, man?

DAN: Was that it?

    [*Silence*]

STAN: What a pig—

DAN: Oh man—
STAN: The pig—
  [*Silence*]
STAN: Christ it's cold—
DAN: I'm cold—
STAN: I'm turning ice-cold—
  [*Silence*]
STAN: The Bomb—
DAN: Those mother-fugs—
STAN: Their Bombs . . .
  [*Silence. It is dark now.*]
DAN [*far away*]: Why do the petals fall off?

CURTAIN

THE ROW

CHARACTERS

Dan Bowman
Longfield
The Warden, His Wife, Their Son
Joe Rachman
Jake Laverne
Romeo
Dudley
Marlowe
Bronski
Roper
Harpo
Officer in Charge ['*The General*']
Various Guards, the Gun Guard
Witnesses, Chaplain, Solomon

THE CELLS
at beginning of the play

Laverne	Romeo	Dudley	Rachman	Bowman
☐	☐	☐	☐	☐

Left

	Bronski	Marlowe	Roper	Unoccupied
	☐	☐	☐	☐

Right

Others offstage complete *The Row*

THE ROW

PART ONE

SCENE: *Death Row, a cell block for condemned men in a large, humanely administered, State Prison, somewhere in the U.S.A. The cells are suspended above the stage, they run from left to right and there are nine of them in sight. All but the last one on the right are occupied. There are a total of twenty-four on The Row. The others are offstage, out of our line of sight. Each cell is approximately 5 feet by 10 feet, and equipped with a bunk, a table, a stool, a washbasin. There are headsets hanging near the bunks. These carry radio programs. A lightbulb covered by a conical shade hangs in each cell. Outside the cells, facing them and above them, is a catwalk, along which a gun guard constantly patrols, back and forth. In the corridor outside the cells lightbulbs burn twenty-four hours a day. There is an office at the Left end of the Row. This is for several Guards and the Officer in Charge. From it, they command a view of the entire Row. The only entrance is near the office. It consists of a large, heavy mesh cage. There is a heavy steel door, barred, at each of the two ends facing us. When someone enters or leaves the Row, one door at a time opens, electrically, one can hear the buzz. A gun guard sits in the cage. As the Curtain goes up, we see not only the Row, and its occupants, but also, below, at Stage level, Center: The Holding Cell, where the Condemned man spends his last twenty-four hours of life, and Right: The Gas Chamber, where the execution takes place. This Chamber is an octagonal, squat, half-glass-enclosed structure. In it are two straight metal chairs, with straps for legs and arms on them. The roof and floor are painted green.*

THE TIME: *The Present.*

For a few minutes, all described above is visible. Then, the Chamber and Holding Cell fade out, and we only see The Row itself.

It is early evening. A number of the condemned men are lying

*on their bunks, listening to the radio via their headsets. One or
two are writing, perhaps letters. One, at the end of the Row,
near the office,* JAKE LAVERNE *is strumming a guitar, singing
softly, cowboy tunes, and blues tunes, mostly. Three or four are
lying down, reading comic books, magazines. Two are sitting on
their bunks, just looking down at the floor, or around their
cells from time to time. One,* BRONSKI, *paces his cell ceaselessly,
those few short steps. And one,* DAN BOWMAN *is seated at the
table in his cell and he is typing. He is surrounded by papers,
books, documents. The cell looks like the cloister of a scholar, a
lawyer, or possibly an author. Bowman is tall, well-built,
a slightly stooping man of about thirty-three. His face is long
and bears the marks of a hard lifetime in it. He has brown hair.
He pauses now in his typing. He picks up one of the books and
looks through it. He finds what he wants and resumes typing.
Soon, he comes to the end of his paper and pulling it out of the
typewriter starts reading it over. As Bowman studies what he
has written, the man in the cell next to him,* RACHMAN, *who has
until now been lying on his bunk reading, rises, looks around,
and walks to the front of the cell. He turns slightly towards
Bowman's cell.*

RACHMAN: How's it going there, man?

BOWMAN [*looking up from his paper, turning toward Rachman's
cell*] : Not too bad. [pause] Not too bad, I guess.

RACHMAN [*with a little laugh*] : You don't want to guess. Not in
this place, man. [*pauses, jerks his head toward the office*]
Those guys don't guess. They never guess.

BOWMAN [*grinning wryly, putting his paper down*] : That's o.k.
[*pause*] Yeh, that's o.k. [*pause*] You have to have some
brains, some, anyhow, to guess. Hell, you ought to know
that. [*He pauses*] Besides, nobody pays them to guess. You
know how it is. Pay them for something, they'll do it. Anything. Anything at all, man. [*pause*] They'll do it.

[*The Gun Guard on the catwalk above and facing the
cells has stopped pacing. He is before Bowman's cell, he
looks down at him.*]

GUN GUARD: I heard that, Bowman.

BOWMAN [*Unruffled, calmly studying his paper again, raises his*

voice slightly, so as to be heard] : Glad to hear it. [*pauses*]
Glad your hearing's o.k., anyway. [*pauses*] I worry about
that. Sometimes I toss around all night here, worrying about
that.

[*There is some laughter along The Row. The Guards in the
Office and in the Cage perk up, on the alert.*]

GUN GUARD: Funny. Mighty funny. O.K., Bowman. Wait until
you're down there. We'll see how funny.

BOWMAN [*laconically*] : Tell me the story of your life. That
should be pretty funny.

[*There is more laughter on The Row. Some of the headsets come off now.*]

GUN GUARD: Don't push your luck, buddy. One of these days
you're gonna do that, old buddy.

[BOWMAN *turns in his cell now, looks up at the catwalk.*]

BOWMAN [*calmly*] : Are they working you overtime again,
Brilliant? [*He pauses, more laughter*] You better see the shop
steward or something, no kidding.

GUN GUARD: Don't push me—

OFFICER IN CHARGE [*from the Office, addressed to the Gun
Guard*] : Knock it off, Mac. No unnecessary talk with the
prisoners.

BOWMAN: That's on page 25 of the Code of Honor, Brilliant.
Got your copy? Read it. You can read, can't you, buddy?
[*More laughter*] Hell, you have a High School Diploma, you
should be able to read. Anyhow. [*More laughter*]

OFFICER IN CHARGE: Knock it off, Bowman.

[*There is no answer from Bowman. There is a long
moment's silence on The Row. Then, the sound of typing.
Bowman has started a new sheet. The Gun Guard resumes his pacing. The men return to their various activities,
silently, gloomily. Rachman, after standing at the bars a
few minutes longer, moves over toward the other side. He
addresses Dudley*]

RACHMAN: Hey, Dudley—

DUDLEY [*lying on his bunk*] : Yeh?

RACHMAN: Get off your ass. I wanta talk to you.

[DUDLEY, *slowly, rises and moves toward the cell door. He
leans against the wall there, near it.*]

95

RACHMAN: Where are you?

DUDLEY: Here.

RACHMAN: O.K. You can hear?

DUDLEY: I can always hear.

RACHMAN: Hey—

DUDLEY: Yeh?

RACHMAN [*after a pause*]: Gettin' much?

DUDLEY [*moaning*]: Oh, man, Oh, Christ, you're a wonder.

RACHMAN [*chuckling*]: Hey, don't go yet.

DUDLEY [*about to lie down again*]: That all you wanted?

RACHMAN: Hell, no. [*pause*] Wanted to ask you somethin'.

DUDLEY: You just did. You just asked me somethin'.

RACHMAN: Man, I mean it.

DUDLEY: O.K. [*pause*] What, then?

RACHMAN [*after a while, quietly*]: Who's next, man?

DUDLEY [*stiffening, growing pale, hesitating, looking around, a haunted, lost look in his eyes. He jerks his head toward a cell at the Right end of the Row, one of those out of our line of sight*] [*His voice slightly above a murmur*]: Solomon.

RACHMAN: When?

DUDLEY: Tomorrow.

RACHMAN: Ten?

DUDLEY: Yeh, ten.

[*There is silence*]

DUDLEY [*louder now*]: How come you never know? How come you keep askin' me?

RACHMAN [*after a while*]: I dunno. [*pause*] Maybe I don't wanta know. [*pause*] *Maybe one of these times it's gonna be mine, and I won't wanta know.* [*pause*] I hope when I ask you, you won't know. For once, maybe, you won't know. I'm hoping that.

DUDLEY: I won't forget. Don't worry.

RACHMAN: Who's worried? Take a look through that wall. *Am I worried?*

[DUDLEY *turns, faces the wall. It almost seems he can see through it. Trying to do so.*]

RACHMAN: *Worried?*

[DUDLEY *continues to stare at the wall, saying nothing.*]

[MARLOWE, *further down the line, to the right, two cells from* BOWMAN, *takes off his headset.*]

MARLOWE: Hey—Roper—

ROPER: Yeh?

MARLOWE: D'you hear that?

ROPER: Ain't listening.

MARLOWE: Man, you shoulda been.

ROPER: Why?

MARLOWE: That guy's gonna be joining us—

ROPER: Longfield?

MARLOWE: Yeh! Who else? Longfield.

ROPER: 'Who else'—there's plenty out there—who else—

MARLOWE: Don't jazz, man—

ROPER: Oh, yeh, Jazz. Oh, man.

MARLOWE: The Judge just lowered him. He'll be here.

[*The news starts spreading through The Row. It goes from cell to cell. The men are not excited, but certainly interested in the piece of news.* BOWMAN *just glances up, hears it, then returns to his work.*]

OFFICER IN CHARGE [*emerging from the Office*]: Keep it down, keep it down, you guys—

MARLOWE [*to the Officer*]: Hey, General—a millionaire on The Row! How about that? D'you hear? Who's gonna keep him down? You? He'll have you canned, man. Ha Ha, oh, man!

[*More along this line spreads through the cells, hits the 'General'.*]

THE GENERAL [*shouting*]: I said Keep It Down! [*They do quiet down now. The General walks up and down the Corridor. He shoots a glance into each cell. Most of the men ignore him. Bowman's typing continues. The General goes by, disappears Right, and later returns, having completed his tour of the Row. He re-enters his Office.*]

RACHMAN [*turning towards Bowman*]: Whadaya think about that, Dan?

BOWMAN [*checking over the sheet he has just pulled out of the typewriter*]: Be a nice change. [*pause*] Nice change, alright.

RACHMAN: Because he has dough?

BOWMAN: Sure, because he has dough.

RACHMAN: Yeh, but how about that, how about it, Dan—pushing the Judge to send him here! How about that! *That's a change!*

BOWMAN: How else could a guy like that get here?

RACHMAN [*after a pause*] [*giving a harsh laugh*]: Yeh. You're right there.

> [*He sits down on his bunk, thinks about it.*]
> [*There is silence on the Row now, except for Laverne's guitar and soft singing. Bowman is studying his papers.*]

BOWMAN [*reading over the papers, to himself*]: 'Petition for Writ of Certiorari . . . [*reads a few lines, his voice inaudible*] . . . Moral Imperative, i.e., Bowman *must* be executed, has been substituted for the legal judgement, i.e., is Bowman held in custody in violation of his rights under the United States Consititution? [*His voice becomes inaudible again, for a while*] . . . Justice Black, dissenting in Beaucharmis v. Illinois, stated, "Urges to do good have led to the burning of books and even to the burning of witches." These same urges led to the publicly threatened burning of one of my books by a Chief Assistant of the State Attorney General. Also, to the seizure by the Prison Warden of other manuscripts of mine, including one possibly worth thousands of dollars. Pauper status has been forced on me because I am not allowed to write a line for publication. The authorities have one aim: guilty or not, Bowman *must* be silenced, forever—a sacrifice to the clamor of the ignorant for gas chamber justice . . . [*again his voice lowers to an inaudible tone, for a while*] . . . The entire case should be reviewed by the Supreme Court. The State law mandatorily requires an automatic appeal to its Supreme Court in capital cases. This appeal is an extraordinary precaution taken by the Legislature to safeguard the rights of those upon whom the death penalty is imposed by the Trial Court . . . The Rules of the State Judicial Council declare that in a death penalty case, the *entire* record of the trial must be prepared and certified as true and correct by the court reporter who stenographically recorded the trial proceedings—[BOWMAN *pauses, makes a note*] . . . Yet, here, with the death of the court reporter, the record was not and could not be prepared in accordance with any existing law or rule governing appeals and particularly the mandatory appeal.

All State-established due process was thrown out and an ad hoc procedure was invented to prepare the record. This was by "human ingenuity", as ordered by the Trial Judge over Petitioner's vigorous objections. For one thing, it so happened that the court reporter in question wrote an old-fashioned type of shorthand mixed with his own invented type of shorthand *which no one else could decipher,* not properly, not without "human ingenuity". Petitioner was never allowed to defend against this so-called Transcript, or to be present, in fact, when it was created, settled, and approved—by "human ingenuity". His motions for a hearing at which he might challenge the validity of this so-called transcript were ignored or denied. Nevertheless, said "Transcript" was used as the basis by which the State Supreme Court affirmed the judgement of conviction imposing *two* sentences of death and fifteen sentences to prison' . . . [BOWMAN *pauses, looks around, grins wryly*] . . . How do you kill a man twice? It takes a Judge to figure that one . . . [*Returns to his reading*] . . . 'The Prosecution in the case had been given authority to select a "substitute reporter" to prepare the "record" of the trial proceedings, and, having selected his own uncle-in-law, kept this fact carefully concealed from the Trial Judge, the Petitioner, and the Reviewing court. Also the Prosecutor and this "substitute reporter", his uncle-in-law, had been given unlimited time to prepare the "record" and used his talks with detectives and key trial witnesses for the Prosecution *as a basis for reconstructing their testimony—* at the suggestion of the Prosecutor. The "reporter" had, out of court, let the Prosecutor check the rough draft of his transcription before it was copied in final form and he had been paid more than three times the statutory fee for his "services" ' . . . [*He reads on in subdued voice for a while*] . . . 'Further, just before I was sentenced to death—*twice*—when asked if there was any legal cause why judgement should not be pronounced, I answered, "The defendant is absolutely innocent of these charges". And I have stated this again and again, and I state it once again *Petitioner happens to be innocent of the crimes for which he was doomed'* . . . [*Bowman sits back, pauses, a short while*] . . . 'In any event, guilt or innocence is not the determining legal factor, for this Court has wisely and soundly repudiated the dangerous doctrine that it may withhold the protection of constitutional safeguards merely as it may deem the litigant guilty or innocent . . . [*Bowman pauses again, makes a note*] . . . The record show, furthermore, as a matter of law, a personal, continuing, and fixed bias on the part of the trial judge against Petitioner and in favor of the State . . . Ever since my arrest six years ago, I have begged for a lie-detector test on the question of my guilt or innocence but have never succeeded in being given one . . . I want to be questioned as to whether I committed the crimes for which I was doomed. If the test reveals that I am lying, when I flatly and unequivocally state I am not guilty of the crimes for which I am awaiting to die, then I shall abandon my six-year-old legal fight for survival' . . . [*Bowman pauses, looks around*] . . . 'Conclusions and Prayer for Writ— The Petitioner respectfully submits the court should hold . . . that the State Trial Court's order approving this challenged "record" must be set aside, as well as the State Supreme Court's affirmation of the Judgement of conviction based on it, and that a new determination of its validity and adequacy must be held in the District Superior Court, with Petitioner allowed to participate therein personally and effectively . . . that he is constitutionally entitled to the release of his unpublished novel and the right to use the products of his mind to defray the costs of litigation and to compensate counsel . . . in this way, once and for all, the case may be resolved decisively and fairly . . . [BOWMAN *pauses*] . . . To make a decision possible at this term of the Court and still give the Court ample time to deliberate, Petitioner and his counsel here stipulate that this petition may be treated as the brief for Petitioner normally filed following the granting of certiorari, and that the case may be decided upon it. Respondent's brief in opposition and answering brief by Petitioner, using the typewritten record. Counsel for Petitioner are prepared to argue the case immediately'. [*Bowman pauses. He picks up a pen and signs his name*] 'Respectfully submitted—Dan C. Bowman, Petitioner per se and Counsel . . .'

[BOWMAN *folds the papers now and puts them in a legal*

envelope. He does not seal the envelope.]
[*The coffee cart is making its rounds. It entered The Row via the Cage a short time ago. The inmate pushing it, Harpo, is an old, wiry little man. He has white hair, cropped quite short. He has been in prison most of his life, one knows, at once.*]
[*Bronski is stirring now. He gets up, starts his pacing again. Bowman rises, stretches, walks to the front of the cell.*]

BOWMAN: Yeh, Longfield. Some change.

RACHMAN [*up near the front of his cell*]: The guy must be one real nut, though.

BOWMAN [*reflecting, watching the progress of the coffee cart. Harpo pours coffee into tin cups and hands them through the bars. He is a friendly little fellow, and chats with everybody. He is not a Condemned man, of course, but a lifer*]: Not necessarily, Joe.

RACHMAN [*also following Harpo's progress*]: How do you figure that?

BOWMAN: He may be tired of living. That's all.

RACHMAN: Wait 'til he spends some time here. He'll snap outa that. Quick.

BOWMAN: That could be.

RACHMAN: What a life, huh?

BOWMAN: I'm not tired of it.

RACHMAN: We're butting a stone wall, Dan. Jesus Christ, what a wall.

BOWMAN: It takes a long time. Maybe it'll never happen. You have to keep butting, Joe. That's their biggest secret, making you convinced it's *just that*, butting a stone wall. That's the way they get you, down on your knees, on your back, flat, out, Joe. Hell, you ought to know that by now. It's that way with everything, *everything*, Joe.

[*Harpo is just a cell away now.*]

RACHMAN: Hell, you'll be here till you're ninety-five, Dan.

BOWMAN: That's o.k. I don't mind at all. Not at all, Joe.

[*Harpo is before* RACHMAN's *cell. They grin at one another.* HARPO *starts to fill a cup. The usual Guard is tagging along with him.*]

HARPO: The usual, son?

RACHMAN: Put a little more hootch in, Pop.

HARPO [*indicating the Guard*]: He won't let me.

RACHMAN: Tell the Warden on him.

HARPO: You mean that?

RACHMAN: Hell, yes. What's he think this is, jail or something?
[*The Guard remains impassive, a few feet from* HARPO, *looking on*]

RACHMAN: Don't he talk, Harpo? [*pause*] Hell, maybe he'll go home and knock off the old lady tonight. [*pause, he watches the Guard*] It could happen. Man, it could. [*pause*] Remember Jeremy? That wasn't too long ago. Remember? Maybe you heard, anyhow. [*pauses, takes the coffee, sips*] Was a Guard, right here. Here, buddy. Went home one night, carved up his old lady. Carved her up, man. They never did find all of her. [*pause*] He took the walk down there. [*pause*] D'you know that, big boy?
[*The Guard says nothing. He nods his head, slightly,* HARPO *starts to move on.*]

RACHMAN: So long, buddy. Give my regards to the Warden for me, old buddy.

HARPO [*grinning, glancing about*]: Be a good boy, son. There's a reward for all good boys here. Remember that, son.

RACHMAN [*grinning*]: How long you been in, anyhow, Pop?

HARPO [*Hesitating, thinking*]: I dunno, son. It was a long time ago. I don't rightly know anymore. This is my home, son.

RACHMAN: Home sweet home. Huh, Pop? [*pause*] Ever have the chance to get out?

HARPO [*moving*]: No use to me, son. No use at all. I'm an old man. This is my home, son.
[*Now he is before* BOWMAN's *cell.*]

HARPO [*grinning, greeting him*]: The usual, son?

BOWMAN: Little more of that rum tonight, Pop.

HARPO [*laughing, the Guard watching him*]: How are you, son? You and me's gonna set the world's record around here. Ever think of that, son?

BOWMAN: I'm not after that prize, Pop. [*pauses, takes the coffee, sips*] I just want to walk out of here, breathe some air, spread my wings. That's all, Pop. Some day. Maybe.

HARPO: Could happen. All the luck in the world to you, son. Just could happen. [*pause*] You won't try takin' me with you, now would you, Dan?

BOWMAN: Don't worry about that, Pop.

HARPO [*sincerely*]: I worry a lot about it. I'm gettin' pretty far on now. I worry one hell of a lot about that.

BOWMAN [*grinning*]: You look it.

HARPO: I don't you mean. That's what you mean. I know, Dan. [*pauses, looks around*] All the luck in the world, son.

BOWMAN: Wish I knew how you meant that, Pop.

[HARPO *stares, then laughs, he gets quite a laugh out of that*]

THE GUARD: Come on, Harpo.

[HARPO *immediately responds, starts to move off*]

HARPO: You're gonna get this Longfield fella. That oughta be something, son—

BOWMAN: Oh, yeh. Something. Oh, yeh, Pop. [*He pulls the legal envelope out of his shirt pocket. He hands it to Harpo.*]

BOWMAN: Here, pass that to the General, Pop.

HARPO [*grinning, taking the envelope, looking it over*] A record, son, a calsarn record, son—[*He moves off.*]

[BOWMAN *grins, sips his coffee.*]

[BOWMAN *sits on his bunk. The coffee cart ritual proceeds. HARPO has a little word with each man. The gun guard paces. The men smoke, drink their coffee. Suddenly, BRONSKI after taking a sip or two of the coffee, hurls the cup out of his cell into the corridor. It clatters on the corridor, its contents spill all over the floor.*]

BRONSKI [*yelling*]: Who wants your coffee? Who wants your goddam coffee? [*Banging on the cell door*] Let me outa here! Mother fuggers goddamn mothers, that's what I want! THAT'S ALL I WANT, MOTHER FUGS, NO COFFEE! [*Becomes more disturbed, the Guards move out of the Office, toward him. The Gun Guard ceases his pacing, looks down at him. The Row is frozen, and silent. The men listen, watch. The Guards move down the corridor. LAVERNE, though he holds his guitar, does not play it. BOWMAN sits on his bunk, as before, quietly. He has heard it all, many times, before. And more.*]

[BRONSKI *does not let up, he continues yelling, banging on*] *his cell door. The Guards reach him and stand before his cell, impassively. After a while,* BRONSKI *quiets down. The General then comes up to the cell door. He looks around, he looks at the coffee mug on the corridor floor.*]

THE GENERAL: You made quite a mess out here.

BRONSKI: Ram it! Why don't you ram it!

THE GENERAL: You better clean it up, I think.

BRONSKI: The fug, Buddy!

THE GENERAL [*giving a signal to the Guards, they unlock and swing open the cell door. They stand there, ready*]: Come on, Bronski.

[*Immediately,* BRONSKI'S *demeanor changes. He becomes quite frightened, cringing, almost. He backs into his cell. He seems to be looking for a way out of the cell.*]

THE GENERAL: I want you to clean it up, Bronski.

BRONSKI: Shut the door—lemee alone—

THE GENERAL: Come on, Bronski—

BRONSKI: I'll call the Warden! Shut the door! Shut the door, General!

[*The General gives another signal. The three Guards jump in and grab* BRONSKI. *He struggles, yells, in terror. Now, all the other men except* BOWMAN, *move up to their cell doors and raise a clamor. They bang and yell. The other Guards are all up and on the alert with their weapons now.* BRONSKI *screams,* 'WARDEN! WARDEN!']

[*The struggle goes on a few minutes, and the clamor. Then, suddenly,* BOWMAN'S *voice is heard above everything, he is at his cell door now.*]

BOWMAN: HOLD IT! HOLD EVERYTHING! NOW!

[*The clamor dies down, the struggle in the cell ceases. The Guards,* BRONSKI, *the General, look around.*]

BOWMAN [*after a pause, calmly*]: You're violating Rule 221, General. You ought to know that.

THE GENERAL [*turning on him*]: Shut up, Bowman! I've had enough out of you, Buddy!

BOWMAN [*again, very calmly*]: I'll have to report this to the Warden, General. I have no recourse, as you know. You're definitely and obviously violating Rule 221, General.

THE GENERAL: Shut your trap, Bowman! You don't run this

goddamn place, buddy! You get away with enough as it is.
I'll slap your ass in isolation, wise boy!

BOWMAN [*as before unruffled*]: You're compounding your
offense, General. You've just violated Rule 392, that's a fact,
General.

THE GENERAL [*turning his attention back to* BRONSKI]: Get that
man out here!

BOWMAN [*above the clamor which has begun again*]: I'll have
to report this, General. I'm sure you're aware of that. There
are twenty-four witnesses here, General. We're civilly dead,
whatever that might mean, but we're witnesses, General.
Bona fide, warm-bodied witnesses, General. [*pause*] He'll be
here in the morning. I'll report it then, General. If I'm not
here, somebody will. *You can't put us all in Isolation,
General!*

[*There is a long moment while the General weighs things.
It could go either way. Then, with an angry gesture, the
General makes known his decision.*]

THE GENERAL: Put him back.

[*The clamor ceases.*]

[*The Guards do as instructed, giving* BRONSKI *a few shoves
in the bargain. Back in his cell, locked in,* BRONSKI *once
again is transformed. He is belligerent. He hurls a stream of
abuse at the guards, the General. A good deal of it is inter-
spersed with the word 'coffee'.*]

BOWMAN [*looking on, nodding his head*]: That's right, General.
That's the only thing you could do, under the circumstances,
General.

[*The General is very angry, but he knows* BOWMAN *has
him. He comes up before* BOWMAN'S *cell, glowers into it.
He assumes a highly belligerent posture.* BOWMAN *remains
unruffled.*]

THE GENERAL [*to* BOWMAN *only*] [*Though the others strain to
hear*]: One day, Bowman—[*pause*] That day's coming, you
can't screw around forever, Bowman—[*pause*] I'll be down
there, I'll watch it alright, Bowman—[*pause*] I'd pull the
goddamn levers if they let me, Bowman—

BOWMAN: I know you would. [*pause*] That would be in clear
violation of Rule 219 though, General. [*pause*] The entire

procedure is carefully, minutely outlined there. [*pause*] You'll never do that, General.

THE GENERAL [*suddenly, shouting*] : By God, somebody will! He sure will! And I'll be there. *Bet your sweet ass I'll be there!*

BOWMAN [*shrugging*] : Maybe, General. [*pause*] Maybe you'll be in the seat next to me, who knows, General. [*pauses, sips his coffee, grins*] We'll hold hands, how about that, General? [*The General wavers. The image affects him, apparently. He turns away. He looks at the Guards. He looks all around. He looks at HARPO, and at the coffee cup, still on the floor. BOWMAN looks at it. So does HARPO, and the Guards. Everybody looks at it.*]

THE GENERAL [*giving a wave of his hand, and in a fairly normal voice*] : Clean it up, Harpo.

[*And he walks away, toward the Office. The Guards, except the one with HARPO, follow him. BRONSKI is quiet now, only muttering to himself. HARPO, soon, moves to clean up the coffee. The men watch him. They sip their coffee, calmy. The General and Guards are back in their office. Soon, LAVERNE's guitar can be heard again. He sings, softly, but clearly, 'The Red River Valley'. The Gun Guard paces*]

FADEOUT, SLOW

SCENE : *The living-room of a comfortably furnished American home. This is at Lower Left. Nothing else is visible to the audience at the moment. A* WOMAN *of about thirty-eight, a rather attractive, healthy and wholesome American woman, is sitting in a chair, reading a newspaper. A boy of about eleven is on the floor, nearby. He is looking through a magazine or comic book. From time to time, the woman glances at her watch.*

THE BOY : Mom, what's a quadrangle?

WOMAN : Quadrangle?

THE BOY [*rolling over, getting up, going over to her*] : Yeh, Mom. See? Here's this fellow talking to this other fellow—

WOMAN : Yes, I see—[*She is thinking about it*] [*It dawns on her*] Why, well—it's very similar to a—a triangle, isn't it? [*She thinks some more*] Yes, dear, think of when someone has Quads—Four—[*she has it now*] Quadrangle—do you see now, dear?

THE BOY [*flatly*]: No.

THE WOMAN [*slightly perturbed*]: Why—well—it's a four sided figure, of course, dear!

THE BOY: Oh?

THE WOMAN: That's so.

THE BOY: Draw me one.

THE WOMAN: Well—[*pauses, thinks*] Well—[*pause*] Well—yes —Get me pencil and paper, dear. [*He trots off, does so. She watches him, fondly. He returns. She sets to work on it. He watches her, not altogether unskeptically*] There—there, you see now?

THE BOY [*practically convinced*]: Oh, yeh, that's simple. It's a rectangle.

THE WOMAN [*thinking about it*]: That's right. [*pause*] It is, isn't it?

THE BOY: Sure Mom. [*pause*] Is that O.K.? Could a rectangle be a quadrangle?

THE WOMAN [*thinking*]: Well—[*considering*] A rectangle— [*pause*] A rectangle would be one form—or type—wouldn't it—of quadrangle—[*pause*] Yes, you see, any figure with four sides has to be a quadrangle.

THE BOY [*after a pause, studying the figure*]: I get it, Mom.

THE WOMAN: Say, 'I see, Mom—'

THE BOY [*embarrassed, somewhat*]: I'm sorry. [*pause*] *I see,* Mom. [*He goes back to the floor. He looks up after a while. She has returned to her reading, after studying the figure herself a while*] Dad going to be late again, Mom?

THE WOMAN: He should be here shortly, dear.

THE BOY: Uh huh.

[*She looks at him.*]

THE BOY: I'm sorry, Mom.

THE WOMAN: Alright, dear. Remember. Always remember.

THE BOY: O.K., Mom.

[*The woman nods her head, returns to her reading.*]

THE BOY: Can I put the television on, Mom?

THE WOMAN: We're going to have supper soon.

THE BOY: I'm hungry!

THE WOMAN: Dad will be here soon. Be patient.

THE BOY: Aw, let me watch television, Mom—

THE WOMAN: Oh, alright. Not loud, now. [*The boy jumps up, crosses the room, flips on the idiot-box. There are some singing advertisements, something about 'tingling-blue' or some such. Then the news. We catch a few lines of it, the word 'LONGFIELD', and later, 'BOWMAN', and 'PETITION'.*] Turn it down, dear, and do you really want that?

THE BOY: Uh uh. [*Flips around to other channels. Comes up with some children's program. A kindly, happy, good man is speaking to a group of children. They respond. The boy sprawls on the floor, enthralled by it. He titters, something funny happened. The Woman goes on with her reading. Shortly, a door slams.*]

THE BOY [*flatly*]: Dad. [*He continues watching T.V.*]

[*The Woman gets up, obviously looking forward to seeing him, her man. He enters. He is a tall and compact man, he wears rimless glasses, he has a kindly manner about him, one might say, or, certainly, gentle. He is slightly balding, in his mid forties. There is an air of responsibility about him. He is the WARDEN of the State Prison whose Death Row we have been seeing*]

THE WOMAN [*Kissing him*]: Hello, dear.

THE WARDEN [*affectionately*]: Hello, hon. [*He returns her kiss, pats her. He turns to the boy*] Hello, son.

THE BOY: Dad, what's a quadrangle?

THE WARDEN [*Taking off his coat, sitting in a chair, unloosening his tie*]: Quadrangle, son? [*pause*] Why, a quadrangle—

THE WOMAN: Pay no attention, I've just told him. [*to the boy*] Go wash now, go on—[*pauses, the boy hesitates*] Go on, now. [*He goes finally. She crosses to T.V., turns it off.*]

THE WARDEN [*after she comes back to him*]: How are things?

THE WOMAN: Oh, fine, dear. [*smiles, gives him another peck*] The Ryans are coming over later.

THE WARDEN: Ted Ryan? Good old Ted.

THE WOMAN: Mildred just wouldn't stop talking.

THE WARDEN: She's that way—

THE WOMAN: Timmy is going to be a Sophomore, imagine that, a Sophomore, dear—

THE WARDEN: Time flies. It just flies, hon. [*pauses, looks around, finds cigarettes*] I can't stay up too late, hon—

THE WOMAN: Oh? [*pauses, glances apparently casually at him*] Early tomorrow?

THE WARDEN [*casually, apparently*]: Yes, I have to get an early start tomorrow.

[*A brief silence. He lights up. They sit there. Then, she rises, she is somewhat nervous.*]

THE WOMAN [*cheerfully*]: Well, I have a nice supper for you—

THE WARDEN: I'm hungry—hungry—hungry, hon.

THE WOMAN [*giving a warm smile, and a low laugh*]: I'll feed my man.

THE WARDEN: How's Mildred? Alright?

THE WOMAN: Oh fine. The doctor said it was nothing. Nothing, nothing.

THE WARDEN [*chuckling, picking up the newspaper, across the front page is sprawled* YOUNG KILLER DIES TOMORROW * APPEAL FAILS] [*He glances at it, opens up, folds the paper*]: She worries too much. I think she's healthy as anything.

THE WOMAN: She is, oh, don't worry. [*pause*] Ever since she came back from Hawaii, I think she misses it too much, don't you? My, it's beautiful there, isn't it, dear? Let's do it again one day.

THE WARDEN [*slowly*]: Would be a nice place to retire—wouldn't it—[*They are looking at one another, they do so for a long moment. Then, suddenly, The Warden's entire mood changes. It is as if a mask has dropped away from him. He is tired, and drawn, and obviously troubled. He turns away from her, slowly. She watches him. She becomes serious, watching him . . .*]

THE WOMAN [*after a pause, knowing his trouble*] [*tenderly*]: What can you do? Who could do more than you? [*The Warden does not move. He stares straight ahead, sombre, quiet. Just at this point The Row becomes visible, dimly gradually.*]

THE WOMAN [*quietly*]: How old is he?

THE WARDEN: Twenty.

[*They remain there, and then, slowly, Fadeout. There is only The Row now . . . though the lighting is dim.*]

[*Gradually, the lighting becomes brighter. It is the next morning. The food trolley has been around. The men have finished their breakfast. Some are washing, shaving. The others, most of them, are out in the corridor, walking up and down, talking. This is their daily two-hour exercise period. They walk back and forth, slowly, along the corridor.* BOWMAN *is in his cell, doing calisthenics, though not very violent ones.* LAVERNE *has his guitar with him, as he paces. He is strumming and singing softly, 'Oh Susannah'. The Gun Guard, the other Guards keep their eyes on the men. The following exchanges take place among the men walking up and down the corridor.*]

RACHMAN: He's down there now.

DUDLEY: Oh, yeh, no kiddin'? I thought he was on the town.

RACHMAN: That ain't funny. Your turn's comin'. Think that's funny?

DUDLEY: Sure, funny. Look at me here, laughin' my guts out, how funny.

[*A silence.*]

RACHMAN: Three hours. Christ. He's just a kid. A kid, Dudley.

DUDLEY: Kids go. [*pause*] You gotta go sometime. [*pause*] No gettin' away from it. [*pause*] Sometime.

RACHMAN: Yeh, but how come some guy can choose my time? I'd like to know that. I don't like that—

DUDLEY: What's the difference? It's all the same, bud. You'll see. You won't know about it.

RACHMAN: Dan's helpin' me out a lot. Maybe nobody'll know about it. Maybe just that.

DUDLEY: All the luck, pal. Here's to ya.

[*A silence. The men walk on.*]

ROMEO: Oh, man, sweet cunt for breakfast.

ROPER: Ha Ha. Don't let the General hear ya.

ROMEO: What's, he got one?

ROPER: Ha Ha Ha. Oh, buddy. [*pause*] That all you think of, anyway?

ROMEO: Sure. What else is there?

ROPER: Too bad. Maybe you wouldn't be here. Too bad, son.

ROMEO: Oh, yeh. What's your excuse?

ROPER: I was framed.

ROMEO: Yeh, think you told me.

ROPER: I was, bud.

ROMEO: Tell the Judge that.

ROPER: I told him. Don't worry. Plenty of times. I told everybody.

ROMEO: Keep tellin' them.

ROPER: Sure I will. Goddamn right I will. Even when they strap me in that chair I will. *The bastards.*

[*A silence.*]

ROMEO: She was no good. No good. The cunt. [*pause*] *What am I here for?*

[*A silence.*]

ROPER: Wonder when Longfield'll show up? That oughta be one. Glad I'm around, anyhow, to see that one.

[*The men keep moving.*]

MARLOWE: G'wan, the guy's a bum. Nothin' but a bum—

BRONSKI: Bum? Twenty game winner! Twenty, man! That's a bum?

MARLOWE: Aw, luck. Pure luck. You get that. All the time you get that. Lookit that Caxton. Lookit his luck. Jesus. Besides, those guys are all bums. The whole damn team, Manager on down—Bums.

BRONSKI [*quite irately*]: Oh, yeh? And every year, practically, who takes the pennant? You tell me that! Who, huh?

MARLOWE: Baw—lookit the League they're in—

BRONSKI: Oh, yeh, o.k., yeh, buddy— *Who wins the Series?* Each year, practically, c'mon, tell me—*you* oughta know—

MARLOWE: Luck. Pure luck. Man, just like you're in here, and I'm in here—luck, that's all— Oh, buddy.

BRONSKI: Luck my ass! Some bastard Judge did that. I'd like him here. I sure would, I'd like him here with me, take the trip with me down there. The bastard.

MARLOWE: Ha Ha. Oh, yeh. OH, yeh, Buddy! [*pause*] Now you take the Cardinals— *There's* a team for ya—

[*The men move on, all the men on The Row, including those we do not see usually. Soon,* BOWMAN *ends his calisthenics and steps out of his cell to join them. He falls in behind* RACHMAN.]

RACHMAN: Whadaya say, muscle-man.

BOWMAN: Oh, yeh.

RACHMAN [*after a while*] [*quietly*]: Won't be long now.

BOWMAN: It's his lawyer's fault. His so-called lawyer's fault. He threw the sponge in. Flat in.

RACHMAN: Sure, why not? What's in it for him?

BOWMAN: That's about it, I guess. Just about it, buddy.

RACHMAN: How come you didn't help him? You could of shown him—

BOWMAN: He never came to me. He got the letter, he gave up. What could I do? [*pause*] A guy has to come to me. Things don't work out at all otherwise.

RACHMAN: He took a screwin' though.

BOWMAN: Sure. We all did.

RACHMAN: Yeh, but him, especially.

BOWMAN: If he had come to me—

RACHMAN: Pretty good, huh—the other guy, *the guy who pulled the trigger*— *Life*! Pretty damn good, huh?

BOWMAN: He should have come to me.

RACHMAN: Well, he's down there now, couple more hours, that'll be it—and how—

    [*A silence.*]

RACHMAN: Think we'll make it? Think we will, Dan?

BOWMAN: I don't know. Who knows? Just keep trying. Hoping. That's all. That's all, Joe.

    [*They keep moving.*]

FADEOUT

SCENE: *The Holding Cell, Lower Center. There is a Guard on each side (4) of the cell, sitting, watching. A young man,* SOLOMON, *sits on the bunk in the cell. He is frightened, very close, in fact, to a state of terror. Presently, a* CHAPLAIN *comes into view. He approaches the cell. The Guards unlock the cell and let him in. The Guards keep close watch.* SOLOMON, *seeing the* CHAPLAIN, *falls to his knees, before him. He starts to sob, the* CHAPLAIN *touches him.*]

SOLOMON: Help me, help me— *Please help me*—[*He sobs. The* CHAPLAIN *soothes him, or tries to soothe him. He pulls out a*

Bible. He prays.] [*Now, briefly, gradually, the Chamber appears, Right.*]

FADEOUT

SCENE: *The Row. about one hour later. The men are all back in their cells now. There is an absolute silence now, even* LAVERNE'S *guitar is stilled. Occasionally, the phone rings in the Guard Office. We hear the brief, muffled conversation of the Guard speaking into the phone . . . Soon, the buzzers sound and the cage doors, one by one, open. It is* THE WARDEN. *All the Guards rise and greet him.* THE GENERAL *comes out of the office.*]

THE WARDEN [*The strain clearly showing on him*]: Good morning, Lieutenant.

THE GENERAL [*falling over himself to please*]: Good morning, good morning. Warden. How are you this morning?

[THE WARDEN *gives him a brief glance, then ignores him. He glances into the office. He looks up and down The Row. The men are all looking at him. After a moment or two he starts walking slowly along The Row.* THE GENERAL, *a Guard, follow.*]

THE WARDEN [*in a low voice*]: How's everything?

THE GENERAL: Fine, fine, Warden. Everything's fine.

THE WARDEN: You've taken care of—his belongings?

THE GENERAL: Yes, sir, Warden. They're all in the office, all packed, ready to go. Just as soon— [*He halts, silenced by a sudden glance from the Warden. They stop before* LAVERNE'S *cell.*] [*They stand there.* LAVERNE, *suddenly, starts strumming his guitar, softly.*]

THE WARDEN [*kindly*]: How are you, Jake, how's everything?

[LAVERNE *strums his guitar a little while longer, then, stops, looks up. He keeps his eyes on* THE WARDEN, *a long moment. Then he turns and looks at* THE GENERAL. *Then, back to* THE WARDEN. *They remain on* THE WARDEN.]

LAVERNE: Just fine, Warden. Fine.

THE WARDEN: Good, Jake. Good. Keep it up.

LAVERNE: I sure will, Warden.

THE WARDEN: Need anything?

LAVERNE [*after a moment, staring at* THE WARDEN]: Uh uh.

[*pause*] Uh, uh, Warden.

THE WARDEN [*after a pause*]: How's the guitar?

LAVERNE: Real good. [*pause*] Warden.

THE WARDEN [*nodding his head, giving a little wave of his hand*]: O.K., Jake. [*pause*] Take it easy.

[LAVERNE *stands there, slowly nodding his head. Then, he resumes the soft strumming. It is barely audible.* THE WARDEN *is before* ROMEO's *cell.*]

THE WARDEN: How are you, Romeo. How's everything?

ROMEO [*On his bunk, not moving, not looking at* THE WARDEN]: You're early, Warden.

THE WARDEN: Yes, I guess so. A little early, Romeo.

ROMEO: Where ya going, little party or something? Warden?

[THE WARDEN *does not answer. He stands there, silently, looking into the cell at* ROMEO. THE GENERAL *shifts around, anxious to be moving.*]

THE WARDEN [*finally*]: You need anything, Romeo?

ROMEO [*after a pause, still not looking up*]: You still got that secretary working for you, Warden? That blonde one?

THE WARDEN: Your lawyer's working hard for you, Romeo.

ROMEO: Best of luck to him. That's all I can say. Warden.

THE WARDEN: Take it easy, Romeo.

ROMEO: Ah ha. I will. All the time in the world for that, Warden. I will. [*pause*] [*now, looks up at* THE WARDEN] Send that secretary up sometime, willya, Warden?

[THE WARDEN *moves on to the next cell.*]

THE WARDEN: How are you, Dudley, how's everything?

DUDLEY [*He is up near the cell door, practically against it. He shrugs his shoulders*]: We gotta go sometime, Warden.

[THE GENERAL *grins. He would like to laugh. But he only grins, briefly.*]

THE WARDEN [*quietly*]: Need anything, Dudley?

DUDLEY [*His eyes looking furtively into* THE WARDEN's *a moment, searching for something. Then, away, quickly*]: Naw, nothin', only nothin', Warden.

THE WARDEN [*nodding his head*]: Take it easy, Dudley.

[*He starts to move on.*]

DUDLEY [*suddenly*]: It's six weeks—six weeks from today—right, Warden?

THE WARDEN [*halting*]: Yes. That's right, Dudley.

DUDLEY: There ain't a chance in a bat's hell, that right, Warden?

THE WARDEN: I don't know, Dudley. [*pauses, gravely*] There's the Governor, there's always a slim chance there, Dudley.

DUDLEY [*with a harsh laugh*]: It's so slim you can't see it, right, Warden?

[THE WARDEN *moves on*].

RACHMAN [*as soon as* THE WARDEN *appears*]: I'm fine, Warden. Everything's just fine. Don't need a thing. How's the wife? You're pretty early this morning, Warden.

[THE WARDEN *stands silently before his cell a few moments. He nods his head.*]

THE WARDEN: Take it easy, Joe.

[*He moves on. He comes to* BOWMAN'S *cell.* BOWMAN *has put down some papers he has been looking through.* THE WARDEN *glances around the cell at the books, the papers.*]

THE WARDEN [*friendly*]: Hello, Dan.

BOWMAN [*gravely*]: How are you.

THE WARDEN: Your latest Petition went out this morning.

BOWMAN: Thanks.

[*A long silence.*]

THE WARDEN [*somewhat uncomfortably*]: What are you looking at?

BOWMAN: They're waiting for you downstairs, aren't they, Warden?

[THE WARDEN'S *composed face collapses. He is visibily affected by this. He puts a hand on one of the cell bars.*]

THE WARDEN [*quicky, to* BOWMAN *only*]: What did you say that for? You know me better than anyone here. You know everything. You know I do the best I can. What else can I do? You know that. I die each time down there, no matter who the man. I give the signal, sure, the law says I have to. It's part of my job, I have to. I hate it, you understand that, hate it, each time I have to.

BOWMAN [*calmly*]: Why do you have to?

THE WARDEN: What kind of a question is that? How can you ask a senseless question like that?

BOWMAN [*shrugging*]: I don't know. [*pause*] One of those things, hard to know, Warden.

THE WARDEN: Think. That's all I ask you to do. Think about it.

BOWMAN [*after a while*]: You could resign. [*pause*] Warden.

[*He is silent. They both stand there, looking at one another.*]

THE WARDEN [*finally*]: Need anything?

BOWMAN: Not a thing. [*pause*] Warden.

[THE WARDEN *moves on to the next cell. As soon as he reaches it,* BRONSKI *jumps up from his bunk. He grabs the bars. He is quite agitated.*]

BRONSKI: I was framed! You know that! A good guy like you knows that! I never done it! The whole thing, a frame-up, the stupid bulls needed someone to hang it on, there I was, dumbjohn! Oh, yeh, yeh, that's right, Warden! I TOLD YOU A MILLION TIMES, didn't I, Warden? *How the hell come I'm still here then, tell me that, Warden?* I'd like the answer to that. When you take me down there, when the hell is it, five weeks from now, it'll be too late, too damn late then. Now! I want it now, Warden! When you give the signal, when those eggs drop, it'll be too late then! RIGHT, WARDEN?

THE WARDEN [*calmly*]: Take it easy, Bronski. You may not go. Your Petition is before the courts, right now.

BRONSKI: Ha Ha! Oh Ha Ha! Tell me another! Jesus Christ, that's a good one! Another!

THE WARDEN: O.K., Bronski. Take it easy.

BRONSKI: Sure, Warden. Easy, easy! Nice and easy. [*pauses,* THE WARDEN *is moving off*] YOU'RE A BOY, WARDEN! A boy and a half, Warden! The General—he's two boys! Two boys and a half, Warden! WARDEN! That makes four of ya! FOUR, WARDEN! How about that! Grab that—WARDEN! GRAB HOLD OF THAT, WARDEN!

[THE WARDEN *is before* MARLOWE'S *cell.* BRONSKI *keeps yelling, pounding his door a while. Soon, he becomes quiet. Looks around. Walks to his bunk. He sits, dejectedly.*]

THE WARDEN [*very quietly, murmuring almost*]: How are you, Marlowe? How's everything?

MARLOWE: Great, Warden. Just great. How are you? Things o.k. with you?

THE WARDEN: Need anything?

MARLOWE [*thinking, rubbing his chin*]: Get Bronski and me couple passes to the next Cardinals game. When they in town again? I gotta show that guy a ball club. He's never seen one. He thinks those bums in New York are, Warden. How about that? We used to have a pretty good ball club here, Warden. What happened? They turn pro on ya? [*pause*] One for me, one for Bronski, Warden. [*pause*] He needs some fresh air. You can see that, Warden. [*pause*] And when's the day? They figured that out yet, Warden?

THE WARDEN [*quietly*]: Your automatic appeal is before the State Court. I wish you all the luck. I can't tell you anything yet. Maybe there won't be a day. Maybe not.

[MARLOWE *nods his head, and is silent.* THE WARDEN *moves off.*]

THE WARDEN: Take it easy, Marlowe.

[*Now he is before* ROPER'S *cell.*]

THE WARDEN: How are you, Roper. How's everything?

ROPER [*staring at him sullenly*]: Tell it to the Judge, Warden.

THE WARDEN: Need anything?

ROPER: Oh, yeh. Lots of things. [*pauses, pulls an envelope out of his pocket*] Thanks a lot for your letter. Nice surprise, Warden. Here, listen—[*starts reading it*] 'Dear Sir' [*pause*] That's me, Warden. Listen. [*goes on*] 'Dear Sir—I have this date received death warrant in your case. Execution of judgement has been fixed for one month from date of this letter, at 10 a.m.— Very truly yours, The Warden' [*pause*] [*waves the letter*] I thought I'd read it to you, Warden, pretty good, huh, Pretty Damn Good Letter, HUH? Ha Ha! Oh Boy Oh Boy! I'll take you out for a drink on that—you and the General, the bastard, the black bastard, step up, General, have a swig, oh yeh, *it's only cyanide!*

[*He tears the letter into a thousand pieces, throws them out through the cell door, they float, they scatter, they fall all about* THE WARDEN, THE GENERAL. *The men watch them, settling.*]

ROPER: OH YEH! STEP RIGHT UP, PALS!

[*Then, quiet.* THE WARDEN *moves on. The next cell is empty, but he pauses before it just a second.*]

117

ROPER: Ain't nobody home, Warden! Nobody at all! He's down there, you'll be seeing him soon! Keep moving, Warden! You'll be late! Move, move along there, Warden! YOU WANTA BE LATE?

> [THE GENERAL *looks as if he will make a move toward* ROPER, *but* THE WARDEN *prevents him. They move along. They are out of sight, moving along the other end of The Row now . . .*]

> [*Silence, except for* LAVERNE'S *guitar strumming and soft singing. The Gun Guard paces.*]

FADEOUT

SCENE: *The Holding Cell, the Chamber.* THE CHAPLAIN *is still with* SOLOMON, *who is sitting on his bunk now, shaking, praying. Presently* THE WARDEN *enters, an assistant is with him.* THE WARDEN *is grim-faced. He nods to the Guards. They open the cell door, he enters.* THE CHAPLAIN *stands to one side. In the Chamber, last minute preparations take place. Witnesses are beginning to file into the room, around the Chamber. On the side of the Chamber opposite the chairs, there is a venetian blind over the window. That is the Executioner's position.* THE WARDEN *will stand beside him, though in full view . . . Now,* THE WARDEN *puts a hand on* SOLOMON'S *shoulder.* SOLOMON *does not look up. He continues praying, shaking . . .*

THE WARDEN [*gravely*]: Solomon—[*He does not move*] It's time, Solomon. [*The Guards move toward the cell door.* THE CHAPLAIN *steps even more to the side.*]

SOLOMON [*looking up, seeing* THE WARDEN]: I don't want to Warden. I don't want to go in there. Please, please don't take me, Warden—

THE WARDEN: I don't want to, Solomon. Nobody here wants to. You know that, Solomon.

SOLOMON: Don't take me—Warden—Please—*Please*, Warden—

THE WARDEN [*quietly, gravely*]: I've got to, Solomon— [*he pauses, the Guards come closer, they enter the cell now*] It won't hurt, Solomon. You'll just go to sleep. [*pause*] That's all it is, Solomon— [*pause*] Going to sleep—

SOLOMON: I don't want to—Warden—Please—Please—

THE WARDEN: Try to get up, Solomon.

SOLOMON: I can't move—I'm paralyzed, Warden— *Don't let them take me*—Warden—*Don't let them drag me in there*— Warden—leave me alone— *Leave me stay here*—Warden— [*The Guards close in, they are all around him.* THE CHAP-LAIN *is outside the cell.*]

THE WARDEN [*softly*]: Come on, Solomon—
[SOLOMON *doesn't move, he sits there, shaking, staring at* THE WARDEN. *Shortly,* THE WARDEN *gives a slight nod. The Guards move, take hold of* SOLOMON, *expertly. They lift him, he starts screaming, struggling, they carry him out, with difficulty, he is fighting, screaming. They carry him out of our line of view now, towards Rear, towards a narrow passageway, which cannot be seen, leading to the Chamber*]

SOLOMON [*screaming*]: Don't Let Them, Warden! They're Taking Me In There! THEY'RE GONNA KILL ME, WARDEN!— Where Is He—Where's That Lawyer—WARDEN—My Mother —WHERE'S MY MOTHER—Stop Them, Warden—I DIDN'T DO IT! Ask the Lawyer—ASK ANYBODY—Warden—THEY'RE TAKING ME!— DON'T LET THEM—My Mother—WARDEN!—WARRRRRR-DEN!—
[*The voice fades away.* THE WARDEN, THE CHAPLAIN *follow. The Witnesses are all gathered . . .*]

FADEOUT

SCENE: *The Row, that evening, and* THE WARDEN'S *Home. On The Row, there is silence. The men have had their supper. They are mainly lying on their bunks, or sitting up, though one or two are doing something.* BOWMAN, *for example, is studying some Law books.* RACHMAN *is playing a game of cards with himself.* BRONSKI *is standing near his cell door, looking in the direction of the Gun Guard, pacing above him.* ROPER *has his headphones on.* LAVERNE *holds his guitar, but does not play it . . . In* THE WARDEN'S *living-room, his wife, wearing an apron, has just entered. The television is on. We hear the last bits of some music, and then an Announcer comes on to give the News.* THE WOMAN, *who has been crossing the room, stops when he gives the first item.*

ANNOUNCER [*sensationally*] : Today in the State Prison, police-killer Robert 'Red' Solomon went screaming and fighting to his death in the State Gas Chamber. Protesting his innocence to his last breath, it required six Prison Guards to carry him in and strap him to the Death Chair . . . [*He goes on in this vein a few moments, and then* THE WOMAN *crosses quickly to turn it off. She stands by the set, white-faced, stiffly. Presently, a door slams, she turns, her son enters the room. He is carrying a football. He looks like he has been having quite a game.*]

THE BOY: Hi, Mom—gosh I'm hungry—

THE WOMAN [*trying*] : You look a sight. Better have a good wash.

THE BOY: Oh, yeh, I will, Mom. [*Puts football down, walks toward T.V. set*] Can I watch T.V. a couple minutes? I won't be late, will I?

THE WOMAN [*nervously, but firmly*] : No, dear. No time for that now. Run along and wash, that's a good boy. Now . . . [*He is disappointed, but does so.* THE WOMAN *stands there, watching him leave the room. She stands there, a long moment, looking after him . . . Then, the outside door slams again. She stiffens, a moment, but then turns, slowly.* THE WARDEN *enters. He stands at the room's entrance. They look at one another, like statues. Then,* THE WOMAN *moves, the moment is broken.*]

THE WOMAN: Hello, dear. [*pause.*]

THE WARDEN [*slowly, quietly*] : Hello, Hon.

THE WOMAN [*tenderly*] : Sit down. [*pause*] I've got a drink for you.

[*He nods his head, slowly.*]

FADEOUT—*of living-room. The Row remains.* LAVERNE *starts to play his guitar now, quietly. He sings 'Lone Prairie', softly.* RACHMAN *lays down his cards, gets up, stretches, walks to the cell door. He stands there. He looks around. He looks toward* BOWMAN's *cell.*]

RACHMAN: What are you doin', Dan?

BOWMAN: Little research. Nothing much. Just a little.

RACHMAN [*grinning wryly*] : You'll be here when the place closes, man.

BOWMAN : You and me both. Maybe.

RACHMAN [*after a while*] : Goodbye Solomon.

BOWMAN : Goodbye.

RACHMAN : Chalk it up, Dan. How many's that now?

BOWMAN : Eighty-four, exactly, Joe.

[*There is a silence.*]

RACHMAN : Think of that poor Warden. Think about that, Dan.

BOWMAN : My heart bleeds for him.

[RACHMAN *gives a wry laugh, briefly.*]

RACHMAN : What kind of research you doin' there, Buddy?

BOWMAN : For my next move, in case the Petition bounces.

RACHMAN : I hope it doesn't, old buddy.

BOWMAN : That makes two of us.

RACHMAN [*after a pause*] : When do you think I'll be hearing something?

BOWMAN : That's hard to tell. You never can tell.

RACHMAN : The latest—

BOWMAN : Oh—three months, I'd say. The latest.

RACHMAN : I'll wait here.

[BOWMAN *grins, a little.*]

RACHMAN : What happened to Longfield, I wonder?

BOWMAN : Maybe he couldn't find the way. Could happen. [*pause*] I've seen it happen.

RACHMAN [*chuckles a little*] : Yeh, does happen.

[*A silence.*]

RACHMAN [*quietly*] : Roper, Dudley, Marlowe—[*halts, pauses*] But I'm gonna be around a while, right Dan? Long as you help me out, long as you're around, that's right, ain't it, Dan?

BOWMAN : Could be. We'll give it a whirl, anyhow. It's Russian roulette up here, Joe. That's all, now.

[*The Row is quiet, save for* LAVERNE'S *guitar.*]

FADEOUT

SCENE : *The Row. The next morning. The men are in their cells.* HARPO *is pushing the breakfast trolley around. He exchanges*

*bits of conversation with the men as he passes their cells, serves
them. He is before* RACHMAN'S *cell when the buzzers sound and
the Cage doors open.* LONGFIELD, *accompanied by two guards,
enters. He is a prosperous looking man in his mid-forties. He is
rather tall, and well-built. He is not bad-looking. His nose is
slightly long, otherwise, he would be handsome. He has dark
brown hair. He has a rather manic air about him, an air of
having dominated people, events, around him, for some time,
perhaps all his life. The second door of the Cage opens, he enters
The Row.*

LONGFIELD [*looking around*] : Not bad. [*pauses, looks at* THE
GENERAL] Not bad at all. [*pause*] Have a cigar, Sergeant. [*He
thrusts a fat cigar at* THE GENERAL, *who stares at it, then,
takes it*] That's right, don't be shy, Sergeant. Who ever got
anyplace being shy? Bet you didn't. I'll just put a bet on that.
You didn't. [*Turns, looks up and down The Row*] How's
everybody? At ease, now. Longfield's here. Of Longfield,
Rowe, and Moore. You name it, we got it—or tell you we
got it. Aha, good, just in time for breakfast. Sergeant, let's
go have a little breakfast.

THE GENERAL : Uh—Longfield—

LONGFIELD : Aren't you hungry?

THE GENERAL : Uh—look—[*pauses, in a low voice*] Those
clothes, Longfield. You'll have to hand them in. We'll give
you Prison Issue.

LONGFIELD [*looking at him, then, shrugging*] : O.K., Sergeant.
[*starts to peel his coat off*] If you say so. I didn't come here to
break any rules. Believe me. No siree, Sergeant.

THE GENERAL : Hold it—there's no hurry—we'll get them later.

LONGFIELD [*putting his coat back on*] : O.K. Sergeant. If you
say so.

THE GENERAL : Follow me, Longfield.

LONGFIELD [*doing so*] : I spent a good stretch in the Army. Those
were the days. This brings it all back. Hello, men. Don't
know how they ever got me out. I nearly died. [*to* ROMEO]
Good morning, there. How are you? [*He greets each man on
the way to his cell, which is next to* ROPER, *the last one in
view*] [*At* BOWMAN'S *cell he stops*] You're Bowman, aren't
you?

BOWMAN: That's right.

LONGFIELD: I thought so. Just like your picture. [*pauses, puts his hand through the bars*] A pleasure. [BOWMAN, *slowly, takes the hand, shakes it*] I'll see you around. I admire you. Have a lot of admiration for you. [*shrugs*] Don't know why.

THE GENERAL: Come on, Longfield.

[LONGFIELD *does so, and at last, reaches the cell.*]

THE GENERAL [*opening it*]: Home sweet home. [*pause*] For a while.

LONGFIELD: Ha Ha! So it is. So you're right, Sergeant.

THE GENERAL [*holding cell door open*, LONGFIELD *walking into cell*]: We'll issue everything later. [*hands him a printed sheet*] Here's the Rules.

LONGFIELD [*taking it*]: Aha, thank you, Sergeant. Thank you very much, Sergeant. [*pause*] What's for breakfast? Joining me?

THE GENERAL: It's coming along here, don't worry.

LONGFIELD: Friend, I'm not worried. What do you think I'm here for—to worry?

THE GENERAL [*looking at him, a long while, then, moving off*]: O.K., Buddy.

[LONGFIELD *looks around his new home. He feels the bed, looks all around. He pulls out a cigar and lights up. He strolls to the front of the cell.*]

LONGFIELD: Man, I've got all the cigars you want, anytime you want any. The best. Just step right up, or something, I'll fix you up. [*seeing* HARPO *coming along*] Don't get lost on your way here, Pop. I'll have two helpings, if you don't mind. [*The trolley is before him now*] Here, have a cigar.

HARPO [*taking it, looking around*]: Thanks a lot.

LONGFIELD: You're welcome. My friend, you're welcome. [*pauses, looks him over*] What are you in for? Are you one of us, Pop?

HARPO: Can't say I am, son. [*pauses, starts filling up the breakfast tray*] I'm with ya, though.

LONGFIELD: All the way?

HARPO [*amused by this, laughs*]: Can't say that, can't say it, son.

LONGFIELD [*taking the tray*]: Your privilege, Pop. Entirely.

[*looks at the food, tastes it*] Good, mighty good. Thank the Warden for me, would you do that, Pop?

HARPO: I sure will, son.

LONGFIELD: What's your name?

HARPO: Harpo, son.

LONGFIELD: Call me Longfield. [*pauses, munches food*] That's my name. [*pause*] How are you, Harpo? How long have you been here? Do you like it here?

HARPO: I sure do. It's my home, son.

LONGFIELD: That's what a man needs. In life, Harpo, a man needs a home. No question of it. I once had a home. Would you believe that, Harpo?

HARPO: Why sure, son, sure. You had a good home, looks to me like.

LONGFIELD [*munching, staring at him a moment or so*]: Right, Pop. Right you are there, my Pop.

 [*There is some clamoring up the line now for breakfast.* HARPO *shouts something to them, then leans in toward* LONGFIELD's *cell a litle more.*]

HARPO: Say, son—[*pauses, looks around*] Say—did it happen—just like the papers say? [*pause*] Did it?

LONGFIELD [*proceeding with his breakfast*]: I don't know. Which paper do you read, Pop? Which one?

HARPO: All of them.

LONGFIELD: All of them? Ah ha. Ha Ha. You don't miss a thing. Right, Pop? Ha Ha. *You* are a well-informed citizen, Pop.

HARPO: Did it?

LONGFIELD: Well, I guess so. They can't all be wrong. Now can they, Pop? What do you think about that? Can they, Pop?

 [*The clamor grows,* HARPO, *shrugging, moves off.* LONGFIELD *chuckles.*]

ROMEO [*after a while*]: Hey—Longfield—

LONGFIELD [*finishing off his breakfast coffee, pulling out a fresh cigar*]: Yeh? Who wants me?

ROMEO: Hey—I wanta ask ya somethin'—

LONGFIELD: Go ahead friend. Go right ahead. [*lights up, puffs his cigar*] Where are you?

ROMEO: Down here—toward the office—

LONGFIELD: Oh, yeh. How are you?

ROMEO: I'm o.k.

LONGFIELD: What's your name?

ROMEO: Romeo.

LONGFIELD: Ha Ha. Shoot, Romeo.

ROMEO: Well, about that cunt—[*He pauses.* LONGFIELD *halts in his lighting up process. He holds the cigar in his hand now*] Was she all they say, buddy? [*pause. A silence*] Hey— what the hell's the difference now—give us the scoop—was she all that way? [*pause*] HEY? Buddy? [*pauses again.* LONGFIELD *remains still, and silent*] Hey—General—Hey, take a look in on our new pal there—he's mighty quiet— Maybe he tied his necktie a little too tight or something—take a look in there, General— We don't want any that kinda stuff around here— Right, General? [*pause*] Longfield? Buddy? *Buddy Buddy?* [*pause*] I gotta hand it to ya. I'd sure like what you had handed to me. Ha Ha. Oh, man. Aha, man. *On a platter.* That's the way, buddy, right on the old platter! How about that? When I get outa here— On A Platter! Buddy? Gonna take care of that for me? [*pause*] General—hey, no kiddin'— take a look in there, Will Ya?

BOWMAN [*quietly, with authority*]: Lay off, Romeo.

[ROMEO *is quiet. He giggles a little bit, moves around his cell, but says nothing more.*]

BOWMAN [*after a while*]: Longfield—

LONGFIELD: Yeh?

BOWMAN: The guy's nuts. [*pause*] A real nut. [*pause*] Pay no attention to him.

LONGFIELD [*grinning slightly now, and briefly, and finally lighting his cigar. Then, quietly*]: He doesn't bother me. [*He puffs, slowly. All is quiet.*]

FADEOUT

SCENE: *Evening.* THE WARDEN'S *home, as before, the parlor. His wife and son are watching T.V. It is a family comedy program. We hear the audience laugh at the funny goings-on.* THE WOMAN *and boy enjoy it. Presently,* THE WARDEN *enters, from the kitchen. He carries coffee. He is in quite good spirits tonight.*

THE WARDEN: Sure you won't have another, hon?

THE WOMAN: Oh, gosh, no thanks, honey.

[*She smiles at him. He sits down. Sips his coffee. Gives a chuckle or two at the T.V. program.*]

THE WARDEN [*finally, after glancing at the boy, seeing he is quite absorbed in the T.V.*]: That Longfield fellow arrived today.

THE WOMAN [*also glancing at the boy, and quietly*]: Did he, dear?

THE WARDEN [*shaking his head*]: My God, it's the limit. The utter limit.

THE WOMAN: Is he insane, dear?

THE WARDEN [*shrugging*]: I wouldn't know. That's not my department, as you know. [*pauses, sips*] According to the Law's definition he isn't.

THE WOMAN: But is he?

THE WARDEN [*looking at her*]: I'd say he is. [*pause*] Just between you and me— [*pause*] I'd sure say he is.

THE WOMAN: It's a pity.

THE WARDEN: It's more than that. [*pause*] A man of that caliber—

THE WOMAN [*glancing over at the boy again*]: It's a real pity.

THE WARDEN: It's grotesque. Absolutely grotesque. [*pauses, puts down the coffee cup*] It's just one more argument against the whole thing. I'm going to utilize it when the time comes. [*pause*] Grotesque. That's the word for it.

THE WOMAN: Awful, really—

THE WARDEN: He's actually forced the State to do his dirty work for him. There's the limit, honey.

THE WOMAN: I think it's awful, awful—

THE WARDEN: That's just the situation it leads to. I'll bang that home, alright.

THE WOMAN: I know you will—

THE WARDEN: He's even tried to stop the mandatory appeal from going through—he had a squad of lawyers on us when he heard about it—

THE WOMAN: God how awful—

THE WARDEN: When I appear before that committee again, I'm going to bang this one home, alright, oh, I will, alright—

THE BOY [*turning*] : Look at that, Pop! Ha Ha—how do they do that anyhow, Pop?

THE WARDEN [*turning his attention to him and the T.V.*] : Say— that's really something—look at that now—[*He and his wife become involved now. They start to laugh, much as the audience is laughing. Soon, the three of them are laughing. It is all laughter . . .*]

FADEOUT

SCENE: *The Row. Next morning. It is Exercise Period. The men file up and down the corridor.* LONGFIELD *is now dressed in prison attire. He smokes a cigar. In contrast to the other men, whose demeanors are grave, he is quite buoyant once again. He is behind* BOWMAN. LAVERNE'S *guitar and soft singing can be heard. One of the tunes is 'Lay That Pistol Down, Babe.'*

LONGFIELD: So there I was, thirty and with my first pile. Not bad. Not bad at all would you say, eh, Bowman? [*pause*] Could have retired then. Not me, though. Too much energy, go. Go, Go. I felt I was carrying the whole damned economy on my back. I had to GO. Keep right on the *Go*. [*pause*] Always been patriotic. Ever since my army days, even more. Ha Ha. Oh Ho Ho. Those were the days. [*pauses, puffs*] That lad's got a fine voice. Fine, fine voice. What's he doing here? He could be making a nice little pile for himself out there. I'd back him all the way, yessiree. Wouldn't you, Dan? Don't mind me calling you Dan?

[BOWMAN *is silent.* RACHMAN, *behind* LONGFIELD, *takes him up though.*]

RACHMAN: That's the way it goes, bud. Some guys just don't wanta get ahead.

LONGFIELD: What's his status, friend?

RACHMAN: Six weeks. That's his status, bud.

LONGFIELD [*after a silence*] : Tough. [*pause*] Tough luck. Wish I could help him. If there was some way, I'd help him. [*pause*] Six weeks, eh, friend?

RACHMAN: That's it, pal.

LONGFIELD: Tough. Damn tough. [*pause*] I'm glad you call me 'pal'. I am your pal. You know I've always been everybody's pal. You know that, don't you?

RACHMAN: Got any more of them cigars—pal?

LONGFIELD [*reaching into his jacket pocket, pulling out one*]: Friend, here you are. [*Hands it to him*] Don't you worry, long as I'm here, you'll have cigars. [RACHMAN *is lighting up*] I've arranged to have several boxes delivered to me each week. I'm glad you like them. Personally, I can't get along without a good cigar. When I get right down to think about it, don't see how anyone can. Don't see it. That's life. That's part of the Vitality of life. [*pause*] What about you, BOWMAN? *Have* a cigar—

BOWMAN: No thanks, Longfield.

LONGFIELD: Aw, come on—

BOWMAN: No, thanks. Can't do it.

RACHMAN: Lay off, pal. He's got stomach trouble.

LONGFIELD: Oh? Oh? Is that it? I'm sorry to hear that. I'm real sorry to hear that. Is it serious?

BOWMAN: It's responding to treatment.

LONGFIELD: Ah, good, good, I'm glad to hear that. Is there a good doctor here?

BOWMAN: Oh, yeh. [*pause*] He told me to take it easy. [*pause*] He said, 'Bowman—*relax*. Just relax'—

LONGFIELD [*Nodding his head, after a while*]: Not a bad piece of advice, that.

BOWMAN: Yeh, I thought so.

LONGFIELD: Not bad at all. [*pause*] He should go places.

BOWMAN: I wish he would.

LONGFIELD: You don't mind if I smoke, do you? Does the smoke hurt you?

BOWMAN: I don't inhale.

LONGFIELD: That's good, that's what causes all the trouble, that inhaling.

RACHMAN: I tell all the guys when they go down there, for God's sake, *don't* inhale.

[LONGFIELD, *after a moment, laughs. He likes it.*]

RACHMAN: Think of it—*if nobody inhaled*!

LONGFIELD [*later*]: You don't mind if I do, you don't mind, do you, friend?

RACHMAN: To each his own, pal.

LONGFIELD [*after a pause*]: They say it's like peach blossoms. Is that right, Dan?

BOWMAN: That's what they say. I wouldn't know. Not yet, anyhow. [*pause*] I'll let you know.

LONGFIELD: Oh, you won't. No fear, you'll never let *me* know. I'll tell you what, I'll let *you* know. I'll send word via the Warden, I mean that.

BOWMAN: Do that.

LONGFIELD: I will, friend.

BOWMAN: Oh, yeh. Just do that.

[*They walk around in silence for a while.*]

LONGFIELD: You're all right, Bowman. *All right.* [*pause*] I've followed your case from the beginning. You got a raw deal, alright. I have a lot of respect for you. All the luck in the world to you. You're a man of my own heart, you're a man who has his mind made up about something, and goes after it. That's what I like. That's it, alright.

BOWMAN: Thanks a lot, pal.

LONGFIELD: Not that there's any sense in what you're doing. Hell, no. But that doesn't matter. What does it matter?

BOWMAN: Thanks, pal.

LONGFIELD: That's alright. [*pause*] You ought to be cheering. Cheering, friend. But, that's how it goes. As our friend behind me pointed out, 'to each his own.' [*pauses, puffs*] What can I say to you? Good luck, that's about it. [*pause*] If you want to make use of any of those jugheads who call themselves my lawyers, you're welcome to. But you don't need them. Far as I can see, you sure don't need them. [*pause*] Do you, friend? [*pause*] I've got a feeling you're going to do it, you're going to walk out of here someday, I can see it, I can see it clearly, my friend.

BOWMAN: That's fine. Wish I could.

LONGFIELD: You have hope, don't you? That's what keeps you going, for God's sake, isn't it?

BOWMAN: Sure I do. [*pause*] That's all I have.

LONGFIELD: That's all you need. [*pause*] And brains. [*pause*] And hard work. [*pause*] How do you think I made my pile?

BOWMAN: I never thought about it.

LONGFIELD: Ha Ha. Why should you? I was nobody to you,

E   129

wasn't I? Before I walked in here, before you heard I was going to be walking in here—what was I to you?

BOWMAN: You said it, pal.

LONGFIELD: Sure I said it. That's how it is, I said it. [*pause*] How much in the way of fees do you figure you've earned for yourself, working on your case? Ever counted that up, friend?

BOWMAN: Good question. [*pause*] It comes to about $150,000, or thereabouts.

LONGFIELD: Think you'll collect?

BOWMAN: A guy can try.

LONGFIELD: It's a nice little bundle to start with.

BOWMAN: With all those taxes?

LONGFIELD [*nodding, puffing the cigar*]: Good point. But see my lawyers. They'll work on that for you. They'll take pretty good care of that for you. You'll wind up with most of it. [*pause*] The little woman, my wife, you know, she's a patriot. She likes to pay taxes. Ha Ha. Nice gal. All the luck to her. Right now the angel is trying to have me certified insane. Did you know that? She's trying to do that. She really thinks she stands a good chance of doing that. Aha. Sweet kid. She wants to *save* me. And at the same time have me put away, and have everything put into her name. That's what they do—did you know that? Hell, it's not even worth it. Not even worth it. What a world. A life. *Life*? Ask the wife. [*chuckles.*]

BOWMAN: What does she want to do that for? Can't she wait?

LONGFIELD [*really chuckling*]: Wait for what? [*pause*] I made a Will. [*pause*] I didn't leave her anything. [*pause*] She's going to have to work for a living. How about that? I can just imagine that, her working for a living. I'd like to see that. I'd like to stay around just long enough to see the angel do that.

BOWMAN: I get it.

LONGFIELD: She doesn't. She doesn't even know she doesn't.

BOWMAN: You're some character.

LONGFIELD: Who isn't? Look around you. Look anyplace. Look at that guy who's going to pull the lever when I go down there. Some character! What do you say? A character?

[BOWMAN *says nothing. They move along, other murmur-*

ings of conversation, LAVERNE'S *guitar and singing, come to us.*]

LONGFIELD [*later*] : What about if I haul in a specialist to check your stomach—

BOWMAN: It's responding to treatment.

LONGFIELD [*shrugging, disappointed though*]: O.K., friend. I'm not forcing him on you. I'm not the guy who operates like that. I don't believe in that. I'm with those guys who wrote the Declaration of Independence, all the way, on that.

BOWMAN: Oh yeh? [*bemused.*]

LONGFIELD: Sure. You've heard of that—right, friend?

BOWMAN: Oh yeh. That one.

LONGFIELD: What do you mean, 'that one'?

BOWMAN: I don't mean anything. Just—that one.

LONGFIELD: Hey—[*pause*] Hey hey— [*pause*] What are you, a subversive? Is that your angle? Is it, Bowman?

BOWMAN [*only chuckles, wryly*] : You talk too much.

RACHMAN: Good cigars though. Hope your stomach's better soon, Dan.

BOWMAN: I'll make a note of that.

LONGFIELD: Ha Ha. A note of that. [*pauses, puffs, becomes worried*] Say, Bowman—

BOWMAN: Yeh?

LONGFIELD: This 'automatic appeal' thing—you know—

BOWMAN: Uh huh.

LONGFIELD: It's just a formality, isn't it? I mean, they don't ever actually reverse anything, do they?

BOWMAN: I've never seen it. ➠

LONGFIELD: Heard of it?

BOWMAN: Never heard of it.

LONGFIELD: Friend, I'm glad to hear that. Takes a real load off my mind. They sprung that on me, you know. My idiot lawyers didn't even tell me anything at all about that. How about that? That would be something. *Something.* I tried to stop it. Nothing doing, they said, the Law's the Law. I'm glad they know it. It was one hell of a job getting here. I'm glad they know it.

BOWMAN: You'll be alright. Don't worry.

LONGFIELD [*after a while*]: Say, Bowman— [*pause*] Say—

How long does it take?

BOWMAN: Down there?

LONGFIELD: Yes.

BOWMAN: Oh—about ten minutes. [*pauses,* LONGFIELD *looks unhappy*] But you don't know it. You take one deep breath, and that's all you know. You get giddy, you black out, your head slumps forward, you're out. Your body fights hard for ten minutes, it just doesn't want to go. Maybe you twitch, but you don't know it. Your heart pounds hard, it's trying to pump a lot of blood to your dying brain. It tries hard. But pretty soon, ten minutes, it's over. You don't know it. The Warden, the witnesses, the doctor, they know it. The guys who unstrap you, cart you out, put you in the cooler—they know it.

LONGFIELD [*after a while, quietly*]: Uh huh.

FADEOUT

SCENE: *The Row, a week later. It is late afternoon, just before supper time. Most of the men are washing up, others lie on their bunks, a few, like* BOWMAN, *are sitting.* LAVERNE *strums his guitar. He sings a soft blues tune.* LONGFIELD *is seated at his desk, cigar in mouth, writing a letter, perhaps.* BOWMAN *is studying his books, and making notes. Soon,* THE GENERAL *emerges from the office. He starts to walk along the corridor. He is making an announcement, and he travels the entire length of the Row as he does so.*

THE GENERAL: Well, you guys, listen—we're showing a movie tonight, it'll start at seven o'clock at the far end of the corridor as usual, and I don't want any trouble. No trouble. No wise guys. I don't want one wise guy. If we have one, just one, that's all, if we have, I guarantee that guy isolation. *I guarantee it.* And for the rest—no more movies, none at all. You get me? Romeo, none of your cornholing, you get me? Dudley, what about you? Bronski—you better stay in your cell if you don't think you can hack it—I mean that, Bronski— [*He pauses, the men whose names he has mentioned mutter, or laugh, or ignore him*] I want every guy here to understand that— Understand that?

[*He is passing* BOWMAN'S *cell.*]

BOWMAN: Subject to the Warden's concurrence, General. Rule 619. You ought to know that, General.

[THE GENERAL *glares through the bars at him.*]

THE GENERAL [*muttering*]: One of these days, Bowman—

BOWMAN [*calmly*]: Are you threatening me, General?

THE GENERAL [*losing control momentarily, shouting*]: Shut Your Trap, Bowman!

BOWMAN [*shaking his head*]: General, tell me one thing. How did they come to appoint you? What have you got, a brother-in-law in the Legislature, or something?

THE GENERAL: I'm warning you, Bowman—

[*The men begin to stir now, they beat their cell doors, they make a clamor. He stands before* BOWMAN's *cell. Soon, the clamor dies down. He remains there.*]

BOWMAN [*quietly*]: Go on, move along now.

[THE GENERAL *does so, presently. He passes* BRONSKI, MARLOWE, ROPER. *He is passing* LONGFIELD.]

LONGFIELD [*up now near the cell door*]: Have a cigar, Sergeant.

THE GENERAL [*halting, glaring at him*]: It makes no difference you're having a pile. No difference at all here, buddy.

LONGFIELD: Go on, have one.

THE GENERAL [*after a pause*]: You're a phoney, Longfield. Wait until we take that walk down there. You'll find out, Longfield.

LONGFIELD: Have two cigars, Sergeant.

THE GENERAL: Stop calling me Sergeant.

LONGFIELD: Ah, well, alright, if you say so. What should I call you? 'General'? Let them, I like 'Sergeant'. You look more like a Sergeant. In my Army days there was a guy in charge of us, a Sergeant, just like you. He was *just* like you! It was a long time ago. Hell, you're in charge here. In the Army, the Sergeants are in charge of everything. *Everything*, Sergeant.

THE GENERAL: You're a phoney, Longfield.

LONGFIELD: Don't you want the cigars? I've got plenty of them. They're for everybody. We're one big family here, you're part of it. What's the matter? They're pretty good, pretty good, Sergeant. I can have a box sent you each week if you're too proud to take them direct from me. How about that?

THE GENERAL: No movie for you, Buddy.

LONGFIELD [*shocked, shaking his head now*]: You've got a problem, Sergeant. A definite, *anti-social* problem, I think, Sergeant. You ought to face it, tackle it. *Work over it*, Sergeant. Talk it over with the Warden. That's it, have a good talk with him. [*pauses, puffs his cigar*] What's the name of the movie?

[THE GENERAL, *humiliated, impotent again, moves off, muttering. He continues to make his announcement and finally disappears from view (far Right), but we can hear him, vaguely.*]

LONGFIELD: That guy worries me. [*pause*] That guy definitely worries me. I wasn't counting on running into a little Napoleon here. No sir, not here.

BOWMAN: Don't let him worry you. Read the rules and throw them at him. They floor him. I'm not so sure he can read, anyhow.

LONGFIELD: What's the movie, anyway?

BRONSKI: Last time it was a Tarzan movie.

LONGFIELD: Tarzan? No kidding? [*pause*] Are you kidding me?

BRONSKI: Whatsamatter, you don't like Tarzan movies?

LONGFIELD: Don't get me wrong, friend—they're alright, *alright*, friend.

BRONSKI: What's the complaint, then?

LONGFIELD: I'm not complaining, friend.

BRONSKI: They don't come better than that, Tarzan movies—

RACHMAN: Take a look at the apes in those movies. Take a good look. Bronski's one of them.

BRONSKI: Pretty funny—

RACHMAN: How much they shell out for that, man? I mean, hell, all you gotta do is sit in the tree, right? That's right, ain't it, man?

[*Laughter.*]

ROMEO: It better not be a Tarzan movie. Christ! I'll ram it down the General's throat, screen and all, watch me!

DUDLEY: Whaddaya want, a girlie show?

ROMEO: Sure! And sure! Why not?

RACHMAN: A lotta good that would do you.

ROMEO: Oh, yeh? How do you know?

BRONSKI [*shouting*]: Yeh, you're sure pretty funny, Rachman old buddy, pretty goddamn funny. We'll see tonight how funny, you wait, buddy.

RACHMAN: Aw, take it easy, I was only kiddin' you there, buddy.

BRONSKI [*still shouting*]: Don't kid around with me, Buddy!

ROPER [*lifting his head from his bunk*]: Can't you guys knock it off? Knock it off a while? Can't ya?

[*The men look around, some shuffle around in their cells. There is quiet. There is* LAVERNE'S *guitar strumming, soft singing, and, far off,* THE GENERAL'S *voice. And quiet.*]

FADEOUT

SCENE: *That evening, The Row. And the Warden's home. The movie is being shown on The Row. It is at the end of the corridor, out of our line of view. The men are seated on their chairs in the corridor. The lights are very low. The guards watch, the gun guard paces. The movie sounds like the Al Jolson film, the story of his life. We can hear Jolson singing his famous songs from time to time, in the distance. At the moment, it is 'Swanee'. In the Warden's parlor there are two men sitting with the Warden and his wife. One is the State Attorney-General, the other is a Judge. They are drinking cocktails, chatting, smoking. His wife leaves the room for a while, perhaps to fix a snack.*

STATE ATTORNEY [*clearing his throat*]: Well—

THE WARDEN: Oh Oh—

STATE ATTORNEY: O.K., you can say that, but look at it from my view—

THE WARDEN [*leaning forward slightly*]: That's what I always try to do—

STATE ATTORNEY: Can't you try a little harder?

THE WARDEN: What can I do?

STATE ATTORNEY: Well, [*pause*] I can appreciate your position. [*pauses, looks around, looks at the Judge, returns to the Warden*] But, you see—the whole thing's getting out of hand. There's an outcry up and down the State, it's the kind of pressure you can't fight. [*pauses, sips, put his glass down*] The Governor has asked me to be clear, perfectly clear—

THE WARDEN: I can appreciate that. It's not a simple issue. I can well appreciate that—

STATE ATTORNEY [*sitting back*]: Well?

THE WARDEN [*gesturing*]: Well? [*pauses, looks around*] Well? What? [*pause*] The fact is, I mean, you can't get away from it, the fellow's simply exercising his constitutional rights— that's all there's to it—

STATE ATTORNEY: Is that it? Is that what the people think? Six years! By God, he's exercised enough constitutional rights to last a lifetime—the sum total of *all* our lifetimes! Come on, Warden— And this latest petition—*eighty-seven* pages— it's a mockery—sheer mockery—and if it's granted—

THE WARDEN: Well, I can't express any opinion there, you know—

JUDGE: *Bah.* The fellow's nothing but a fiend, a *known fiend.* Don't hand me that, Warden. He's making monkeys out of all of us, the entire State, the Judiciary, everything. A first class laughing-stock out of us. It doesn't matter much to you. You're just his Custodian, aren't you? [*pauses, leans forward*] But I sentenced him, I'm the fellow who's supposed to have given him a 'rigged' trial and 'wrongfully' sentenced him. Here I am. It's my name, my career, to bring it down to a personal level, that's involved, in addition to everything else, everything. [*pause*] Can you see that?

THE WARDEN: Well—Judge— [*shifts around*] Well, as you know, I always try to see everything—

JUDGE: Sure you do, so do I, that's why the people elect me—

THE WARDEN: And you do a fine job, a mighty fine job, Judge—

STATE ATTORNEY: That doesn't solve our problem—

THE WARDEN: Well, no, it doesn't—I never said it does— [*pause*] I can see the spot you're in, all you fellows are in—

JUDGE [*nodding his head, pleased somewhat*]: Sure you can, I'm sure you can— [*pause*] Everybody knows the good work you do there, everybody—you don't have to worry a minute about that, Warden—

STATE ATTORNEY: You'd like to continue doing it, we'd like to see you continue doing it, we only wish there were more like you around, that's what we wish—

JUDGE: But this is something, really something—it's— [*pause*] it's one of those 'once in a lifetime' things, that's how to look at it, Warden—

STATE ATTORNEY: Look at his record—just look at his record— [*There is a silence.*]

THE WARDEN [*finally, quietly*]: What can I do? Just what do you expect me to do? He's only exercising his rights, his *simple, constitutional rights*, gentlemen—

STATE ATTORNEY [*leaning forward*]: You're appointed by the Governor, Warden. The people elect me. The Sovereign people of this Great State elect me. *And the Governor.* [*pause*] Bear that in mind, Warden.

JUDGE [*nodding his head*]: It's something, just something you ought to bear in mind, Warden—

STATE ATTORNEY [*quietly*]: We have to get down to earth. We have to get our feet on *good, solid* EARTH. [*pause*] Warden.

[*There is silence. The three men sit there in silence. The room* FADES OUT.]

[*Up on The Row, there is a burst of laughter. Something very amusing no doubt, on the screen.*]

BRONSKI [*suddenly, though we do not see him clearly*]: YEEOW! He's Got Me! GENERAL! Hey, General! THE GODDAMN QUEER'S GOT ME!

[*There is a violent struggle in the dimly lit corridor, chairs start flying, the men punch, grab, wrestle, the guards rush in, alarm bells ring. There is pandemonium . . .*]

BRONSKI [*screeching*]: THE GODDAMN QUEER! THE QUEER! GET OFF ME!

[*And in the background, the movie runs on, its sounds break through, sporadically.*]

FADEOUT

SCENE: *The Row, a week later. There is only silence. Laverne is strumming his guitar, but very quietly, and he is not singing, or humming. The men sit quietly, or stand, very quietly.* ROPER *is the only active one. He is packing his few belongings in a sheet.* LONGFIELD *is up near the cell door, smoking a cigar, leaning toward his cell. Soon, the Cage doors buzz and open, one by one. A party of Guards enters. They nod to the General, hand over and sign some papers. They start to walk down the corridor.*

RACHMAN [*grimly, quietly*]: Here we go.

DUDLEY: So long, Roper.

ROMEO: Sweet dreams, buddy, sweet dreams, boy, don't let them kid you—

[BOWMAN *rises from his desk. He watches the guards walk by, as does everyone else on The Row. The Guards reach* ROPER's *cell. The one in charge steps forward, unlocks the door.*

GUARD IN CHARGE [*quietly*]: It's time, Roper.

[ROPER *nods his head, he has finished with his things. He leaves them on his bunk. He looks around the cell.*]

ROPER: Let's go.

[*He holds out his hands. The guards put a strap around his waist, and handcuffs on his wrists. A chain leads from the handcuffs to the belt. The guards step back.* ROPER *steps out of his cell. He looks up and down the corridor. He starts to move along now, some of the guards in front, others behind.*]

LONGFIELD: So long, son. [*pause*] Don't worry about anything. [*pause*] Not a thing.

[ROPER *halts a moment, in response to this. He looks back, half-way. Then, walks on. As he passes each cell he murmurs, 'So long' or 'Be seeing you' or 'So long, pal.' The men respond, similarly. At the office he speaks to* THE GENERAL.]

ROPER: So long. See you some day.

THE GENERAL [*nodding his head*]: Good luck, Roper.

[*Now* ROPER *is led into the cage, and far door opens, he passes through, the guards pass through. The door closes. He has disappeared.*]

[*There is silence on The Row. Then,* LAVERNE's *guitar, softly, can be heard. He hums an old cowboy song, 'Lone Prairie'*]

FADEOUT

[*And, slowly, the Holding Cell, the Chamber appear, for a long moment.*]

FADEOUT

THE ROW

PART TWO

SCENE: *The Row. Morning, a few days later. There is quite a lot of activity. It is linen-exchange day. The men are removing their old sheets and hanging them over the bars of their cell doors. Presently, a cart, pushed by* HARPO, *enters. It contains a pile of clean sheets. He goes from cell to cell, handing them out, collecting the old ones, which he drops into a large canvas bag hanging alongside the cart.* LONGFIELD *has moved up one cell toward* BOWMAN. *He is in fact in the cell formerly occupied by* ROPER. *His old cell is vacant. He is smoking a cigar, as usual.*

MARLOWE [*looking around, thinking, looking toward* LONG-FIELD]: Don't you feel funny in there, pal?

LONGFIELD: No, friend. Not at all.

MARLOWE: You could of stayed in your own cell.

LONGFIELD: I know that, friend.

MARLOWE: How come you had to move there, huh?

LONGFIELD: Look at it this way— Life is all movement, *movement*, friend. You never stand still, not for a moment, friend, are you ever still. You know that?

MARLOWE [*shrugging, shaking his head*]: Have it your way, pal. [*pause*] Any cigars?

LONGFIELD: Friend, plenty of them. [*He steps back, grabs a fistful from a box, and thrusts them toward* MARLOWE] Pass them along. Do that, will you, friend? Take a few, enough to hold you a while.

MARLOWE: Thanks, pal. Thanks a lot. That's what I like, a good cigar. Oh, yeh. Real good cigar.

LONGFIELD: Friend, that's good to hear. That puts a glow in my heart, that's mighty fine to hear.

MARLOWE [*lighting up, issuing clouds of smoke*]: Longfield—

LONGFIELD: Here. Always here. Twenty-four hours a day, friend, right here.

MARLOWE: Yeh, well, been meaning to ask ya something—

LONGFIELD: Go ahead, friend. At your service.

MARLOWE [*puffing, then a pause*]: Are you nuts?

LONGFIELD: Friend, that's an interesting, but ungrateful thing
to say. Ungrateful, friend. That's a cardinal sin, did you
know that? Know anything at all about that, my friend?
[*pause*] Don't you like your cigar?

MARLOWE [*somewhat flustered*]: Hell, don't get me wrong, pal.
I like them fine. Fine, fine. I didn't mean a thing ungrateful
there—

LONGFIELD: Is that right?

MARLOWE: That's right.

LONGFIELD: You just wanted to know—

MARLOWE: Yeh, that's right, I just wanted to get things straight,
I wanted to know—

LONGFIELD: You figured I'd know—

MARLOWE: Yeh, I did, I figured you'd know—

LONGFIELD: You wanted information, that piece of information.
You wanted me to communicate it to you—

MARLOWE [*after a pause, scratching his head, shrugging*]: Yeh,
guess so—

LONGFIELD: Well, friend— [*pauses, puffs*] I'll tell you what.
I'm just going to tell you what. [*pause*] You keep your eye
on me. You keep your one good eye on me. You decide. I'm
going to leave it up to you to decide. How about that?

MARLOWE [*not happy*]: Aw, hell. *Me* decide—

LONGFIELD: Sure, why not? You ought to be able to do that—
Decide.

MARLOWE: Would I ask, if I could decide?

LONGFIELD: Think it over.

MARLOWE [*absorbed, after a pause*]: You're here. A guy like
you, here. You asked them to put you here. [*pause*] Hell,
you'd never have been here!

LONGFIELD: You're right, friend. It's not so easy getting here.
I almost *didn't* get here.

MARLOWE: That's what I mean—

LONGFIELD: What do you mean?

MARLOWE: You get me—a guy like you—you really get me—

LONGFIELD [*smiling*]: You don't want to worry about it, friend.

You can really get yourself in one hell of a knot there, worrying about it. I mean it.

MARLOWE [*suddenly, coming as close as he can to* LONGFIELD]: I've got two weeks, two more weeks, Longfield—

LONGFIELD [*after a pause*]: That's not long. Keep yourself busy. Listen to your radio there. There's always good stuff on the radio. Read. Talk to me anytime you want to. Enjoy those cigars. Before you know it—two weeks. [*snaps his fingers*] two weeks, friend. In terms of the earth's journey through time, space— *What the hell's two weeks, friend?* You tell me that—can you, my friend?

MARLOWE: Don't hand me that! It's a hell of a long time to me, Buddy!

LONGFIELD: Well, what can I do? Ask them to move it up? You think I can do that, friend?

MARLOWE: You *are* nuts! You don't get me at all, man!

LONGFIELD: Oh, don't I? OHO! *Don't I?*

MARLOWE: Wait, buddy!

LONGFIELD: That's all I've got to do here, friend—

MARLOWE: Well, wait, oh yeh, just wait, buddy—I'd like to see it. It's too bad I won't see it— *When They Come For You, Buddy!*

LONGFIELD: I'll be here.

[*A silence,* MARLOWE *broods in his cell.*]

LONGFIELD: Friend? [*pauses, puffs*] What's the matter? [*pause*] Don't you think I will? Don't you?

[*Meantime, the linen exchange has been proceeding smoothly.* HARPO *chats with the men.* LAVERNE, *soon, starts strumming his guitar.*]

HARPO [*before* DUDLEY's *cell*]: There y'are, son.

DUDLEY [*flatly*]: Yeh, thanks a lot, buddy.

HARPO [*looking around first*]: They turn you down? Governor turn you down too, son?

DUDLEY: Flat down.

HARPO: Aw, I'm sorry. I'm mighty sorry.

DUDLEY: Then take my place, buddy. [*pause*] Want to do that? [HARPO *is embarrassed, only stands there.*]

DUDLEY: You're sorry, ain'tcha? If you're sorry, you're sorry, buddy!

[HARPO *still stands there.*]

DUDLEY: One more week—that's all you gotta be sorry for! Think of that, Buddy!

[HARPO *does not move.*]

DUDLEY: Go on, move, buddy. You ain't sorry. Ain't one goddamn person's sorry. You don't give a goddamn, Buddy!

HARPO [*low-voiced*]: You're doin' me wrong son—I'm real sorry—

DUDLEY: Move along, buddy—

HARPO: I din't put you here! Don't jump me, son! I din't do it!

DUDLEY [*loudly*]: *A Guy A Lot Like You Put Me Here*! Oh, Yeh—*He Did*, Buddy! Maybe it even *Was* you— How would I know? *How Would I*, Old Buddy?

[*He is quite disturbed now.* LAVERNE'S *guitar stops a moment.* HARPO *moves along. He shoves the sheets in quickly to* RACHMAN, *barely looking at him, takes the old ones. He pulls up before* BOWMAN'S *cell.*]

HARPO [*quietly*]: Dan— [BOWMAN *is facing him*] Dan—

BOWMAN: Yeh, Harpo—

HARPO [*barely murmuring, his voice quavering*]: He's got me wrong—all wrong— You know that— *You* do, don'tcha, Dan?

BOWMAN [*after a while, taking the clean sheets*]: Sure, Harpo. [*pause*] Sure. I know that.

[*They remain there, looking at one another. Then, quickly,* HARPO *turns away, moves off*] [LAVERNE'S *guitar is heard again.* DUDLEY *starts to make his bunk up.*]

FADEOUT

SCENE: *The Row, two weeks later.* DUDLEY *is gone. So is* MARLOWE. LONGFIELD *has moved into his cell. He is much as before, high spirited, smoking a cigar.* LAVERNE'S *guitar and soft singing, as before.* BOWMAN *is at his table, writing.* BRONSKI, *in the next cell, is in bad shape, restless, pacing his cell, back and forth, like an animal.*

LONGFIELD [*listening to the pacing, and after a while*]: What's the matter, friend?

BRONSKI: Mind your own business, pal.

LONGFIELD: Aw, come on, have a cigar. That's what you need, m'friend.

BRONSKI: Lay off, Crackpot. I mean it!

[LONGFIELD *shrugs his shoulders, relaxes on his bunk, puffing away at his cigar.*]

LONGFIELD [*expansively*]: Friend, you're lucky. Look at me! Four more weeks. *Four.* There's no way I could get them to speed it up. I even put a request in writing. *My own personal handwriting.* No soap, *Nyet.* And those so-called lawyers of mine— How about that? How's that for a prize pair of clowns, eh? Legal clowns! Hell, one of them should make a judge some day! Five more days for you, friend. You're lucky! I'd trade places with you anytime, Anytime! What a pair of clowns!

BRONSKI: Lay Off, Buddy!

[LONGFIELD *grins, shrugs again, puffs his cigar, and keeps quiet now. There is silence on The Row.* BRONSKI *paces a while longer, then comes to the front of his cell. He is near* BOWMAN's *side.*]

BRONSKI: Dan—

BOWMAN [*looking up*]: Yeh, Bronski—

BRONSKI: They won't get me down there.

[BOWMAN *is quiet.*]

BRONSKI [*quietly*]: I got a $10,000 government insurance policy. It's made out to the old lady. If they get me down there, she gets nothing. [*pause*] If I go before they get me down there— she collects. [*pause*] I found that out. The guy that was here yesterday, that guy was the insurance man. I found out. Oh yeh, he told me.

[BOWMAN *is quiet.*]

BRONSKI: I wanted to tell ya, Dan. [*pause*] You won't monkey me around, will ya, Dan . . .

BOWMAN [*quietly*]: How come you don't file a Writ? I can show you how. [*pause*] Want me to do that?

BRONSKI: What's the use?

BOWMAN: You'd be surprised, Bronski.

BRONSKI: That's what the D.A. said. *A big surprise.* You're in for a Big Surprise, Bronski. Oh yeh. He sure was right. Old Buddy

Boy D.A., *right*, alright.

BOWMAN: Think about it, Bronski.

BRONSKI [*after a while*]: You won't try anything—you won't monkey around—willya—Dan—

BOWMAN: I'll be here. Right here. Think about it.

BRONSKI [*soon*] [*quietly*]: I been doin' that a long time. [*pause*] Thinking about it.

[*He remains near the cell door. He is quiet.* BOWMAN, *shortly, turns back to his work. The Row is quiet, save for* LAVERNE'S *guitar.*]

FADEOUT

SCENE: *The Row, a few mornings later. It is Exercise Period.* LONGFIELD *is behind* BOWMAN.

LONGFIELD [*puffing his cigar*]: It surprised Hell out of me, Dan. I don't surprise easily.

BOWMAN: Uh huh.

LONGFIELD: I have to hand it to him, though. How'd he do it? Hell, it must have taken an hour at least! I couldn't do it when I had a second! A split second! Bang, that's all I had to do! But I couldn't, I had to turn myself in, force the State to do it. And here's this guy—Jesus, *I have to hand it to him—*

BOWMAN: Uh huh.

LONGFIELD: Not your first one, is it?

BOWMAN: Uh uh. [*pause*] One, two a year—at least.

LONGFIELD: *How'd he do it?* That's one for the books alright. I'll never get near to understanding it. Believe me. [*pause*] Believe me, Bowman—

BOWMAN: I believe you.

LONGFIELD: Think there might be a little stinko about it?

BOWMAN: Maybe.

LONGFIELD: His relatives ought to sue Hell out of the State. They could really cash in—yes sir, they ought to do that.

BOWMAN: Maybe they'd prefer him back though. You can't tell. Could just be that way, Longfield.

LONGFIELD: What about your pal, the Warden? Think he'll come through it alright? They might be hot after him, eh? Hasn't been around today. Maybe they've started already, what do you say?

BOWMAN: That could be, Longfield.

LONGFIELD [*after a while*]: You've been here too long. Too damn long, Dan.

BOWMAN: I agree there.

LONGFIELD: I admire you, I've told you that a hundred times if one. But what's the point of it? You tell me. I'd like to know the point of it.

BOWMAN: That's your problem, Longfield.

LONGFIELD: Oh?

BOWMAN: Sure. Sure it is. When you lost your nerve, when you couldn't pull that trigger, that problem became yours. All yours, old buddy.

LONGFIELD [*thinking over that one*]: I've always paid my taxes. Not that I wanted to, goddamn it, but I paid them. *A good part of them.* So, let the State do it for me. It's about time they did something for me. Am I asking too much? It's the least they can do for me.

[THE GENERAL *steps out, calls* 'TIME', *and the men file back to their cells.* LONGFIELD *now occupies the cell next to* BOWMAN. *He looks around, up and down The Row.*]

LONGFIELD: The place is thinning out, Bowman.

BOWMAN: That could happen. Once, about three years ago, it got down to seven.

LONGFIELD: Just *seven?*

BOWMAN: That's right. [*pause*] Then, a couple of months ago, full house. Thirty cells, thirty tenants. Maybe a few more waiting outside. Who could tell?

LONGFIELD: Where would they wait—outside? [*He chuckles over that one. Then, lowers his voice, comes near to* BOWMAN's *side*] When's that guitar boy going?

BOWMAN: Next week.

LONGFIELD: I'm going to miss him.

BOWMAN: We all will. [*pause*] You ought to take over his guitar. You'd be doing us all a favor, Longfield.

LONGFIELD: Maybe I'll do that. [*pause*] I used to play a clarinet once, the High School band. I might just do that. [*pauses, puffs his cigar*] Always have liked the guitar.

[BOWMAN *is silent.*]

145

LONGFIELD: Know anything about a guitar?

RACHMAN: Hey, Longfield—

LONGFIELD: Yeh, friend?

RACHMAN: Pass one down, willya?

LONGFIELD [*grabbing some cigars, handing them to* BOWMAN *to pass along*]: At your service, friend. [*pause*] Hey, Sergeant, relax, it's only a few cigars— Have one—

THE GENERAL [*from the office*]: Cut the jazz, Longfield.

[LONGFIELD *laughs,* THE GENERAL *mutters something.* RACHMAN *has his cigar. He passes a few to the guard nearby, for* ROMEO, *and* THE GENERAL. LAVERNE *does not smoke them.*]

RACHMAN [*lighting up*]: Thanks a lot, buddy. I hope you'll be around a while.

LONGFIELD: Don't worry if I'm not. I've made arrangements to keep you boys supplied.

RACHMAN: Is that right?

LONGFIELD: Sure. What do you think my lawyers were here for the other day?

RACHMAN [*after a pause*]: That's nice of you.

LONGFIELD: I do what I can, I always have, friend. What good is life otherwise? There's not a damn bit of satisfaction in life otherwise. Believe me.

[*There is a silence.* RACHMAN *enjoys his cigar, nods his head.*]

LONGFIELD: What are you doing there, Dan?

BOWMAN: Writing.

LONGFIELD [*after a pause*]: What are you writing?

BOWMAN: The story of my life. I think.

LONGFIELD: You think?

BOWMAN: Yes.

LONGFIELD: Why don't you know?

BOWMAN: Don't ask me. I just started something here, and it looks like it's turning out that way.

LONGFIELD: Write mine too, while you're at it. [*pause*] No kidding, would you like to? [*pause*] It's fairly interesting.

BOWMAN: I don't doubt that. [*pauses, looks around*] [*casually*] What happened, anyway, Longfield?

LONGFIELD: Don't you read the papers?

BOWMAN [*shrugs*]: Well, if you don't want to tell me—

146

LONGFIELD: Oh, yeh, I want to tell you. Don't get me wrong there. [*pauses, lowers his voice, comes nearer to* BOWMAN'S *side, stands there a while*] She was my secretary.
   [*A silence. He looks around.*]
BOWMAN: Uh huh—
LONGFIELD: I fell head over heels for her, I ran around a lot with her. [*pause*] She liked me too. [*pause*] To put it mildly, friend.
BOWMAN: Uh huh—
LONGFIELD: Oh, yeh, uh huh. [*pause*] Trouble was, she was married too. [*pause*] And neither her husband nor my angel wife would spring us loose, *No Divorce*. [*pause*] You get those types, *real types*. Oh, yeh. [*pause*] I moved we just went off together, you know, just took off and set up a new life, somewhere, together. It was like that. [*pause*] But she wouldn't do that. I don't know, funny girl that way, she just wouldn't do that. [*pause*] She quit her job, she was going to break up with me.
   [*A silence.*]
BOWMAN: Uh huh—
LONGFIELD: So—one day—after a week without her—I came to the conclusion, this lousy life wasn't worth a damn without her. *Not one damn.* [*a long pause*] I figured out a way I could have her for all time— [*pause*] All, *the whole of Time*— [*pause*] *I'd put a bullet through her head, and one through mine.*
   [*A silence*] [LAVERNE'S *guitar strums, the gun guard paces.*]
LONGFIELD: It came to me, just like that. [*snaps his fingers*] I didn't have to sit in a room, in the dark, a long time, maybe night after night, thinking, figuring. Nothing ever came to me that way the whole of my life anyway. That's the secret of my success, friend! [*pause*] Yes, the whole idea, the whole beautiful idea just popped into my mind. [*pause*] Well, you know the rest. I did half the job, and then I found out I couldn't do the other half—my half. Don't get me wrong, friend, I tried. I sure tried! [*pauses, looks around*] I sat there six, seven hours, trying . . . [*pause*] So I turned myself in, I said, Let the State complete. Let this Great Sovereign State, friend, Complete! [*pause*] It wasn't easy, I'll tell you, friend,

I almost didn't make it, I had to fight like hell every step of the way, believe you me, my friend—you think it's hard getting out of here for something you say you didn't do, something I believe damn well you didn't do—well, you ought to see the job it is getting here when you want to, and for something you did do! That's funny, huh? That's like the whole of life, pretty goddamn funny, huh? Hell, even now they've got that damned automatic appeal business hanging over me, and that angel of a wife of mine trying to get me in a nuthouse. Oh, yeh, some job!

BOWMAN [*after a while*]: Well, you don't have to worry about that appeal, Longfield.

LONGFIELD: You don't know, I'm just the one guy it might happen to—

BOWMAN: Don't worry.

[THE GENERAL *emerges from his office. He puffs a cigar.*]

THE GENERAL: Nice cigar, Longfield.

LONGFIELD: I thought you'd like it, Sarge. The first time I laid eyes on you I knew damn well you were a man of taste, judgement. I knew that. There's just something about you that told me that.

THE GENERAL [*chuckling, in good mood today*]: You must of looked a long ways for this.

LONGFIELD: You're right, friend. I have a man who does nothing else for me.

THE GENERAL: That a fact?

LONGFIELD: It sure is.

THE GENERAL: Well, I'm obliged. Anytime you can spare one—

LONGFIELD: Don't you worry, friend, I'll see you're taken care of.

THE GENERAL: Anything you need there?

LONGFIELD: Not a thing, not one single thing, my friend.

THE GENERAL: Just give a holler. [*Re-enters the office. Opens comic book.*]

BOWMAN: You've got a friend for life.

LONGFIELD [*chuckling*]: That's what I need.

[*There is silence a while.* LONGFIELD *moves about his cell.* BOWMAN *continues his writing. After a while,* LONGFIELD *moves to the front of the cell again.*]

LONGFIELD: What are you doing now?

BOWMAN: Still writing.

LONGFIELD [*after a pause*]: What's your story, anyhow?

BOWMAN [*shrugs, looks around*]: It's just like you heard it.

LONGFIELD: *I'd like to hear it from you.*

BOWMAN: It's not much.

LONGFIELD: Let's hear it—

BOWMAN [*after a pause*]: You think that's going to do you any good hearing it?

LONGFIELD: Hell, friend, I'm interested, real interested, I have a lot of respect for you—

BOWMAN: Well— [*pause*]

LONGFIELD: Well?

BOWMAN [*sighing*]: Put it this way— [*pause*] I'm still pretty young. I'd like to live a few years longer. I don't mind dying, but I don't like the idea of anybody figuring out for me when I should die. I'm funny that way. I just don't. Well, the State disagrees with me. The State thinks I've lived long enough, and also thinks it knows the date, the time, it should prove that. They want me to come along peacefully into that chamber, have a seat there, take a deep breath—my last deep breath. [*pause*] And I don't want to. Somehow, I just don't want to. First of all, because I'm not sick of living. You'd think I would be, but I'm not. Funny thing, huh? Secondly, because I happen to be innocent. I was framed. I was tried in a court where the Judge was a son of a bitch and everything was stacked against me. [*pause*] I didn't have the dough to get hold of a lawyer, either. I had to play games with some dope of a court-appointed one. Oh, yeh. [*pause*] And there's politics. It's pretty complicated. I'm still working it out. Maybe that's why I'm writing this book. It was election year, they needed someone real bad to pin this on to. The papers, the public was screaming for it. And there I was. [*pause*] So now, I'm a fiend. You have mobs howling out there, whipped up by those same papers, for the State to get rid of me. Maybe the Governor, one or two of the top dogs, who knows, maybe they'd like to turn me loose. But it's a vicious circle. The mobs they whipped up, or helped to whip up, now control them. *Bowman Must Go.* [*pause*]

That's it, and then, yeh, I've had lots of time to think, maybe you'd like to know what I think— [*pause*] This whole set-up, the whole thing, stinks. Know what you're in? *An Abattoir*. That's a good word for you. Look it up sometime, I'll loan you my dictionary. Sure, a *social abattoir*. That's what it is, that's all it amounts to. And I don't like it. Not just because I happen to be caught up in it. I just, on general principles, based on specific thinking, observation, *don't like it*. [*pause*] Hell, I'm not even the only one. The Warden is one of them. Anyhow, he claims to be. He's always making speeches about it, or testifying before some legislative committee about it. Did you know that? He'd really like to see the whole thing go. He would, just ask, he'll tell you so. [*pause*] If ever I make it out of here, that will be my crusade. [*pause*] If I ever make it out of here, that will be my crusade in life. [*pause*] Well, Longfield, that's it, that's about all there is to it. Here I am, six years later. Not bad, huh?

You'll make it out of here.

BOWMAN: Trying to lower my guard?

LONGFIELD: Hell no, I'm for you. I'm all for you.

BOWMAN: Oh, yeh. I can believe it.

LONGFIELD: Hey, you ought to. I mean it. [*pause*] Maybe, deep down, I can't see any sense in what you're doing, knowing what I do about what's out there—but I mean it. I sure do mean it.

    [*A silence,* BOWMAN *gives a wry grin, returns to his writing.*]

LONGFIELD [*later*]: About your Warden—

    [BOWMAN *looks up.*]

LONGFIELD: He's a phoney.

BOWMAN [*reflecting*]: Well, maybe. Maybe so. That's not an easy thing to tell. [*pause*] A job like he's got, it's damn hard to tell.

LONGFIELD: How could the guy hold the job, otherwise?

BOWMAN: Yeh, I've thought a lot about that. A hell of a lot. [*pause*] But he's a good man. I mean, he has a good prison, he really tries hard to do his best, maybe even straightens a lot of guys out. Educates them, teaches them trades, you'd be surprised. [*pause*] He seems pretty hard hit every time somebody takes the walk down there. He's made a lot of facilities available to me, enabling me to carry on my fight. True, they're my constitutional rights, but he didn't have to. You know what those rights amount to when a guy in his job doesn't want you to have them. Or when people, in general, don't want you to have them. You know, don't you. [*pause*] Of course, it's hard for him to stop me now, even if he wants to. I don't think he likes all the support I've built up, all over. He likes the limelight himself. Maybe he would like to stop it. Maybe he can't though. Just maybe.

LONGFIELD: Your life has a lot of maybes in it. There's no maybe in mine, not about this guy. He's a phoney. I know one a mile off.

BOWMAN: Alright, what does it matter?

LONGFIELD [*shrugs*]: I guess it doesn't. [*pause*] Far as I'm concerned, it doesn't at all matter. I just thought you might like to know.

BOWMAN: A guy in your shoes wouldn't think otherwise.

LONGFIELD: *Whose* shoes? [*pause*] Friend, there's a good one to think about— Just *Whose* Shoes? [*pause*] Anyhow?
   [*There is silence, a while.*]

LONGFIELD [*quietly*]: How's the stomach? What did that pill-pusher have to say this morning? You were quite a while with him.

BOWMAN: Making progress. Slow, steady progress.

LONGFIELD: I'm glad to hear that.

BOWMAN: 'Relax'—he keeps saying to me.

LONGFIELD: That's great. Have a cigar—

BOWMAN: Keep the cigar.

LONGFIELD [*after a pause*]: You won't have to put up with me much longer, Dan.

BOWMAN: You're not hard to put up with.

LONGFIELD: There's going to be hell to pay if that damn court up there jazzes me around, you know.

BOWMAN: I told you, don't worry a minute about that, pal.

LONGFIELD: I always used to say, before all this, before any of it, I used to say, to hell with all courts, all law, to hell with it all. When I saw a cop I used to laugh, or want to puke.

I was quite the Anarchist, you might say. But then they did me that favor and I can see some sense in the whole set-up after all.

[*He puffs away at his cigar, contentedly.*]

BOWMAN: They haven't done it yet, Longfield.

LONGFIELD: They better, that's all I can say.

BOWMAN: You sure have an interesting mind, Longfield.

LONGFIELD: Well, thanks a lot, friend.

BOWMAN: Don't thank me, I'm just making an observation.

LONGFIELD: What's so interesting about it? I'd like to know?

BOWMAN: Take a look at what you've just said—

LONGFIELD: What did I say?

BOWMAN: Take a look—

LONGFIELD: You're the guy, you've got the interesting mind. Look at what you're up to. What you've been up to. What you're prepared for the next twenty years, if necessary, to be up to. That's really interesting, friend.

BOWMAN: What's interesting? Trying to stay alive? What's so interesting about that, I wonder?

LONGFIELD: What's the point in it? Just what in hell's the point in it?

BOWMAN: When you had the chance, you didn't pull the trigger. Maybe now, maybe though you don't even know it, you're hoping for that court up there, or your wife, to do the same. Just maybe, Longfield.

LONGFIELD: Are you kidding? [*pause*] You're not just kidding, friend?

BOWMAN: You lost your nerve. You think you'll have it when your time comes?

LONGFIELD [*after a pause*]: It won't make any difference, will it?

BOWMAN: Well, what's all the malarkey about then? A guy like you always finds someone to do his dirty work for him. You've found the State, the Law. Not bad, pal. What does it prove?

LONGFIELD: What's it supposed to prove? What the hell's it supposed to prove?

BOWMAN: You tell me. Send me a message from down there. When your time comes, do that, Longfield.

LONGFIELD: Alright, I will. [*pause*] You sit here and wait, see if I don't! [*pause*] Friend, *I will!*

BOWMAN [*quietly*]: I'll be here. I'm not going anywhere.

[*There is silence.*]

ROMEO: Hey, Rachman?

RACHMAN: Yeh, boy—

ROMEO: It won't hurt—will it? You don't feel a thing—do ya?

RACHMAN: Nothing, man. [*pause*] The eggs plop in the pan. You smell something funny. You're lookin' at the Warden. He gives a signal. You take a deep breath. [*pause*] That's it, pal.

ROMEO: Jesus, Holy Jesus, Rachman—

RACHMAN: Take it easy. They ain't got you there yet. Not yet, pal.

ROMEO: They will though! I got that feeling—things ain't gonna work out at all, they'll get me there, sure they will! You watch and see, THEY WILL! Jesus Christ, Rachman—THEY WILL! *They're not kiddin', they're out to do it to me,* THEY WILL!

[*Silence on The Row.* ROMEO *is white, shaking.* LONGFIELD *puffs his cigar.* BOWMAN *writes.* LAVERNE *strums his guitar, sings quietly.*]

FADEOUT

SCENE: *The Row. Afternoon. A week later. The Cells on the Right, near* LONGFIELD, *are occupied now, by nameless, silent men. They may have been moved up from the other end. They may be new arrivals. One paces his cell, ceaselessly. The other sits in his chair, the third, on his bunk.* LAVERNE'S *guitar and singing, as usual.* THE GENERAL *strolls down the corridor. He looks in at the men. He stops before* LONGFIELD'S *cell.*

LONGFIELD [*after a while*]: Have a cigar.

THE GENERAL [*taking it*] [*grinning*]: Thanks, my friend. [*pauses, smells it, savours it in his mouth*] I'm breaking the rules every time I take one of these, Longfield. Your friend Bowman knows that. He's a great one for rules, yet for once he says nothing. I wonder why.

LONGFIELD [*shrugging*]: Maybe he hopes one might be poisoned.

THE GENERAL [*somewhat alarmed, looking over the cigar*]: Hey, I never thought of that—

LONGFIELD: You *didn't*? [*pause*] That's the sort of thing you always ought to be thinking of—friend, how have you lived so long?

THE GENERAL: Here, maybe you better take it back—

LONGFIELD: Hell, I don't want it!

THE GENERAL: You better take it back—

BOWMAN: You better keep it. I'll turn you in sure as hell for all those others you received—and enjoyed, General.

LONGFIELD: He's got a point, Sergeant.

THE GENERAL: You guys can't get away with this—

BOWMAN: Better keep it, General.

THE GENERAL [*looking over the cigar again, sniffing it*]: I don't think it's poisoned. [*pause*] I think you're pulling my leg—

LONGFIELD: You won't know until you've tried it though, will you?

THE GENERAL [*tossing the cigar in at* LONGFIELD. *It hits the cell floor*]: You better keep it!

LONGFIELD [*picking it up, tossing it back out at him*]: I don't want it! It's for you, Sergeant. Enjoy yourself!

[THE GENERAL *stands there, staring at it, on the floor, beside him.*]

BOWMAN [*after a while, calmly*] [*with authority*]: Pick it up, General.

[THE GENERAL, *after a long moment or two, a glare or two, under the steady gaze of all the men on The Row, bends down, slowly, and picks it up. He looks at it, shoves it in his pocket, shoots one final glare at* BOWMAN, *and moves off, down the corridor.*]

[LAVERNE'S *guitar and singing resume.*]

[BOWMAN *chuckles.*]

RACHMAN: Beats me why you hand out cigars to that ape, Longfield.

LONGFIELD: Friend, he's like the rest of us. Only like the rest of us.

RACHMAN: Glad you think so.

LONGFIELD: A fellow human, friend. *Have you no feeling for your fellow humans, m'friend?*

BOWMAN: Don't take it so hard, Joe.

RACHMAN: It burns me, man.

LONGFIELD: You've got the wrong outlook, friend—think about it—

RACHMAN: Hell, they're your cigars, man.

BOWMAN: The guy's got a lousy job, Joe. That keeps his sunny side from coming out. That happens when a guy has a lousy job.

RACHMAN: Oh, yeh? Lousy guys take the lousy jobs.

LONGFIELD: Friend, don't condemn him! A man's got to have a job! How do you know, he may have a lovely wife, two lovely children, how do you know, friend? Consider that! Maybe he couldn't find any other job. Maybe the guy has talent for the job. It must take talent, Jesus, I couldn't handle it! Look at all those comic books he gets through! Consider that, friend. Consider the job. Could *you* handle it?

RACHMAN: No, friend.

LONGFIELD: There you are. Think about it. You'll see what I mean. It may take a while, but you'll see what I mean.

RACHMAN [*after a pause*]: You wouldn't wanta put a bet on that, pal?

LONGFIELD: No sir! I'm against gambling. Except in business, I'm against gambling.

RACHMAN: You never played the horses?

LONGFIELD: Don't get obscene, friend.

RACHMAN [*in a low voice*]: What's that, Dan?

BOWMAN: Dirty.

[RACHMAN *laughs, puffs his cigar.*]

BOWMAN [*later*] [*to* LONGFIELD]: Well, you had your good news this morning. How do you feel?

LONGFIELD: Fine, just fine, now that you mention it.

BOWMAN: Is the wife still trying?

LONGFIELD: She won't give up.

BOWMAN: That was a nice letter they sent you. See how polite they are? Ever since they stopped dancing guys on air, they've been polite as hell. Hell's hell.

LONGFIELD: Why not? They're civilized. They're only doing a job. That's all it is, a little old job. [*pause, puffs cigar*] Your Warden had tears in his eyes when he handed it to me.

BOWMAN: Uh huh.

LONGFIELD: Maybe though that was because of the investigation. Think they've been giving him a hard time there?

BOWMAN: Who knows? [*pause*] If you don't see him around anymore, you'll know.

LONGFIELD: Next time he comes around, I'll ask him point blank, *How's it going? Or, Is it over?* How would I know, it might be over. It just might be over. I'd like to hear him on that.

> [THE GENERAL *comes back into view now, heading for his office, after his stroll up The Row. He makes a few notes in the office. He puffs his cigar, pulls out a comic book, sets to work.*]

BOWMAN [*to* LONGFIELD]: His favorite is 'Superman'. You can bring in a ton of 'Superman', he wouldn't get bored by it. [*pauses, raises his voice*] That's the kind of mentality it takes to run or work in a place like this, that's just it, buddy.

> [*The Gun Guard halts, looks down at him.* THE GENERAL *glances up from his reading, glares at him.*]

THE GENERAL: You're beggin' for isolation, Bowman—

LONGFIELD: Ho there, Sergeant, take it easy now. You just want to concentrate on your reading material there and take it easy. Hell, I'll cut off the cigars!—

> [THE GENERAL *looks angry, then puzzled, then returns to his comic book. He looks up occasionally. The Gun Guard paces.*]

BOWMAN [*chuckling*]: What was your line, anyhow, Longfield?

LONGFIELD [*expansively*]: Why, *you don't know?* You didn't know, *friend?* [*pause*] Inspiring people! Uplifting them! My organization did that, over the years, we built up a fortune doing that! We sold Culture, you know, that was our *main* activity, Culture, the Humanities, friend, to the People, you didn't know that, my friend? [*pause*] This is a Democracy, the world's Greatest, we're the Pillar of Western Civilization, we have to let the People know all about the Great Ideas, that's what we sold, friend, and we *Uplifted* the People! [*pauses*] [*chuckles*] See what a cigar can do? Another secret of my success, friend. I made my first pile through a cigar! I didn't have a penny in the bank, I had to influence the

Chairman of a certain Board, and he loved cigars. I borrowed a few bucks to buy a box of the best. I brought them along with me. He appreciated that. A man who likes cigars, of that quality, there's a man you could depend on! I had to depend on him, Faith, that's what it was, that's what made our whole wonderful Organization work anyhow! Things worked out, mighty fine, and I've always had a box or two along with me since, no matter where. Never failed! It's a great secret, friend. It's a bond, a Great Bond, between men. If you make it out of here, try to remember that. I'll stake you, if you like, I don't mind. You'll see what I mean. [pause] I'm even going to take one in there with me. [*pause*] Who knows what's in the *Beyond*? [*pause*] Maybe they'll try to stop that though, but I've already got my legal clowns working on that. I have, Friend! They'll get a Court Order, if necessary! [*pause*] Inspiration, Uplifting, friend. That's the greatest Service one man can render another, believe me, that's what makes Mankind, my friend. [*pauses, puffs*] Say, did I tell you about the wife? She tried to pry the contents of the Will out of them! [*pause*] How about that? Some honey, eh? [*pause*] So they said, *Nothing Doing*. Now I hear she's trying to get the matter into court. And she's still trying to get me in the nuthouse! *How about that?* Ever hear the likes of that? [*pause*] Ha Ha, that's my little angel, alright, alright, though . . .

[*He trails off puffing his cigar.*]

RACHMAN: They won't get you down there, Longfield. [*pause*] You'll talk yourself to death before that, pal.

[LONGFIELD *likes that, chuckles.*]

LONGFIELD: Couldn't think of a nicer way to go.

BOWMAN [*after a pause*]: So you sold books, that it, Longfield?

LONGFIELD: Only *part* of our Operation, Friend! We had a Great, a Vast *vision*, friend, the Uplifting, the Inspiration of the Whole Nation, my Friend! Western Civilization counted on us, needed us, *We heard Its Call*, my Friend!

BOWMAN: Was that the *only* Call, Longfield?

LONGFIELD [*after a pause*]: HA HA. [*pauses again*] Ha Ha Ha! [*pauses once more*] Friend!

BOWMAN: Ever read any of those books, Friend?

LONGFIELD [*His laughter disappearing*] [*suddenly*]: You're a wise guy, you're one of those Wise Guys, friend—

BOWMAN: Yeh, but *did* you?

LONGFIELD [*shouting*]: *What's that got to do with it,* FRIEND?

BOWMAN [*pressing*]: You think *anybody* who buys those books reads them— *Friend?*

LONGFIELD [*quite agitated*]: You're needling me—you're going too far— *I'll Turn The Sergeant on you, Friend!*

BOWMAN: *What the hell do you think they buy them for,* Friend? Ever stop to think about that, one minute maybe, *one*—Friend?

LONGFIELD: I can see why you're in here, I can see now, Friend!

BOWMAN: And you? What about you? [*pause*] *What About It,* FRIEND?

[LONGFIELD *calms down, he turns, walks about his cell. He sits on the bunk.*]

LONGFIELD [*quietly*]: You've had a pretty rough life, haven't you, Dan?

BOWMAN [*also, quietly*]: You might call it that.

LONGFIELD: I know, I know all about it—

BOWMAN [*after a while*]: I was pretty crazy. It didn't have to be that way. [*pause*] Things in me, and out there, got together, and I turned out that way. [*pause*] [LONGFIELD *sits quietly on his bunk, listening*] [*Soon,* BOWMAN *resumes*] When I first came here, I fought everything with my fists. I spent more time in Isolation than you could dream of. [*pause*] I wouldn't recommend you dream of it. [*pause*] I began to change, it was that first time I got a stay— [*pause*] I was actually down in the Holding Cell—I had an hour to go— [*pause*] Yeh, when they brought me back up, I went into a hell of a shake. Inside, I mean. It lasted a long time. [*pause*] And then, I began to change. [*pause*] I calmed down. I saw a lot of things. About myself, about everything. [*pause*] Yeh, Longfield, I sure did. [*pause*] I don't mean I quit. Don't get me wrong, I don't mean that at all. [*pause*] I mean I knew, now, the things I had to fight against, I knew them all—the *real* things—and after a while — [*pause*] How to do—*just that.* [*pause*] Longfield.

LONGFIELD [*after a while*]: What are you telling me for? [*pause*] You trying to get me to be like you? [*pause*] You banking on something like that happening to me? [*pause*] Friend?

BOWMAN: I couldn't tell you. Maybe you'll let me know.

LONGFIELD: Sure, I'll do that. [*pause*] You've got a weird sense of humor, friend.

BOWMAN: You know where you are? [*pause*] Try appreciating that. [*pause*] You might get that way.

LONGFIELD [*after a while*] [*quietly*]: How many jails you been in anyway, Dan?

BOWMAN: I don't know. I never counted them.

LONGFIELD: No kidding, Dan?

BOWMAN: Would I kid you—Friend?

LONGFIELD [*soon*]: Next time your pal comes around, I'm going to ask him, Dan.

BOWMAN: If he doesn't tell you, don't blame me, pal.

LONGFIELD [*after a pause*]: I wouldn't dream of it, friend.

[*A silence.* LAVERNE'S *guitar, the Gun Guard. Men in their cells.*]

BOWMAN [*after a while*]: What do you dream of?

LONGFIELD [*looking around, surprised, and affected by this*]: I dream of a lot of things. [*pause*] [*quietly*] It all comes down to one thing— [*pause*] Seeing her again.

BOWMAN [*very quietly*]: Good luck, buddy.

LONGFIELD [*after a while*]: I was dreaming last night about a pain in my shoulder I once had. It was a hell of a pain, it lasted a long time. It was just after my mother died. It was about fifteen years ago. That's a funny thing to dream about. [*pause*] Isn't it?

[BOWMAN *nods his head, slightly, but says nothing.*]

LONGFIELD: I went to a lot of pill-pushers about it. A hell of a lot. Jesus Christ, the bull they fling you. They said, some of them, anyhow, it was a 'Rotator Cuff Syndrome'. Ever hear of that, Dan? I know you're mainly a legal-eagle, but I thought you might have come across that somewhere, sometime, in your research, who knows. Who knows what's in those lawbooks, friend! [*pause*] What it is, Dan, what it is, the Fibrous tissues harden in there, oh yeh, I had it all explained to me. It's the shoulder muscle, one of the shoulder muscles. The *Spinegus*—that's it—I think. And then when it gets into that state it grates on the other muscle surfaces, the normal ones, they're softer, you know. That's where the pain comes in. It's one hell of a pain, friend! You have painful abduction of the arm, 'supra spinegus', that's it. 'Tenderitis'. Check that. [*pause*] Ever hear of it, Dan?

BOWMAN: No, I haven't, Longfield.

LONGFIELD: That's it, alright.

BOWMAN [*after a while*]: Cleared up, did it?

LONGFIELD: Finally! I saw about a dozen pill-pushers, I had physiotherapy, shots, drugs, vitamins, minerals, infra-red, ultra-violet, X-ray, supersonic subsurface diathermy—you name it, I had it! The works, brother! None helped, not one, friend! [*pause*] One day, after about two years, one morning, I woke up—and it wasn't hurting. Just like that, Dan, just about when I had given up. [*pause*] I had given up! I had stopped all treatments completely! [*pause*] What do you make of that? Think it was all in my mind then?

BOWMAN: Could be, just could be.

LONGFIELD: Those damn pill-pushers. Damn them!

BOWMAN: They tried their best.

LONGFIELD: Oh yeh, didn't they! You should have seen their bills—that was the best! Hell, I retired three of them, put a bet?

BOWMAN: Well, you don't have that worry now, Longfield.

[*A long silence.*]

LONGFIELD [*strangely*]: I'm going to be buried next to her. [*pause*] I've already made arrangements for that. [*pause*] I guess that doesn't interest you much. [*pause*] To me, that means everything. [*pause*] Everything, everything.

BOWMAN: All the luck, pal.

LONGFIELD [*after a pause*]: What I like, most of all, Dan, what I've always liked—far back as I can remember—what I liked was walking in a small, church graveyard. [*pause*] Yeh, there's the church, and the graveyard. [*pause*] I've always liked it. [*pause*] There's real quiet, real peace, my friend. [*pause*] I took her, sometimes. [*pause*] That's where she is now, that's where I'll be, it won't be long. [*pause*]

When I was a kid, there was a real nice, real old one near us. The little church on it must have gone back a couple hundred years—at least. [*pause*] I grew up in a small, sleepy town, a dreamy, warm, dusty little town, Bowman. I can see it, I can see everything in it, before me, now. [*pause*] We were poor, Bowman, poor as poor, that's putting it mildly! But what we had, I appreciated. I had only one sister. She's still around, down there. She married some guy from that town, he's a shoemaker. [*pause*] I lost contact with her, after my mother died. I was too busy, too damn busy. I was Inspiring people, I was making my pile! You might know how it is, Dan. I didn't have time for anything like that. I was moving, going, seven days and nights a week, friend, eight, if I could have squeezed it in. I handed out cigars, beaucoup. I made my fortune. [*pause*] Well, she's still down there, I know. And she's got a surprise coming. [*pauses, lights up another cigar*] Know what it is, Dan? [*pauses, puffs*] I left her everything. *Everything*! [*pause*] That's some little surprise she has coming, right, Dan, right, my boy?

BOWMAN: I hope she gets over it.

LONGFIELD: So do I. [*pause*] I thought about that. So— She won't be getting it all at once. Small chunk the first year, little more the next, more yet the next, and so on, building her up for it, you see? It'll take a long time, but she's got children. I thought about it a lot. I came to that conclusion, it was the best way. [*pause*] What do you say?

BOWMAN: Good idea.

LONGFIELD: One of her boys has a good head on him. He's in High School.

BOWMAN: I'm beginning to like you, Longfield.

LONGFIELD: Well, don't fall in love with me! Jesus, don't do that, will you, friend? [*pause*] And call me Jack!

[BOWMAN *chuckles. A silence.*]

LONGFIELD [*finally*]: Another thing I like is Opera. [*pause*] Italian Opera. I have a record collection home of all the Operas. Whenever I had some free time, you could find me in my den, locked away there, listening to them. I don't mean some of those crappy singers, either. I had the best, all the best, Bowman. De Los Angeles, Tibaldi, Callas—all of them.

Unless you get the best, so far as Opera is concerned—like anything else, I guess, but especially Opera—you get corn, nothing but corn. I'll tell you. Once they sent me a couple wrong albums. I think it was 'Tosca'—the one they sent me was in English. How about that, English! It was made in England, English orchestra, singers—imagine, *singing it in English!* I could have rolled off the chair when I heard it. It was about the lousiest thing I've ever heard. [*pause*] I didn't even bother sending that album back. I smashed it to pieces. Pieces, Dan! I phoned up that damn store the next day and gave them hell. They sent me down the right album—free. That was a store with Initiative, Imagination, alright, Bowman! [*pause*] I think I owned about a quarter of the shares in it, at least. [*pause*] I even took a couple of trips to Italy to hear the Operas, Dan! Business trips, yeh, but what I went for was the Opera. [*pause*] Milan's the best place. [*pause*] You like Opera?

BOWMAN: Sometimes.

LONGFIELD: Yeh, but have you heard the best? You have to hear the best, friend! Anything else, brother—don't let me mention it. [*pause*] Just don't let me, Dan!

[*A silence.*]

LONGFIELD [*later*]: The Warden tells me I'm allowed to invite five people.

BOWMAN: That's right.

LONGFIELD [*after a pause*]: I'm inviting the wife. [*no answer*] How about that? [*pauses, no answer*] Think she'll come?

[BOWMAN *says nothing.*]

LONGFIELD [*getting up*]: Dan?

BOWMAN [*finally, quietly*]: I wouldn't know.

[LONGFIELD *stands there.* BOWMAN *turns to his desk. Resumes writing. The Row is as before.*]

FADEOUT

SCENE: *The Row. The following morning. Exercise Period.*
LAVERNE *strumming his guitar, is singing, softly, 'I'm Just Drivin' Nails In My Coffin'. All the men, except* BOWMAN *and* LAVERNE, *are smoking cigars.*

ROMEO: Maybe we'll hear something today.

RACHMAN: That's what you say every day.

ROMEO: Yeh, but, one of these days—

RACHMAN: I'll be here.

ROMEO: Oh, yeh, I know—

RACHMAN: Now you're talking, pal.

ROMEO: Man, *whatever happened?* I thought I had it made—for life!

RACHMAN: When was that, pal?

BOWMAN [*to* LONGFIELD, *in front of him*]: How come you married her, anyway?

LONGFIELD [*puffing away*]: It's one of those things, one of those things you run across all the time in life, friend. Anyone's life. [*pauses, puffs*] There she was, waiting for me, who would have known it? I never knew it. My uncle? Sometimes, uncles are the ones, they seem to know everything, they tell you. Well, this one didn't. He never told me—if he knew. I could ask you a dozen similar questions anyhow, Dan. What would you answer? [*pause*] I don't know, I must have been about twenty-two, I guess. I was getting my feet on the ground. I was full of life, the whole world was out there for me, I was going after it. Well, I don't know. I met her. I started running around with her. Don't ask me what happened. I woke up one morning, friend, and I was married to her. Not that I minded. She was a good-looking gal, maybe you even saw some pictures of her in the papers, those were taken quite a while ago, but she still looks pretty good. She's held her own. Let's put it that way. [*pause*] What am I talking about? I don't want to make the whole thing too complicated, because it wasn't, after all. She and I were just a couple of minds apart, that's all. We found that out too late. [*pause*] I did, anyhow. Can't speak for her. [*pause*] Who can? Oh, yeh, who can? [*pause*] Our minds collided—Wham, Friend! Don't ask me why she wouldn't let me go, I just wouldn't know. Maybe she liked me. You can't tell, a gal like that—yeh, she just might have liked me. [*pause*] We didn't have children. Maybe that would have helped, if we did. Just maybe. It's another one of those things. [*pause*] One day, when I found out I'd made my first pile, I just didn't want her anymore. Not in *any way, anymore.* It was just that simple. [*pause*] How's the stomach?

BOWMAN: A lot better, coming along real fine.

LONGFIELD: Glad to hear it! Just say when you want the cigar—

BOWMAN: I will.

[*A silence.*]

LONGFIELD: Maybe you'll hear something today. The Man might bring some news. [*pause*] I'm pulling for you all the way, you know that, don't you?

BOWMAN: Sure, I do.

ROMEO: I'm going to ask him today.

RACHMAN: All the luck, man.

ROMEO: He's not a bad guy. He will.

RACHMAN: Ask him nice, real nice, man.

ROMEO: Sure. Sure I will.

RACHMAN: Put in a good word for me.

ROMEO: Sure.

RACHMAN: Do that, man.

LONGFIELD: I'm glad I ran into you here, Bowman. You're a guy I can talk to.

BOWMAN: Is that what I am?

LONGFIELD: Hell, yes! Most people are walls, did you know that, Dan? *Walls.* Who can talk to a wall? [*pause*] When I talk to you, I know you're receiving. I know that, friend. You might not believe or go along with what I say, but you're receiving, it doesn't matter. That's the important thing, *to be received,* Dan. [*pause*] Walls, they're all Walls! What you say, I mean, what you really say bounces off. It just bounces off! [*pause*] That was a great thing about her—she received—oh, friend, did she receive! [*pause*] It's a hell of a thing to talk about to you, Dan, but I'll tell you something—you would have gone for her. Friend, she was *a girl-and-a-half.* She was something. They make them like that once in a million. I knew that first time I saw her. [*pause*] When she came for her interview, when she walked into my office there, Friend—I looked up, and I forgot about interviewing her. [*pause*] That's the way I was, Dan! Faith, Faith, you've got to have Faith! [*pause*] I hired her. And

she stood there, looking at me. [*pause*] Corny, Dan? Pretty
corny? [*pause*] Maybe so, but if it had happened to you, if
you had been me— Would it be? [*pause*] That's how it was.
That's what I wanted you to know— *How it was.*

BOWMAN [*soon*]: So here you are.

LONGFIELD: Don't say it that way—

BOWMAN: You've got a couple of more weeks—unless your wife
springs you— What *should* I say?

LONGFIELD: She'd better not! The silly bitch, she sure better
not!

BOWMAN: What Should I Say?

[THE GENERAL *calls out, '*TIME*'. The men break up, amble
back to their cells.*]

LONGFIELD [*after a while*]: All my life, Dan, I've been lonely.
Inside me, deeper than any well, or ocean—all the oceans.
That lonely. There were people all around me, all the time,
all kinds of people around me—and I was lonely. I knew it!
Especially at night, I knew it. [*pause*] I was never alone,
hardly ever a minute alone— [*pause*] And I was lonely.
That's how it was, Dan! It was inside me, nothing could
touch it— [*a longer pause*] I met her, friend, and it was the
first time I could ever recall—except—*except maybe a long
time ago, way back there, in the beginning*—not being lonely.
[*pause*] Do you know anything about that? [*pause*] Maybe
you can tell me, my time's coming soon, I wish you'd tell me.

BOWMAN: When they've all turned me down, if it comes to
that, when I take that final walk down there, Longfield, if it
comes to that—I'll be able to tell you. [*pause*] I will, Longfield.

LONGFIELD: That's too late. Too damn late, Friend.

BOWMAN: What can I do? That's how it is, buddy.

LONGFIELD: You're holding back! There's a *hell* of a lot you
can tell me. [*pause*] A guy can't spend six years here and
not have something on that to tell me!

BOWMAN: That's time, Longfield. You're talking about time now.
Who would know about time—here? You tell me, Longfield.

LONGFIELD [*after a while*]: When I was younger, I thought the
pile, when I made it, and I was sure I'd make it, would
take care of things. I thought, sure as hell, That will take

care of things! [*pause*] Well, I was wrong, it didn't. It didn't
help a bit. It kept me running, busy, to put it mildly. Kept
me, a good deal of the time, away from it. [*pause*] But that
was it! I couldn't do any more than that with it! [*pause*]
You can't get away from yourself at night— Not in your
bed, at night—

BOWMAN: You can dream.

LONGFIELD: My dreams—[*halts*]

BOWMAN [*after a while*]: Last night I dreamed the Warden
was standing at the entrance to the Chamber handing out
ice cream cones. That nice, soft ice cream, Longfield. Don't
ask me what flavor. [*pause*] Then, when he opened the door
I saw my mother and father in there, in the chairs. I turned,
I said to him, 'There's no room, Warden.' [*pause*] I still
held the ice cream.

[*There is a silence. Then, the cage doors buzz, open, one
by one, and* THE WARDEN *enters. He stops for a while in
the office. Then, with* THE GENERAL, *he starts his tour.*]

THE WARDEN [*before* LAVERNE's *cell*]: How are you, Jake, how's
everything? [LAVERNE *stops strumming his guitar. He looks
up, stares at* THE WARDEN] I've got some news, Jake. [*pause*]
[*takes out an envelope*] You've got a stay. [*Hands the envelope to* LAVERNE] The Governor's reviewing your entire case.
[*pause*] Don't build your hopes too much—but, it looks good.

LAVERNE [*after opening the letter, perusing it*] [*murmuring*]:
Thanks a lot, Warden.

THE WARDEN: I hope things work out, son.

[LAVERNE *nods his head, says nothing.*]

THE WARDEN: Need anything?

[LAVERNE *shakes his head.*]

THE WARDEN: Alright, Jake.

[*He moves on to* ROMEO.]

ROMEO: Heard anything? Anything at all, Warden?

THE WARDEN: Not a thing, not yet, son.

ROMEO: That's good, there's still a chance, right, Warden?

THE WARDEN: That's right, son.

ROMEO: Boy, will I take you out on the town if that day comes!
I sure will—I guarantee it, Warden—

THE WARDEN: Well, I hope it does. You know that, son.

ROMEO: Sure, Warden, sure I know—

THE WARDEN: Need anything?

ROMEO: Only one thing, that's all, Warden—

THE WARDEN [*nodding*]: I hope you get it, son.

> [*He moves on*] [*Glances in at the empty cell, moves to* RACHMAN.]

RACHMAN: How are you, Warden?

THE WARDEN: No word yet, Joe.

RACHMAN: Uh huh.

THE WARDEN: How are you, Joe?

RACHMAN: Oh, yeh. Just too good. Warden.

THE WARDEN: You have a chance, Joe.

RACHMAN: That's all I need, once chance, Warden.

THE WARDEN: Take it easy, Joe.

> [*Moves on to* BOWMAN.]

THE WARDEN: Nothing yet, Dan.

BOWMAN: They're taking their time. That's good, Warden.

THE WARDEN [*nodding, standing there*]: What are you doing there, Dan?

BOWMAN [*glancing over his books, papers*]: Nothing much. Same old stuff.

THE WARDEN [*after a while*]: Need anything?

BOWMAN: Not at the moment, Warden.

THE WARDEN [*after a pause*]: Take it easy, Dan.

> [BOWMAN *nods his head,* THE WARDEN *moves on.*]

THE WARDEN: How are you, Longfield, how's everything?

LONGFIELD: I had an answer for you.

THE WARDEN: Need anything?

LONGFIELD: Have a cigar—

THE WARDEN: I don't smoke them, Longfield.

LONGFIELD: I know, you keep telling me that. You ought to try one though. Maybe you'd change your mind, Warden.

THE WARDEN: I think it might be a little too late for that now, Longfield.

LONGFIELD: Warden, no kidding, you've never tried one?

THE WARDEN: That's right, Longfield.

LONGFIELD: By God, that's something. That's really something. [*pause*] I still think you ought to try, Warden.

THE WARDEN: I'll have to pass on that, Longfield.

LONGFIELD [*puffing his cigar, eyeing him, lowering his voice, later*]: How'd you come out on that investigation, Warden?

THE WARDEN [*uncomfortable, taken by surprise*]: I can't talk about things like that with you, Longfield.

LONGFIELD: Yeh, but I bet you came out way ahead, Warden. I'd put a good sized bet on that, Warden.

THE WARDEN: I wouldn't worry about things like that, Longfield.

LONGFIELD: What would you like me to worry about, Warden? [*pause*] You're not going to let me down, run out on me, are you, Warden? You're not thinking of doing that—are you? Warden?

THE WARDEN: I don't anticipate that, Longfield.

LONGFIELD [*nodding his head*]: Good. Good, Warden. That's how to keep things, Warden.

THE WARDEN [*after a pause*]: Take it easy, Longfield.

[*He moves to the next cell, and so on, until he is off Right. We only hear him murmuring, though, after* LONGFIELD.]

ROMEO: He's a pretty good guy, Joe.

RACHMAN: Thanks for telling me.

ROMEO: How long can they keep us waitin', Joe?

RACHMAN: Just relax, take it easy, buddy. Keep thinking of the Warden, what a nice guy he is. Think about that. Put yourself to sleep there or something, thinking about that.

ROMEO [*ignoring that, indicating* LAVERNE's *cell. He has started strumming his guitar again*]: He's lucky, man.

RACHMAN: Maybe you'll be luckier.

ROMEO: I should be! What the hell am I here for? What good was she? You got an answer to that? How'd I wind up here, Joe?

RACHMAN: Somebody has to, Romeo. [*pause*] That's what it's here for. [*pause*] What the hell you think they have it here for? Buddy—

[*A silence.*]

LONGFIELD: How are you, Dan, how's everything?

BOWMAN: Just fine, everything's fine, Sir.

[*They have a chuckle.*]

LONGFIELD: Friend, where do they make them like that, anyhow?

168

BOWMAN: It's all the same place, Longfield. [*pause*] Things could be worse around here.

LONGFIELD: Sure, I don't doubt that— [*pause*] He could put you out of business pretty quick, for instance, couldn't he?

BOWMAN: Not that quick. I have friends outside. I drop them a little note once in a while, once a week, just to say Hello. Nothing more. If they don't get it, they start asking why. He's the man who will have to answer that question, and fast. He knows it. I made damn sure, a long time ago, he knew it. [*pause*] Maybe that's why I'm still in business, Longfield. It could be.

LONGFIELD: You've thought of everything, friend.

BOWMAN: This is a jungle. I have to, if I'm going to stand a chance.

LONGFIELD: You've got a chance.

BOWMAN: A chance in a hundred, but it's a chance.

LONGFIELD: They sure have given you a rough time, though.

BOWMAN: Sure. I don't go crawling to them on my belly. I never have. I stand up and fight them, on their own ground. They don't like that. They don't see why anyone should do that, least of all, me, a 'known fiend'. I don't fit into their plan, their scheme of things. They said I should die, what am I making all this fuss about, *dying*? What do I want to go rocking their boat for? It might make monkeys out of them, something even more out of a certain court. It might show them up for what they are.

LONGFIELD: You should have crawled, maybe. A long time ago. You might have made it by now. Hit them with a block-buster later on, but first—*crawl*. Just maybe, Dan.

BOWMAN: I gave that some thought, once. [*pause*] I came to the conclusion it was no good. Not good at all, Longfield. [*pause*] I have to beat them, on their own ground. Otherwise, it's no damn good. Not at all. I'll tell you.

LONGFIELD: They can play with you for years, though.

BOWMAN: That's o.k. I'm ready for it.

LONGFIELD: You should have turned religious! There's a great thing alright, you would have had it made, the Religiosos on your side! Think of all those holy boys, marching to see the Governor, think of that, it should appeal to you. What politico could resist that pressure? That's quite a chunk of votes, there!

BOWMAN: There's only one way I can get out of here and hold my head up. You ought to know that.

LONGFIELD: I'm only trying to point out ways you could have made it out of here, maybe long ago.

BOWMAN: You know better than that, Longfield.

LONGFIELD: Friend, I know the world. I didn't get where I was not knowing it. I've mixed with all kinds of people, I've seen a lot of life. On the basis of that, I'm offering you my advice. [*pause*] That's all I can do, right? I've got a little date to keep, it's not far off—it's the least I can do, right?

BOWMAN: You're crazy, but you know better, Longfield.

[LONGFIELD *shrugs. There is a silence.* THE WARDEN *comes back from his tour of The Row. He nods farewell to the men as he passes their cells. He has a brief word with the guards.* THE GENERAL. *He departs.*]

LONGFIELD: So long, friend.

BOWMAN: Ice cream cones. Name your flavor, Longfield.

[*A silence.*]

FADEOUT

SCENE: *The Row, a week later.* THE WARDEN *is there. He strolls to* LONGFIELD'S *cell.*

LONGFIELD: You're early, Warden.

THE WARDEN: I came to tell you your wife's Writ has failed.

LONGFIELD: O.K., that's fine. Thanks for telling me.

THE WARDEN: We'll take you down to the Holding Cell to-morrow morning. You'll be there for twenty-four hours, Longfield.

LONGFIELD: Is that necessary, Warden? Couldn't I just as well stay up here?

THE WARDEN: I wish I could allow that. However, the rules of procedure are very strict. I'd be breaking the law if I left you up here. I wish I could. I'm very sorry about that, Longfield. I have to follow the rules of procedure.

LONGFIELD [*nodding his head*] [*quietly*]: You want to try and do what you can for Bowman. He's innocent, you know.

There's no doubt of it.

[THE WARDEN *says nothing.*]

LONGFIELD: He's writing a book. I think it's the story of his life. He hasn't told you that, has he, Warden? [THE WARDEN *says nothing*] Poverty, Warden. There's between forty and fifty million in this great country of ours right now living in poverty, did you know that, Warden?

[*Pause, silence.*]

That's all going to be in his book. Because both of us know something about poverty. Our backgrounds were pretty much the same. Pretty much, Warden.

[*A silence.*]

LONGFIELD [*nodding*]: It's hell of a world, a hell of a life, Warden. I'm glad to be getting out of it. This is one time you don't have to waste a minute worrying, Warden. Don't waste one minute feeling sorrow for me. I'm only too glad to get out of it. Just give me the signal, I'll know what to do. I'll give you a big thank you. And you can sleep that night. I mean it, Warden. You'll see me there. [*pause*] Forty to fifty million, Warden. This great, rich country. Think of it. Imagine the rest of the world! Just try to imagine, what must things be like, Warden? Maybe there's an excuse there, but what about our country? You tell me, Warden.

[*A silence.*]

THE WARDEN: I'll see you tomorrow morning, Longfield.

LONGFIELD: I'll be here.

THE WARDEN: Alright, Longfield. So long for now.

LONGFIELD: See you in the morning, Warden. [*pause*] Did you send out all those invitations alright, Warden?

THE WARDEN: Now that you mention it— [*pause*] I couldn't send the one to Bowman. That's prohibited.

LONGFIELD: Too bad. [*pause*] The wife?

THE WARDEN [*hesitantly*]: Yes, I did.

LONGFIELD: Think she'll be there?

THE WARDEN: I don't know.

LONGFIELD: You hope she won't—

THE WARDEN: I don't mind telling you, I hope she won't.

LONGFIELD [*nodding his head*]: Sleep tight, Warden.

[THE WARDEN *leaves.*]

[LAVERNE's *guitar is heard. His soft singing.* LONGFIELD *puffs his cigar.* BOWMAN *sits at his desk, writing.*]

LONGFIELD [*coming towards* BOWMAN's *side*] [*standing there*]: Still at it?

BOWMAN: Hu huh.

LONGFIELD: Don't forget what I told you. Did you make a note of it, Dan?

BOWMAN: I did.

LONGFIELD: You're the kind of a guy who could do it, if anyone could. It's a disgrace, a national disgrace. There's no two ways about it. It's been on my mind more and more. *Fifty million!* You have to think about that, Dan. They have no voice, no pressure, nobody gives a damn about them, they're just swept under the carpet, nobody knows or cares about them, that's the way things are here, this great country of ours—you know that, you know that damn well, Dan—

BOWMAN [*after a pause*]: A funny thing for you to be worrying about, Longfield. It took you a long time, your whole life, I'll bet, to start worrying about it.

LONGFIELD: Better late than never, friend. That's what this place has done for me, I guess! I see a little bit now what you were talking about a few weeks ago. Maybe everybody ought to spend some time here. That might be the answer, Bowman. Ever think of it that way? Might just be the answer —to everything! I'm serious, Dan.

BOWMAN: Maybe. [*pause*] Maybe you're right, Longfield.

LONGFIELD: I think I am, Friend!

BOWMAN: If you didn't have that appointment to keep tomorrow, you could do something about that problem.

LONGFIELD: I'm counting on you! As long as I know I can count on you, I know I'll have done my part! [*pause*] All my life I never gave a thought to the problem—I was poor myself once, wasn't I? When I made my pile, I forgot all about that— Far as I was concerned, they were there, would always be there, and to hell with them—I had made it— they weren't part of me anymore—if they were still down there, why didn't they do something about it? Yeh, friend, that's how I thought—just like that, Dan— [*pause*] I don't see it that way now. I feel pretty damn bad, I realize how

her husband— [*pause*] I did, Dan! [*pause*] The Warden
helpless they are, that's what I think now—that's a fact,
Dan.

BOWMAN [*after a while*]: I believe it, Longfield.

LONGFIELD [*after a while*]: What are you going to do with
yourself if you ever get out of here, Dan?

BOWMAN: That's a fair question. [*pause*] The answer has a lot
to do with *when* I get out of here. [*pause*] I've got a lot of
ideas brewing. [*pause*] I'll write. [*pause*] I'll work hard to
get rid of this abattoir. [*pause*] Maybe I'll dedicate my life
to it. [*pause*] [*grins wryly*] Maybe I'll run for Governor on
it. Think I'd have a chance, Longfield?

LONGFIELD: Sure, I'd vote for you—

BOWMAN: That's fine. I'll have a chance, then—
     [*A silence.*]

LONGFIELD: I tried to get the Warden to invite you. [*pause*]
You didn't know that, did you? [*pause*] I almost succeeded.
I had you down on the list, with my wife, my legal clowns,
said it was against the Rules. [*pause*] Would you have come,
Dan?

BOWMAN: No, Longfield.

LONGFIELD: Even if I asked it as a last favor?

BOWMAN: No, Longfield.

LONGFIELD [*after a while*]: That's a blow, Dan. [*pause*] I really
feel it.

BOWMAN: I'm sorry about that.

LONGFIELD: A real blow, Dan—

FADEOUT

SCENE: *The Row, that evening. The Gun Guard paces.* LAVERNE
strums his guitar, softly. The men are quiet. Finally, ROMEO
*walks toward the front of his cell. He looks around. He stands
there. He turns toward* RACHMAN.

ROMEO [*quietly*]: I'm gonna miss the guy.

RACHMAN: You'll get used to it.

ROMEO: Twenty-two hours a day in this bin, that was something to get used to. And now, no more cigar-man. That's too

much, bud! That Warden better bring me some good news soon!

RACHMAN: What more do you want? You're off the hook.

ROMEO: For how long? How long, buddy?

RACHMAN: Would I know? [*pause*] Anyhow, stop worrying. When he goes, you still get cigars. Sure, he's taken care of that. You didn't know that, man?

ROMEO: Yeh, but here? Why here? Did I ask for it? *Did I ask to be born? Did I?*

RACHMAN: Your mother was good to you, wasn't she, Romeo?

ROMEO: Sure she was. Sure! She's still around, if I went home even now, she'd still be good to me! I shouldn't of left the place, that's where I went wrong buddy, leaving that place—

RACHMAN: We all got to sometime—

[*A silence,* ROMEO *mutters.*]

RACHMAN: If you make it outa here, lay off the broads, Romeo. See what they brought you to?

ROMEO: Oh yeh? Think so? Yeh?

RACHMAN: Yeh.

[*Their conversation fades away.*]

LONGFIELD [*puffing a cigar, just finishing a letter*]: There. That does it. That takes care of everything, friend.

BOWMAN [*after a pause*] [*looking up from his desk*]: I might even try the Bar Examination, Longfield.

LONGFIELD: Are you eligible?

BOWMAN: That's a question for a specially convened committee to decide. [*pause*] I'd probably pass it, though.

LONGFIELD: All the luck, friend!

[*A silence. Time passes.*]

LONGFIELD: You're not tired, you're not going to sleep soon, are you, Dan?

BOWMAN: You want to talk to me?

LONGFIELD: Would be a pleasure, Dan.

BOWMAN: I'll be here all night. Talk all you want, Longfield.

LONGFIELD: I probably won't talk all night.

BOWMAN: I'll be here.

[*A silence.*]

LONGFIELD: Have you travelled much, Dan?

BOWMAN: No.

[*A silence.*]

LONGFIELD: Have you ever had a job, you know what I mean, a bona fide job, as they say, Dan?

BOWMAN: No.

LONGFIELD: Too bad I'm taking that trip tomorrow. I'd hire you right away, I'd give you a top exec job—

BOWMAN: I believe you would, Longfield.

LONGFIELD: Sure I would! Would you take it?

BOWMAN: If you gave me a reasonable amount of time off.

LONGFIELD: You could have all you want, Dan!

BOWMAN: There's only twenty-four hours in a day, and I have to sleep at least six.

[*A silence.*]

LONGFIELD: Think of all the hours I'll be sleeping soon! [*pause*] It feels funny. I want you to know that.

[*A silence.*]

LONGFIELD: I'll be with her. I'll be buried by her side. The legal clowns have taken care of that. Nobody could stop it. It's all taken care of.

BOWMAN [*quietly, after a while*]: What did she do when you pulled the gun out?

LONGFIELD [*looking up, after a pause*]: She stared at it.

BOWMAN: Then what?

LONGFIELD: She asked me what I was going to do. [*pause*] She didn't know what I was going to do. It was all my idea, Dan.

[*A silence.*]

LONGFIELD: I told her, and she got scared, she said she didn't want me to do it. [*pause*] I said it would be over quickly, very quickly. She said it didn't matter. She didn't want me to do it. [*pause*] She told me to put the gun away, and later, throw it away. [*pause*] That's what she said.

[*A silence.*]

BOWMAN: And then?

LONGFIELD [*after a pause*] I pulled the trigger. [*pause*] There was an explosion. [*pause*] The gun jumped. It jumped like hell in my hand. [*pause*] I pulled it four times, Dan. [*pause*] That's a funny thing. [*pause*] Ever shot anybody, Dan?

BOWMAN: Not that I know of.

LONGFIELD: The blood spurted all over. Like a fountain. I don't know what I was expecting. It surprised me. It spurted and spurted, all over. She was soaked in it. [*pause*] I stood there a long time. Watching her. [*pause*] She went right away, the first shot, I'm sure. [*pause*] Right through the heart. [*a longer pause*] Then, I don't know when, a hell of a long time later, I raised the gun, I had it pointed to my head. [*pause*] Nothing happened. [*pause*] My hand started to shake. That happened. [*pause*] I tried and tried, for hours, Dan. [*pause*] At last, I found it wasn't a gun I was holding any-more. A phone. I was phoning the cops. [*pause*] They were there pretty quick—ten, fifteen minutes, I think.

BOWMAN [*after a pause*]: They move pretty fast, sometimes.

LONGFIELD: They were decent to me.

[*A silence.*]

LONGFIELD: I'm really hoping hard for you, Dan.

[*A silence.*]

LONGFIELD [*taking out a piece of paper*]: Take this paper, Dan. [*He hands it out of cell door,* BOWMAN *takes it*] I've written down where we'll be buried. You come to see me. Promise me that, Dan. Say Hello to me. Say a nice big Hello to me, I'll appreciate that.

BOWMAN: I'll do that. If I make it out of here, I'll be sure to do that.

LONGFIELD: Thanks a lot. That's nice. Real nice of you, Dan . . .

FADEOUT

SCENE: *The Row. About midnight. The men are all asleep, except* BOWMAN *and* LONGFIELD. *The Gun Guard paces.*

LONGFIELD [*after a while*]: Still awake?

BOWMAN: Right.

LONGFIELD [*after a while*] [*quietly*]: You never get to anything. You could think and think about things. You could spend all your life doing that. You never reach anything. You just have to accept it—everything—

BOWMAN [*after a while*]: I'll tell you what I do a lot of the time. I try to go over my life, year by year, every step of it. At night, mostly, lying in my bunk. I've been doing that these last four years. Here. I'm trying to remember everything, everything. When you consider all that's stored in a brain, anyone's brain, it's pretty fantastic. There doesn't seem to be a limit to what it can store. Nothing is forgotten. It's all there, somewhere. If you can work hard enough, long enough, everything comes back to you. [*pause*] I went way back. I got back to when I was a baby. I got stuck there. It's hard work. If I work hard enough, I'll break through.

LONGFIELD: And then what?

BOWMAN: Don't ask me. I'll have the answers, maybe. Anyhow, I'll have my life back. That's what I want most of all, the whole of my life—back. It was all over the place, it was here, there, everywhere. Now I want it back. It's taking me a long time, it's hard work, but I'm getting there, I'll have it back. [*pause*] What am I talking about myself for? That's a hell of a note, I'm sorry, Longfield.

LONGFIELD [*after a pause*]: You don't have to be, friend, believe me.

BOWMAN [*a pause*]: What I know for sure is, I sure wish you weren't taking that trip down there. I have to say that, Longfield. That may be another dumb thing to say, but that's it, I have to say it.

LONGFIELD: I'll be alright. I'll have company, Dan. [*a pause*] I put a request in to the Warden to play a tune that she and I liked a lot. We danced to it a lot. They were playing it the first time I took her out, we went to a roof garden club, they were playing it, an orchestra with a sort of Sammy Kaye style. [*pause*] We danced, that was the first time I had her in my arms . . .

[*A silence*]

LONGFIELD: She liked jazz a lot too. We used to hit the jazz clubs. 'The Saints', she was crazy about that one. And so was I. So was I, Dan. [*a pause*] I asked him to play that one too, just before I went in. I want to hear it, good and loud, one last time, Dan. I want to go out with it. I'll be one of them, one of the Saints, how about that, Dan, marching in—

[*A silence*]

LONGFIELD [*suddenly*]: I got to the top! From nothing, I got to the top! And I found the best girl in the world! What more could a guy ask for? What more could a poor jerk of a human being ask for? In this horses ass of a world— what more could any guy ask for?

[*The Gun Guard stops pacing. He looks down at them. The Guards in the Office look up.*]

BOWMAN [*slowly, looking up at the Gun Guard*]: Keep walking, Brilliant.

GUN GUARD: No jazz, Bowman—

BOWMAN: Keep that carcass moving, Buddy. You heard what the Warden said. Even a fathead like you must have heard what he said. Didn't it penetrate?

GUN GUARD [*muttering*]: One of these days, Bowman—

[*He moves on, soon, he does not bother them again*]

LONGFIELD [*watching him*]: There's a nice life, Dan.

BOWMAN: Oh yeah. Perfect.

LONGFIELD: Keeps him busy, out of trouble—maybe.

FADEOUT

SCENE: *The Row, about* 3 *a.m. As before,* BOWMAN *and* LONGFIELD, *awake, talking.*

LONGFIELD: All governments, all big organizations— That's right. A clean sweep. All of them.

BOWMAN: That would be okay—in theory. But think about it— I mean, the present level of humanity—just think about it. What would you have? [*pause*] A real jungle, Longfield. You say, that's pretty well what we have now. I don't deny it. But at least, I'm still alive, for instance! At least I have a sixteenth or a hundredth of a chance, just that, of getting out of here alive, Longfield!

LONGFIELD: You wouldn't have been in here at all, my friend—

BOWMAN: Don't get me wrong—it's great, just great—in theory.

LONGFIELD: Maybe you'll live to see it. When they start throwing their Bomb around, after that, if anything's left, if you're left, you might just see it—

[*A silence*]

BOWMAN [*finally*]: I don't want to see it. Not that way. If it has to come that way, I don't want to be around to see it.

[*A silence*]

BOWMAN: I've been here a long time. If I get out, that's not what I want to get out for— [*pause*] You think that's anything worth getting out for?

[*A silence*]

LONGFIELD [*quietly*]: All the luck, friend. [*pause*] All the luck in the world to you, friend . . .

FADEOUT

SCENE: *The Row. 9.30 a.m. The men are in their cells, sitting or standing, quietly.* HARPO *is just finishing collecting the breakfast trays. He is up to* LONGFIELD'S *cell. He stands there a moment, he murmurs, 'So long, son.'* LONGFIELD *nods his head, smiles, responds, 'Have a cigar, Pop.' He hands him one.* HARPO, *reluctantly, takes it. Moves on. He leaves The Row. Presently, Guards come for* LONGFIELD. *The usual preparations. He stops by* BOWMAN'S *cell.*

LONGFIELD: So long, friend. Thanks for everything. It's been a pleasure. A real pleasure. [*pauses, they shake hands*] So long.

BOWMAN: So long, Longfield.

LONGFIELD: Don't forget.

BOWMAN: I won't. [*pause*] Don't worry, Longfield.

[LONGFIELD *nods. They stand there, a long moment. Then, with the Guards, he moves off. The men murmur 'So Long', and similar things to him, he responds. He says 'So Long' to* THE GENERAL. *He steps into the Cage. He is gone. There is silence. Absolute silence. The men stare after him.* BOWMAN, *after a while, stares at the wall of his cell . . .*]

FADEOUT

SCENE: *The Holding Cell. The Chamber. The next morning,* THE WARDEN *is approaching the area . . . The Warden's Home, also. His wife enters the parlor. Her son follows soon. She is tidying things up.*

THE BOY: Can I go out and play football, Mom?

THE WOMAN: You'll be home in time for lunch?

THE BOY: Yes, Mom—

THE WOMAN: You're all caught up on your homework now?

THE BOY: Oh, yes, Mom—

THE WOMAN: Your Arithmetic?

THE BOY: I did that last night, just after supper, Mom—

THE WOMAN [*smiling, kissing the boy*]: Go on then—
[*He dashes out*]

THE BOY: I'll be here right on time, don't worry, Mom! Dad's bringing me that new missile model, did you know that, Mom? See you! [*He is gone*]
[THE WOMAN *looks after him, smiling. She glances at her watch. She resumes her tidying up. She has stopped smiling.*]

FADEOUT

[*In the Holding Cell,* LONGFIELD *smokes a cigar. There is a record playing. It is 'Put Your Arms Around Me, Honey'. It is a Sammy Kaye-ish version. It goes on and on.*]

LONGFIELD: Turn it down a little bit, Friend. That's it, that's perfect. I hope you haven't been bored too much listening to it. I can only apologize, if you have, men. That's all I'm in a position to do, I'm afraid. It's a nice tune, though. I appreciate your playing it for me. I appreciate it a lot, men.
[THE WARDEN *is near. A Guard unlocks the cell.* THE WARDEN *approaches.*]

LONGFIELD: Good morning, Warden. Nice to see you. What's the news of the world today? This is Longfield's day! This is what I was born for, Warden. If you think about it, well, maybe you will think about it . . . You'll see it. What all of us were born for—that's an absolute fact, Warden—think about it—give it a good think tonight, talk it over with the wife, Warden—
[*A silence. The record plays on*]

THE WARDEN [*quietly*]: It's time, Longfield—.
[LONGFIELD *nods, starts to move out of the cell. He waves goodbye to the Guards.*]

LONGFIELD: So long, boys. Best of everything to you. [*They respond, quietly*] [*As he walks out, on his way to the Chamber,* THE WARDEN *following, they put another record on.*]

*It is 'The Saints'. Preparations are going ahead now in the
Chamber. Witnesses are beginning to file around it.*]

LONGFIELD [*disappearing into the shadows around the Chamber*]: Louder! A little louder, boys—I want to hear it in
there!

[*The music becomes louder. He is in the narrow passageway leading into the Chamber. We cannot see him.*]

LONGFIELD: LOUDER!

[*The music grows even louder. It is quite powerful now.
Soon, LONGFIELD re-appears, in the Chamber. Guards strap
him to the chair.*]

THE WARDEN [*quietly*]: Watch me, I'll be out there, directly in
front of you. When I raise my hand, take a deep breath.
[*pause*] It will be better that way. [*pauses, LONGFIELD nods*]
Good luck, Longfield.

[*He stands there a moment. LONGFIELD stares at him.*]

LONGFIELD [*finally*]: So long, Warden. [*pause*] Thanks for
everything. Don't worry about anything. Anything at all,
Warden. [*pause*] They're not out there— Are they?

THE WARDEN: No, Longfield.

[*A silence*]

LONGFIELD: Give Bowman the breaks, Warden. He deserves
them.

[*THE WARDEN nods, slightly. He stays a moment longer.
Then moves out. The Guards follow. The Chamber is
sealed. Now, The Row appears. The men are on their feet,
very quiet. There is a clock in the office on the wall. They
are looking at it. THE WARDEN appears outside the Chamber.
He stands next to a section of the glass that is covered with
a blind. He nods his head. We hear the 'eggs' drop into
the pan of acid under LONGFIELD's chair. Thin wisps of
white fumes begin to rise. LONGFIELD sniffs. The music is
still playing, though not so loudly.*]

LONGFIELD [*just as THE WARDEN is raising his hand, loudly*]:
WARDEN!

[*The music stops. The witnesses stir and stare. LONGFIELD
struggles to speak. The fumes have hit him, but he fights
hard to speak.*]

LONGFIELD [*finally*]: IT'S NOT PEACH BLOSSOMS!

[pause] *TELL BOWMAN!* *[pause]* *ROTTEN EGGS!*
[fights hard] *IT'S LIKE ROTTEN EGGS* *[pause]*
WARDEN! *[pause]* *TELL HIM!*

[*His head falls forward, on his chest. He starts dying. The
music resumes, though not loud. Up on The Row,* BOWMAN,
*slowly, turns away from the clock. He sits on his bunk. He
gets up, after a while, slowly. He goes to his table. He starts
to write . . .*]

[*The music increases in volume.* IT IS A ROAR.]

FADEOUT

— CURTAIN —

THE PARTNERS

CHARACTERS

THE MAN
THE CARD PLAYER
THE THIRD MAN

THE PARTNERS

SCENE: *A room, very plain, austerely furnished. There are two tables, which might pass as desks; a large wardrobe-type cupboard; two bunks, at far Right of the room; a large screen at Left, behind which, possibly, is a washbasin, a bath—in short, a place for ablution. There is a window over the bunks. There is a door in Center wall . . . A man,* THE CARD PLAYER, *sits at the table set to the Left, so that he is in profile to the audience. The other table is to the Right, nearer the bunks, and faces the audience. There is quite a space between the tables . . . He is in the room alone, and he is playing a game of cards. He plays patiently, lovingly, he appears to have been playing for hours, days; it is timeless. He is not a very large man, he could be in his late thirties or early forties. He has a good appearance, in a manner of speaking, that is to say, he is not ugly, he is clean, modestly, though nicely, attired, almost elegant, yes, there is a touch of elegance about him; in any event, some indefinable something, a certain superiority about him—not open, but there, somewhere, lurking; one is aware of it, lurking . . . He wears a bow tie. He has his hair. A nice head of hair. Yes, definitely superior—a certain—it's hard to say—almost—aristocratic—casual—immutable—superiority about him . . . Presently, while* CARD PLAYER *is jotting down his score on a notepad beside him,* THE MAN *enters . . . He is, one quickly notices, a different cut of the cake entirely—though not entirely; he is tall, thin, a touch of ungainliness about him, a touch of having rubbed often, and hard, possibly, against, and among, that which is called —humanity. But he is not ugly. And he too is fairly well, that is to say, modestly attired. He wears an ordinary tie. He has his hair . . . He stands in the doorway a minute, shooting a quick glance at* CARD PLAYER, *who looks up at him. Then, he closes the door, and starts to cross the room, toward the bunks. He crosses slowly. The* CARD PLAYER *watches him, with his eyes—follows him.* THE MAN *reaches the bunks, halts, looks up at the window. There is silence. Then, he starts to*

185

whistle, slowly, carefully, 'I'm Forever Blowing Bubbles'. He whistles it all the way through, to the end. He does not move. Somewhere, far off, a bell tolls, it is a deep-throated bell, almost a gong. It strikes a number of times, then— silence. The CARD PLAYER *does not take his eyes off him.*

THE MAN [*finally*] [*quietly*]: I got there on time. [*pause*] As usual. [*pause*] I looked up and down the line, I looked all around. [*pause*] I walked. [*pause*] I walked up the line, the usual distance, all the way up the line. [*a longer pause*] As usual. [*pause*] I came to the spot, the exact spot, fifteen feet from the signal boxes. [*pause*] As usual. [*pause*] I paced off exactly—[*his voice is becoming a little stronger, firmer*]— There's no question at all in my mind about that—Exactly— [*pause. A long pause. A silence. The* CARD PLAYER *stares, awaits, expectantly*]

THE MAN [*finally, his voice dropping again*]: And there was nothing. [*pause. He whirls about, faces* CARD PLAYER, *quite agitated*] Nothing. [*pause, he is growing more agitated, his voice stronger, louder*] Nothing! Nothing! [*pause*] Do you comprehend that? Are you—capable of understanding that? [*pause*] Nothing! As Always—Absolutely—Nothing!

[*Complete silence. He is rigid. The two stare at each other. They are statues. Finally,* CARD PLAYER *moves, slightly*]

CARD PLAYER [*quickly, quietly*]: Did you walk to the right?
THE MAN: Yes!
CARD PLAYER: Twenty-five feet? Twenty-five? To the right?
THE MAN: Yes!
CARD PLAYER: And left?
THE MAN: Yes!
CARD PLAYER: *Ten-feet—left?*
THE MAN: Yes! Yes!

[*A silence. They remain there, tense, looking at one another, immobile. Finally,* CARD PLAYER *moves, he sits back in his chair, something seems to have gone out of him, he stares at his cards, he picks them up, he nods his head, slightly*]

CARD PLAYER [*barely audibly, drawling it out*]: Yes—
THE MAN [*sharply*]: What?

186

CARD PLAYER [*as before, slightly louder*]: Yes. Yes . . .

THE MAN [*becoming more tense, moment by moment, the whole of him, heading for an explosion point, clenching his fists, then suddenly*] What do you take me for?

[*Silence. The* CARD PLAYER *looks up, calmly, almost listlessly, though somewhat quizzically*]

THE MAN [*angrily*]: Just what do you take me for? [*pause*] Damn your card game! God D'AMN your card game! I'm putting it to you quite seriously, I don't want any nonsense, any evasive, clever clever maneuvering from you, oh no, not any more. Not This Time! I want an Answer! [*pause*] *What Do You Take Me For?*

[*The* CARD PLAYER *continues to gaze at him, mildly, an almost hurt look creeping into his face now*]

THE MAN: Well? [*pause*] Well, *Well?* [*pauses, waits*] Look here—I want to know! [*pause*] I'm not a brute, a machine, a-a—I'm a human being! A sensitive, living, genuine Human Being! [*pause*] Understand that? [*pause*] Is it possible for you to Comprehend that? [*pause*] [*becoming somewhat entreating as well*] You owe it to me—it's the least you can do for me—[*pause*] [*bursting forth*] I WANT TO KNOW!

[*A silence*]

CARD PLAYER [*finally, calmly*]: You haven't filed your report—

THE MAN: Report! [*pause*] [*A definite look of pain comes over the* CARD PLAYER] Damn the Report! Your damned Reports! Dozens, hundreds, hundreds and hundreds, *thousands*— your damned Reports! Look—Look Here—Your Reports! [*He crosses violently to the Cupboard. It is a large Cupboard, rather beautifully made, the only item of any quality at all in the room. It is against the wall. He wrenches the door open. Inside, there are many shelves, and they are piled high with paper, sheets of paper, neatly stacked, arranged— Reports. The Cupboard bulges with them.*] Look Here! *Will* you look? [*pause,* CARD PLAYER *does so, turning slowly, calmly quite composed again now*] *Where* would I put the Report? There's not room! There's not even Room for *one more* Report!

[CARD PLAYER *continues to gaze at the cupboard, mildly put off now; this is clear*]

CARD PLAYER [*after a while, calmly*]: You're right. [*pause*] We need another one.

THE MAN: *What?*

CARD PLAYER [*somewhat louder*]: Another one. [*pause*] [*looking up*] We've no choice. [*pause*] It's all filled up, you're quite right. [*pause*] We'll just have to do that—get another one.

[THE MAN *stares at him, incredulously*]

CARD PLAYER [*with a slight shrug, calmly*]: We've no choice—you can see for yourself—

THE MAN [*sarcastically, yet, desperately*]: What are you going to do—*Requisition* it? [*pause*] [*his voice rising*] Going to put one of those *Requisitions* in?

CARD PLAYER: Why—[*pause, slightly puzzled*] of course—[*pause*] That's the procedure—[*pause*] Isn't it?

THE MAN [*tightly, controlling himself*]: And I suppose—I suppose—[*pause*] I'm to—take care of it? [*pause*] Fill out the form for it?

CARD PLAYER [*mildly*]: Why—

THE MAN [*exploding*] [*crossing to* CARD PLAYER, *facing him, standing before him, leaning with his hands on the table*]: *I'm Sick Of It!* [*hammers the table*] Sick, Sick, SICK of it! [*pause*] Look Here! You've taken my life, the best years of my life, the Whole of my mature life, practically, from *its apex*, yes, that's where it was, At Its Apex—for all practical purposes—practically [*pauses*] *What Do You Take Me For?* Let's get back to it! I'm not budging from here until I've had an answer from you—It's time I knew! It's time—Time—The Cards Were On the Table! [*pause*] Yes! [*pause*] Oh Yes! [*pause*] *What Do You Take Me For?*

[*A silence.* CARD PLAYER *maintains his calm gaze on him, though the hurt look again crosses his face*]

CARD PLAYER [*finally*] [*calmly*]: You're tired—

[THE MAN *stiffens, as if kicked in the back suddenly*]

CARD PLAYER: You're obviously tired. [*pauses, a somewhat worried looking coming into his face*] Upset. [*pause*] Something must have happened. [*pause*] Something you left out of your verbal Report. [*pause*] What—

THE MAN: Oh No—

CARD PLAYER: What was it?

THE MAN: *Don't try That one*—

CARD PLAYER: Everything generally goes—smoothly. [*pause*] Why, I can't—I can't ever remember—

THE MAN: *Don't Pull That One On Me!*

CARD PLAYER: But—

THE MAN: No!

CARD PLAYER: You—

THE MAN: *No! No!* I say NO! [*pause*] I want to know [*pause*] Thousands, thousands of times, down there, For You! Reports! I've filled that cupboard with Reports! Neatly, alphabetically, chronologically in order—Those Damned Reports! My whole life, Dedicated to You! Now—NOW—I want to Know! I'm not moving from here Until I Know!

[*A silence. The* CARD PLAYER *keeps gazing on him, mildly, the slight worry, and now a certain sadness, almost on his face*]

CARD PLAYER [*finally*]: What—What do you want to know? [THE MAN *does not answer. He stands there, leaning on the table, petrified*]

CARD PLAYER [*a very slight anxiety now as well*]: What is it you want to know?

THE MAN [*grimly*]: You're going to try all of them, are you—

CARD PLAYER: I—

THE MAN: It won't make any difference! Go ahead! Try them all, the whole spectrum, the lot, All Of Them!

CARD PLAYER: But—

THE MAN [*slamming the table*]: *What Do You Take Me For?* [*pause*] Let's have the answer! Now, straight away, Pronto! What do you think of that? Have you ever heard that? *Pronto!* You know?

[*A silence. They remain there.* CARD PLAYER, *finally shifts a bit*]

CARD PLAYER [*sitting back in his chair, quietly*]: I haven't even seen your Report.

[*Silence.* THE MAN *trembles.* CARD PLAYER *turns, slowly, surveys the cupboard. He surveys it a long while, looking it up and down. He turns, at last, to* THE MAN *again*]

CARD PLAYER [*mildly, kindly*]: Don't you have any Forms?

THE MAN [*a shot*]: What?

CARD PLAYER: Have you run out of Forms? [*pause*] Is that it? [*pause*] Do you think you've run out of Forms?

[*A silence.* THE MAN *stares at him*]

CARD PLAYER [*pedestrian*]: I checked your desk while you were out. The drawers were all empty. [*pause*] There wasn't a single Form. Not one. [*pause*] The drawers were all empty.

[*A longer pause.* THE MAN'S *eyes are fixed on him wildly*]

CARD PLAYER: I filled them.

[THE MAN *stiffens, as if kicked again*]

CARD PLAYER: All of them. [*pause*] If you'll look—if you'll just go over and take a look—[*pause*] You'll see. [*pause*] Plenty of Forms. Nice, fresh supply of them. [*pause*] I filled your desk drawers right to the top with them.

[*A silence.* THE MAN *is a volcano, rapidly coming to eruption. He stands there, staring, the volcano boiling, gathering momentum in him. At last, he bursts forth, violently, lunging across the table, seizing the* CARD PLAYER *in a stranglehold, both hands about his neck*]

THE MAN: I'll Kill You! I'll Kill You! I've Had Enough! I Don't Care Anymore! I Don't Care A Damn Anymore! YOUR TIME HAS COME! [*And, in fact, he is throttling him, arching him to the side and over the chair, so that his head is nearly touching the floor. The* CARD PLAYER *struggles.*]

CARD PLAYER [*alarmed*] [*amid gurgling, strangled sounds*]: I —I assure you—thousands—Thousands—Fresh—Forms—

THE MAN: You're Through Now! Oh Yes! This is the End! Your End! Why Did I Wait So Long? Why Did I Let You HUMILIATE Me So Long! I'd Like to Know! Maybe You Can Let Me Know! You're Just The Sort Of Monster Who Would Know! [*Grunting, squeezing*] Aren't You? [*Pause, More*] Just Aren't You? Eh? Eh Hey? Why Did I Wait So Long? What Sort Of A Fool Was I Waiting So Long? Can I know? SO LONG! Yes, Now, You Fiend—SO LONG! It's All Gone! All Those Years, MY LIFE, Gone, Gone! *Those Stupid Tracks! Those Stupid Trips Up Those Tracks!* Well, Now—You're Gone! Going Fast— [*pause*] Fast—[*pause*] UP THOSE TRACKS—

[*They struggle violently,* CARD PLAYER *gurgles, fights for his life. Suddenly, a phone starts to ring. There is one in the room, not far from the bunks, on a little table. One would never notice it. It is there. It rings, just like any ordinary phone. Twice, pause, twice more, and so on. The struggle ceases. For a moment they are absolutely frozen, still. Then,* THE MAN's *grip relaxes. And, finally releases* CARD PLAYER, *who starts to breathe again, at first, gasping.* THE MAN, *still bent over* CARD PLAYER, *turns slowly toward the ringing. Gradually, he straightens up. He is obviously frightened. The* CARD PLAYER *eventually pulls himself up, caresses his throat, re-arranges, re-composes himself. Soon, he is much as before. He too looks toward the ringing.*]

CARD PLAYER [*finally, calmly*] : Answer it.

[THE MAN *does not move*].

CARD PLAYER: Please answer it. [*pause*] [*No movement*] It will ring all day, all night, you know that. [*pause*] I do ask you, Answer it.

THE MAN [*finally*] : Why don't you answer it?

CARD PLAYER [*amazed*] : I? [*pause*] I, Answer it? [*pause*] Have I —ever answered it?

[*A silence*]

THE MAN [*stiffly*] : It hasn't rung for a long time—

CARD PLAYER: You're right, it hasn't—

THE MAN [*after a pause*] : It saved your life. [*pause*] What a remarkable coincidence. [*pause*] Remarkable, you know—

CARD PLAYER [*shrugging, lifting his hands off the table*] : These things happen. [*pause*] They've been known to happen. [*pause*] Perhaps you've heard of them—happening. [*pause*] I, for one—I'm glad they happen.

THE MAN [*after a pause*] : I'm sure you are.

CARD PLAYER: Not for my sake—believe me.

THE MAN: Remarkable. Just—remarkable, you know— [*pause, turning, facing* CARD PLAYER] Almost—a bit too remarkable. [*pause*] *You know?*

CARD PLAYER: What do you mean? [*pause*] You don't suppose *I* set it ringing? [*pause*] You don't suppose *that,* do you? [*pause*] Look here, you don't suppose there was a button, or some such, just under my head—on the floor—*Do You?*

[*pause*] Take a look, take a look, if you like. [*pause*] *Do You?*

[*Silence.* THE MAN *does not move.*]

THE MAN [*finally*]: Why don't you answer it?

CARD PLAYER: But I— [*pause*] It's cut and dry—crystal clear— [*pause*] I've *never* answered it.

THE MAN [*finally*]: *Why?* [*pause*] *Why haven't you answered it?*

CARD PLAYER: It's not my job! [*pause, explaining now, patiently*] We're a team—*Partners*—each has his job— [*pause*] You know that. [*pause*] You're perfectly aware of that. [*pause*] Why—why if I were to answer that—

THE MAN: I don't care. [*pause*] Hasn't that occurred to you? [*pause*] I *no longer care.*

CARD PLAYER: You said that last time—

THE MAN: Don't hand me that one! [*pause*] *Last time*—

CARD PLAYER: It's ringing—

THE MAN: I nearly finished you. Another minute—just one more minute— [*pause*] I would have finished you! [*pause*] Imagine? Finished You!

CARD PLAYER [*calmly, though a little worried, too*]: Well, there it goes. That's how it goes. [*pause*] These are complex matters. Highly complex. They're *far above us.* [*pause*] Who are we— [*He halts, trails off, looks at* THE MAN *a while longer, then, picks up his cards, proceeds with his game.*]

[*The phone keeps ringing,* THE MAN *stands there, staring at him. The tension mounts. He is approaching explosion point again. Then, suddenly, he reaches into his pocket, whips out a pistol. He points it at* CARD PLAYER]

THE MAN: *Answer it.*

[CARD PLAYER, *presently, looks up. He is somewhat surprised, but he looks steadily at the weapon*]

CARD PLAYER [*finally*]: What have you got there?

THE MAN: What do you think?

CARD PLAYER [*after a pause*]: Is it real?

THE MAN: *Real?*

CARD PLAYER: It looks real—

THE MAN: I can try it out. Shall I do that?

CARD PLAYER: Where did you get it?

THE MAN: What?

CARD PLAYER: *Where did you get it?*

THE MAN [*Distinctly thrown, thinking*] [*pause*]: What's the difference? [*pause*] What *is* the damn difference?

CARD PLAYER [*finally*]: Have you a licence for it?

THE MAN: *What?*

CARD PLAYER: A licence. [*pause*] Have you taken out a licence for it?

    [*A silence.* THE MAN *stares*]

THE MAN [*finally*]: You're funny.

CARD PLAYER: No.

THE MAN: You're trying to be funny.

CARD PLAYER: No.

THE MAN: That warped sense of humor of yours, oh yes, I know it well. You always bring it into play, when everything else has failed—Don't You? [*pause*] It's pulled you through a thousand and one nights, just like the fairly tale—Hasn't It?

CARD PLAYER [*seriously*]: I'm not trying to be funny.

    [*Silence*]

CARD PLAYER: I'm stating a *fact.* [*pause*] The whole world knows it's a *fact.* [*pause*] And so do you. [*pause*] Don't you? [*pause*] [*very seriously*] You must have a licence for it.

    [*Silence*]

THE MAN [*finally*] [*grimly*]: *Answer it.*

    [CARD PLAYER *does not move*]

THE MAN: I'll count to three—

CARD PLAYER [*suddenly*]: It's—shocking, really! It's just—It's just—unheard of, Really! [*pause*] Why—you—Where would we be? A pretty mess of a pickle it would all be—Eh? Wouldn't it? [*pause*] No licences! Think—all sorts running around with those things—Without Licences! Think, think of it! What—what sort of a world would it be—Tell Me! Where would—where would civilized, Our civilized society be—Eh? I ask you! [*pause*] It wouldn't be safe venturing out onto the street—Would It? [*pause*] Answer me that one now— [*pause*] *Would It?*

THE MAN: One—

CARD PLAYER: *Would it?*

THE MAN: Two— [*The pistol is levelled menacingly. A pause. Then, slowly, very slowly, the* CARD PLAYER *rises. The two face one another in a long, tense moment. Then,* CARD PLAYER *moves, turns, heads for the phone, very slowly.* THE MAN *turns, watches him, the pistol all the while on him. He is very relieved, and trying not to show it.* CARD PLAYER *is near the phone. He stops. His hand reaches out, touches the receiver. He looks at* THE MAN. *He looks away from him. He manages it, he picks up the receiver. The ringing stops. He holds the phone to his ear a long while, he says nothing.*]

    [THE MAN *puts the pistol back into his pocket*]

CARD PLAYER [*finally*]: Quite. [*pause*] Quite. [*long pause*] Oh, yes. Quite. [*pause*] Here. [*pause*] Clear. [*long pause*] Quite clear. [*pause*] Absolutely. [*pause*] Yes. [*pause*] Right. [*long pause*] Right. [*We hear a click, then a dial tone, from the other end. He hangs up, slowly. He stands there. He turns, faces* THE MAN. *They stand silently, facing one another.*]

THE MAN [*in whom tension has been mounting*]: *Well?*

CARD PLAYER: Intensify efforts.

    [*A pause*]

THE MAN: *What?*

CARD PLAYER [*starting to move, noting the pistol has disappeared*]: We're to intensify efforts. [*Pause, he is crossing the room, heading for his table, his game.* THE MAN *watches him. He reaches the table. He sits. He glances at his cards. He looks up at* THE MAN. *He looks down, picks up his cards, studies them.*]

THE MAN [*finally*]: How? [*long pause*] How do we do that— I wonder? [*pauses, waits. No answer*] I say—I'd like to know [*pause*] Were you told? [*pause*] I make one round trip every day as it is, it takes me most of the day— [*pause*] Just what's involved? [*pause*] How do we—'*intensify efforts*'?

CARD PLAYER [*looking up, finally*]: You're to make two trips a day now. [*Head down again on his game*] [*A pause*]

THE MAN [*finally*]: *What?*

CARD PLAYER [*Up again*]: Two trips—Monday through Friday— [*pause*] Now.

THE MAN [*finally*]: That's mad! [*pause*] Absolutely, Mad! [*pause*] Are you serious?

CARD PLAYER [*Up again*]: Yes.

[*Pause*]

THE MAN: I should have answered it myself. [*pause*] I don't think you could have heard right. [*pause*] You couldn't have heard right!

CARD PLAYER [*Up again*]: And one trip, as usual, on Saturdays and Sundays.

[*A long pause*]

THE MAN [*exploding, finally*]: *That's incredible!* [*pause*] *Absolutely Incredible!* You couldn't have heard right! You couldn't possibly have heard right!

[*The* CARD PLAYER *proceeds with his game*] [THE MAN *stares at him*]

THE MAN [*finally*]: The Reports! [*pause*] My God, think of the Reports! [*pause*] Doubled! [*pause*] Do you know that? [*pause*] Are you aware of that?

CARD PLAYER [*without looking up this time*] [*calmly*]: You haven't made out the one for today yet. Have you?

THE MAN: No! I haven't!

[*Pause*]

CARD PLAYER: I wouldn't delay too long. [*pause*] I wouldn't, you know.

THE MAN: No?

CARD PLAYER: No.

[*Pause*]

THE MAN: Why?

CARD PLAYER: You've got to go out again.

THE MAN: *What?*

CARD PLAYER [*looking up now*]: Intensification efforts start today.

THE MAN [*after a pause*]: *Today?*

CARD PLAYER [*calmly*]: Today.

[*And in a moment he resumes his game*]

THE MAN: You couldn't have heard right! [*pause*] That—That's inhuman! [*pause*] You couldn't possibly have heard right! [*pause*] I've wondered about your hearing for some time now. [*pause*] I've been—*very suspicious* about your hearing—I'll put it to you bluntly—for some time. [*dropping his voice very low*] Some time. [*Raising it*] Did you hear that?

CARD PLAYER: What?

THE MAN [*snapping his fingers not far from him*]: That!
[*The phone starts to ring as soon as he has said that.
Again, they are frozen. This time, stunned, almost*]

CARD PLAYER [*finally*]: Answer it.

THE MAN: What—What's going on—

CARD PLAYER: It's ringing—

THE MAN: I know! [*pause*] I know that! [*pause*] *The second
time!* What's going on around here? Things are certainly
taking a *very funny* turn around here!

CARD PLAYER: You ought to answer it—

THE MAN [*after a while*]: It may stop—
[CARD PLAYER *gives an ironic, yet not unfriendly, smile to
him*]

THE MAN [*sharply, and somewhat plaintively*]: Why not?
[*pause*] Why not? Eh? [*pause*] Strange things are happening
around here today—It May Well Stop! It wouldn't surprise
me At All if it stopped! [*pause*] You know?

CARD PLAYER [*shaking his head, slowly, sadly*]: I don't know,
I don't know. [*pause, murmurs*] Things went so smoothly,
they used to go so smoothly— [*pause*] Then you became
difficult— [*pause*] So difficult— [*pause*] Why are you difficult? [*He looks at* THE MAN *now, almost entreatingly, certainly, mildly, sadly*] Why have you become difficult?
[*Pause. They look at one another. The phone starts to ring
in bursts of three rings now.* THE MAN, *finally, wavers, cuts
the air with his hand, turns, and goes to the phone.* CARD
PLAYER *relaxes, sits back, resumes his game*]

THE MAN [*after a while, into the phone*]: Here. [*pause*] Yes,
Here. [*pause*] Well— [*pause*] As a matter of fact— [*pause*]
You see— [*pause*] Yes— [*pause*] The fact of the matter—
[*pause*] Yes— [*pause*] I see— [*pause*] Yes— [*pause*] Of
course— [*pause*] Quite, yes, Of Course— [*pause*] Certainly—
[*pause*] I see— [*pause*] Yes, of course— [*pause*] Without a
doubt— [*pause*] There's not the slightest doubt— [*pause*] Beg
pardon? [*pause*] Of course! [*pause*] I understand! [*pause*]
I'm sorry. [*pause*] I'm terribly sorry— [*pause*] Of course—
[*pause*] No, no— [*pause*] Never— [*pause*] I assure— [*pause*]
Yes! [*pause*] Yes, Yes! [*pause*] Certainly! [*pause*] Thank

you. [*pause*] Thank you very much. [*pause*] I see! [*A longer pause, a click, and then, he hangs up*] [*He stands there*]

CARD PLAYER [*looking up finally*]: Well?

THE MAN [*quietly*]: They're sending another one.

CARD PLAYER: One?

THE MAN: Just one.

CARD PLAYER [*A pause. He stands there*]: Well, good! [*pause*] That's very good! [*pause*] Don't you think so?

THE MAN [*after a silence*]: We're to keep— [*his hand raised briefly in direction of the cupboard*] that one. [*pause*] We're to keep it right here. [*pause*] A lock's to be put on it. [*pause*] It's coming. [*pause*] It will be inside the new one. [*pause*] It should arrive—today. [*pause*] Sometime today.

[*A silence*]

CARD PLAYER [*finally*]: Well, good! Fine! That takes care of that! [*pause*] Doesn't it? [*pause*] Very, very nicely. Doesn't it? [*pause*] Anything else?

THE MAN: The phone.

CARD PLAYER: What?

THE MAN: There was quite a little thing there—about the phone. [*pause*] *Your* answering the phone.

CARD PLAYER: Aha, was there?

THE MAN: Yes.

CARD PLAYER: You see?

THE MAN: Quite a to-do. [*pause*] Quite.

CARD PLAYER: I knew there would be.

THE MAN: You're not to again—under *any* circumstances.

CARD PLAYER: You see? You see? [*pause*] I could have told you so!

THE MAN [*turning, slowly*]: How did they know it was you? [*pause*] Our voices are very similar. Yes. As a matter of fact —very, very similar. [*pause*] Aren't they? There's hardly anything at all between them— Is There? [*pause*] If we were to make a record of your voice—then mine—reciting the same line— I know I wouldn't be able to tell the difference! [*pause*] Would you?

CARD PLAYER [*after a pause*]: There is a difference.

THE MAN [*after a pause*]: Is there?

CARD PLAYER: Yes.
>[*A pause*]

THE MAN: Can you tell the difference?

CARD PLAYER: I've never thought about it.

THE MAN: Well, think of it. [*pauses, gazes hard at* CARD PLAYER] Are you thinking of it?

CARD PLAYER [*looking up from his game, meeting his gaze, finally*]: Your Report. [*pause.* THE MAN *does not move, though he winces a little*] I really must have your Report. [*pause*] You'll have to go again, soon. [*Gazes a little longer at him, then returns to his cards*] [THE MAN, *after a while, surrenders. He goes to the other table, sits at it glumly for a while, then, listlessly, pulls open a drawer and hauls out a blank form. He starts to write his Report. He is murmuring, mulling over it, writing, resenting it.*]

THE MAN [*finally*]: Right! [*Slams the desk, rises, holding the completed Report*] Right! There you are! Signed, sealed—now for Delivery . . . [*He crosses the room, lays it down before* CARD PLAYER, *who, barely glancing at it, picks up a large rubber stamp and, with a vigorous thump, stamps it.*]

CARD PLAYER: Right! [*pause, picks it up, hands it to* THE MAN] File it.

THE MAN [*standing there, staring at it*] [*finally*]: You haven't read it—

CARD PLAYER: I know.

THE MAN: What?

CARD PLAYER: I'm not to.

THE MAN [*quite troubled*]: Why not?

CARD PLAYER: New Instructions.

THE MAN [*comprehending*]: Since when?

CARD PLAYER: Since the phone call.
>[*A pause*]

THE MAN: The one you took? *That* phone call?

CARD PLAYER: Right.
>[*A silence*]

THE MAN [*finally*]: Preposterous! [*pause*] Why—you won't know what I've written! No idea at all! [*pause*] It could be—anything at all! Anything! [*pause*] Why—that makes nonsense of your position! After all—that's what you're here for! [*pause*] Basically— [*pause*] When you get right down to it— [*pause*] Isn't it? [*pause*] You're the reviewing, approving Authority—prior to filing! [*pause*] How am I going to do any more filing?

CARD PLAYER [*giving another little shrug*]: The instructions were quite clear. [*pause*] I'm not to.

THE MAN: *And what about the filing?*

CARD PLAYER: There's no change there. [*pause*] [*nodding at Report*] File.

THE MAN [*after a pause, quietly*]: I'll have to wait for the cupboard. [*pause*] The new cupboard. [*pause*] I'll—leave it on my desk, [*pause*] until its arrival—

[*A pause*]

CARD PLAYER: That's alright.

[*Another silence*]

THE MAN [*finally*]: What will you do with your time now? [*pause*] That's a strange departure. [*pause*] I tell you, things are certainly, certainly taking strange departures. [*pause*] Why—you'll have nothing whatever to do with your time now!

CARD PLAYER [*good humoredly*]: Oh, don't you worry. [*pause*] I'll manage. [*pause*] I've got my cards—time passes—I'll manage.

[*A silence*]

THE MAN [*finally*]: I say—

CARD PLAYER: Yes?

THE MAN: I've just thought of something—

[CARD PLAYER *looks up at him, slightly pained, mildly rebuking*]

THE MAN: Why couldn't *you* go down there? [*pause*, CARD PLAYER *really frowns*] Yes, why couldn't we take turns going down there? After all, the workload is doubled—for all practical purposes. Doubled— [*pause*] You've nothing to do now— Nothing Whatever, so far as one can tell, To Do Now— [*pause*] Why couldn't you—

CARD PLAYER [*quite startled, but controlling himself, as if addressing a madman*]: That— [*pause*] Those weren't the Instructions.

THE MAN: Devil the Instructions! [*pause*] We're allowed to

make local interpretations of Instructions! [*pause*] Aren't we? [*pause*] Couldn't we? [*pause*] I mean—Who's To Know? [*pause, lowering his voice, leaning forward*] That time—that little business about the bunks—

CARD PLAYER [*uneasily*]: We may have a visit.

THE MAN [*scoffing*]: A visit! Ho Ho! [*pause*] When have we had a visit?

CARD PLAYER [*shifting*]: Well, that's it—that's the point— [*pause*] *You never know.*

THE MAN: We won't have a visit! I don't believe for a minute in visits! Not here! You won't see a visit! [*pause*] You're shirking. You're just shirking. You can't fool me, you know! [*pause*] I know you! [*pause*] A visit!

[*A long silence. They stare at one another*]

THE MAN [*quietly*]: I haven't had my tea, you know.

CARD PLAYER [*finally, calmly*]: You'd better go now.

CARD PLAYER: There will be an extra big supper for you, when you get back.

THE MAN: Will there?

[*A pause.* THE MAN *likes the idea. He smiles*]

CARD PLAYER: There certainly will.

THE MAN: Will there be curry?

CARD PLAYER: What?

THE MAN: Beef curry! [*pause*] Do you remember that time? [*pause*] It was wonderful! [*pause*] Oh, it's been some time —You remember! [*pause*] Simply—Wonderful! I've not had the pleasure of anything quite so satisfying—no, not quite— Since! That was a pleasure. A real Treasure of pleasure! [*pause*] Are we?

CARD PLAYER: I'm not sure. [*pause*] You know that. [*pause*] I'm never told the menus before hand. [*pause*] I'm sure you know that.

THE MAN: True! [*pause, reflecting*] I've never been happy about that arrangement. [*pause*] Have you?

CARD PLAYER [*shrugs*]: We've never been disappointed.

THE MAN: Yes—well—

CARD PLAYER: Has any meal, any one meal, ever disappointed us?

[*A silence*]

THE MAN: Well—

CARD PLAYER: So?

THE MAN: Well—[*pause*] You see—[*pause*] that is to say—[*pause*] It would be nice to *Know*. [*pause*] Even to have—to have a—certain voice in the matter—possibly submit requests, suggestions—[*pause*] You know? [*pause*] I mean, as things stand, well, as you say, all well and good—[*pause*] But—[*pause*] Well, after all—everything's—*so arranged*—cut and dry—[*pause*] We simply take what's offered—and that is that—[*pause*] Like it or not, hope for something other or not—[*pause*] That is that!

CARD PLAYER [*after a pause*]: I always like it.

THE MAN: It's not the point! [*pause*] I wish we had Curry tonight! I'd be—absolutely—Thrilled if there were Curry tonight!

[*A silence.* THE MAN *walks toward the door. He is near it. He turns*]

THE MAN: Are you having tea?

CARD PLAYER [*chuckling*]: You know I never take tea—

THE MAN [*after a pause*]: Do I know what you do when I'm not here?

CARD PLAYER [*bonhomie*]: Of course you do!

THE MAN [*after a pause*]: Do I?

[*This time,* CARD PLAYER *says nothing. He returns to his game*]

THE MAN: What do I know? [*pause*] You might get up to anything! [*pause*] You might—make a call! Yes, you might get up, edge your way over to the phone—Make A Call!

CARD PLAYER [*patiently*]: You know very well this phone handles only incoming calls.

THE MAN: That's what you tell me, I know *that* very well.

CARD PLAYER [*lifting his eyes*]: Well, go on over and try to make a call—[*pause,* THE MAN *does not move*] Go on—[*pause*] Dial 999, dial anything, TIM, something simple like that—[*pause*] Go on then—

[*A silence.* THE MAN *looks at the phone. He looks away from the phone. He looks at* CARD PLAYER. *He pulls a cap out of his pocket. He places it on his head.*]

THE MAN: I'll see you later.

CARD PLAYER: There'll be a fine supper waiting for you.

THE MAN: I know.

CARD PLAYER: It may even be Curry—[*pause*] Who knows?
[*A silence. They look a long while at each other*]

CARD PLAYER [*finally*]: Have you still got it?

THE MAN: What?

CARD PLAYER [*good humoredly*]: You know—[*pause*] What
you were waving at me before—[*pause*] When I answered the
phone—[*pause*] You know?

THE MAN [*finally*]: I've got it.

CARD PLAYER [*solemnly*]: You must get a licence for it.

THE MAN: I—

CARD PLAYER: You can stop off on your way down there, I
really think you ought to, you should have a licence for it—

THE MAN [*after a pause*]: Where would I—stop off?

CARD PLAYER [*after a pause*]: Make inquiries! [*pause*] Don't
you pass a Police Station on the way? I believe I once saw
that in a Report. [*pause*] One of the early Reports. [*pause*]
Yes. Stop in there. Inquire. They're bound to know. [*pause*]
They'll put you right.
[*A silence*]

THE MAN [*finally*]: I may not keep it.

CARD PLAYER: What?

THE MAN: I may decide not to keep it.

CARD PLAYER [*obviously unprepared for this turn*]: What will
you do with it?

THE MAN: I don't know. [*after a pause, shrugging*] Dispose of it.
[*A silence*]

THE MAN: Do you want it?

CARD PLAYER: I? Good Heavens! I, Want it—? [*He is amused,
a little horrified*] I don't want it!

THE MAN [*shrugging again*]: That's what I'll do, then.

CARD PLAYER: Dispose of it?

THE MAN [*opening the door, taking a final look back*]: Yes.
[*pause*] I'll dispose of it.
[*He closes the door, he is gone, we hear his footsteps
echoing along what might be a long hallway. Then, des-
cending stairs. Then, far off, an outer door, it seems, slamming. The CARD PLAYER plays a few more hands, totals up
his score, then rises. He crosses the room. He pauses before*]

*the cupboard, which is still open. He stares at its contents,
the thousands of Reports, piled neatly, filling the cupboard
completely. He crosses to the phone. He is humming something, we cannot make out what it is. He picks up the
phone, he dials a sequence of numbers—three numbers,
four numbers, two numbers, three more numbers, four
numbers, finally, one number—then hangs up. This takes
some little while. He does not move. He is waiting.
Presently, the phone rings. He picks it up. He speaks, after
a brief pause, into it]*

CARD PLAYER: Beef Curry.

*[There is a click, a dial tone. He holds the phone a moment
longer, then hangs up. He turns. He yawns, he stretches.
He starts toward his table again. He halts as he passes THE
MAN's desk. His eyes fall on the Report. He glances at it.
Then, he resumes his walk to his desk. He sits down. He
stares at the cards. He deals himself a new hand. He
holds them, studies them. Slowly, carefully, almost lovingly,
he starts to whistle. He whistles nicely. The tune is
'Together'. He whistles a good part of it. He studies his
cards . . .]*

FADEOUT, SLOW

SCENE: *The same. Some hours later. Only, there is a second
cupboard in the room now, exactly like the first, and it is placed
near the first. There is also a dining table, and on it are several
large silver trays, covered, several bottles of wine, glasses, silver-
ware, plates, a salad, and other accoutrements usually found
at a good table. Two chairs are before the set places. They await
their occupants. The CARD PLAYER is still at it, though at the
moment he is busy totalling up his score. Presently, the door
opens. It swings wide open. THE MAN stands in the doorway.
The CARD PLAYER looks up, expectantly. THE MAN looks right, he
looks left, he surveys the scene. Outside, far off, somewhere, the
bell, which sounds like a gong, tolls—twice. THE MAN looks at
the dining table. He looks at the new cupboard. He looks a long
time at it. Then, he turns to the CARD PLAYER, who awaits his
verbal Report]*

THE MAN [*finally*]: The same.

[*The* CARD PLAYER *does not move. He is poised to ask his battery of questions*]

THE MAN: *Don't ask any questions! Don't ask One! I won't answer! I won't, I Won't Answer!* Do you hear? I'm speaking fairly loud now, You Should Hear! [*pause*] No Change! [*pause*] The Same! [*pause*] Everything, as always, every single detail—[*pause*] *The Same!*

[*Silence*]

THE CARD PLAYER [*struggling with himself, he wants to ask the questions*] [*finally*]: Are you sure?

THE MAN [*bursting forth*]: YES!

[*They remain thus, looking at one another, a while. Then, finally, the* CARD PLAYER *relaxes, he sits back in his chair, he grins, he is a completely relaxed person, he chuckles, expanding all the while*]

CARD PLAYER [*very good humoredly*]: Well, don't worry, don't worry about it, that's how things go—we've done our best! As always, God knows, our very best! No, don't let it get you down at all—Not At All! You've had a hard day, we've both had a day—Eh? Ha Ha. Don't let it get you down, don't take another minute letting it get you down. What more can we do? That's all we have to ask ourselves, right? [*pause*] The answer is obvious. Completely obvious! What more could we possibly do? [*A silence.* THE MAN *remains standing there, staring at him*] Put it all behind you! [*pause, gestures now toward the food*] Look! Just look here! [*sniffs*] Marvellous, isn't it? Haven't a clue what it is—but it certainly smells marvellous, doesn't it? It's just arrived. You're just in time! [*pause*] Don't worry! [*pause*] Look—go and wash up, wash up a bit—why don't you—and we'll tuck in. Yes, tuck right in! [*pause*] How about that? Oh, you'll enjoy it, I'm sure—whatever it is! I know I will! Indeed! I will! [*pause*] And wine! Have you noticed? It's been some little time, hasn't —some good little time, since we had wine! There you are— Wine!

[THE MAN *surveys it all, then, slowly, turns and stares at the new cupboard*]

THE MAN: It's arrived.

CARD PLAYER: Yes, only a short while ago.

THE MAN: It's just like the other one.

CARD PLAYER: Yes, come to think of it. [*Looks at it*] It seems to be. [*pause*] I haven't had time to examine it closely.

THE MAN [*after a pause*]: There's no doubt about it. Exactly like the other one. [*He looks it over. He sniffs.*] Brand new. [*pause*] What kind of wood, do you think?

CARD PLAYER: Why—well—[*pause*] I wouldn't know—

THE MAN: Beech. Beech and elm. Same as the other. [*pause*] Shelves are elm. [*pause*] Lovely. [*pause*] Lovely wood, isn't it?

CARD PLAYER: Elm?

THE MAN: Both. [*pause*] Beech and elm.

CARD PLAYER: Yes.

THE MAN [*suddenly, becoming somewhat rhapsodical*]: They look wonderful out there, too— Growing! Why—what's more exciting, I ask you, than looking out upon beech—a vast, lovely wood of beech! I ask you! Golden beech! Acres, acres of beech! [*pause*] Do you know Burnham Beeches?

CARD PLAYER: Why—

THE MAN: Of course you do! Who doesn't? What a place! Magnificent! [*pause*] And elm— [*pause*] I used to live near a large elm wood— Did you know?

CARD PLAYER: The shelves are elm?

THE MAN: Definitely, Elm. [*A long pause. He clouds over. He looks hard*] My God, the room in it!

CARD PLAYER [*in his element*]: It holds thousands! [*pause*] It's specially designed! [*pause*] Like the other!

[*A silence*]

THE MAN [*slowly, quietly*]: Yes. [*pause*] The other. [*He stares at that one. It has a large padlock on it now*]

[*A long silence*]

CARD PLAYER [*all bonhomie now*]: Well—what do you say? [*indicating the dinner*] Shall we? [*pause*] Go on, have a wash, don't take too long—I wouldn't want to wait too long! It smells—Delicious! [*pause*] Hungry?

THE MAN [*coming up again*]: Very hungry.

CARD PLAYER: That's fine! Aha, that makes two of us! Fine! [*He rises, goes to the dining table*] Look, I'll just mix the salad, shall I? Take a look at that salad! Look—Will You? [*pause,* THE MAN *peers*] Is that a salad? Have you ever seen such a salad?

THE MAN: Not in years.

CARD PLAYER: It's a Salad!

THE MAN: Ha Ha. [*pause*] You're right. [*pause*] *Some* salad.

CARD PLAYER: Run along, go on, now—

THE MAN: Right!

CARD PLAYER [*cheerily*]: And don't worry about your Report! You can make it out later! [*pause*] Right?

> [THE MAN *halts in his tracks. He is immobile a moment. It is in doubt whether he will proceed.*]

THE MAN [*finally*]: Right. [*pause. He starts to move*] Right. [*He disappears behind the screen*]

> [CARD PLAYER *is very busy, humming, buzzing around the dining table, arranging things, peeking in at things*]

> [*Over in the corner, behind the screen, sounds of water running, splashing*]

THE MAN [*muffled, behind the screen*]: I'm actually—Ah— Quite Hungry—you know— Aha—[*pause, splashing*] I've —worked up quite an appetite, yes—[*pause*] Yes, that's quite so—you know— [*pause*] Aha— [*pause*] What kind of an appetite have you? [*pause*] It's amazing, really—what kind of an appetite I've got—That's what the increased workload leads to! [*pause*] Ha Ha! [*pause*] How are you? [*pause*] Are you peeking? Are you going to take a little peek? [*pause,* CARD PLAYER *starts mixing the salad*] What's that? What's that you're doing now? [*pause*] It sounds grand! It sounds just grand! [*pause, splashing*] Wait till I'm out there? [CARD PLAYER *is working on the wine, he pops a cork*] Aha! The Wine! Ha Ha Ha. What's it like? I can smell it from here! I can, you know! [*pause*] Yes—I'd say, indeed, I will say, tonight, this evening—I'm doubly hungry! [*pause*] Appetite, it seems to me, is directly proportional to the Work Load! [*pause*] This is something—in my experience quite true. You know? I would formulate it—a formula— One could [*splash*] positively make a formula of it—[*pause*] A-P . . . W-L . . . [*pause*] What lovely smells! Aromas! Something that nice is not a smell! [*pause*] Is it? [*pause*]

Now, is it? [*pause*] Due recognition will, I hope, be extended
us—[*pause*] You haven't lifted the lids? [*pause*] The aroma
is—Wonderful! [*pause*] I believe you have lifted the lids, you
know—? [*pause, final vigorous splashings, rubbing*] Absolutely—wonder—wonderful—you know—[*He emerges from
behind the screen, scrubbed, fresh and ready.*] I'll soon know!
[*He crosses the room and halts a few feet from the table.
CARD PLAYER, with a flourish, removes the lid from the
largest tray*] [*THE MAN beams. He is absolutely stunned with
joy*] Beef Curry! [*pauses, tries to find words*] My God—
Only God—[*pause*] Can it be? [*pause*] Am I dreaming?
[*pause*] Give me a pinch—Is it Really—

CARD PLAYER [*grinning*]: It's curry.

THE MAN: Marvellous! Wonderful! How Very Wonderful!

CARD PLAYER: Ha Ha. Isn't it?

THE MAN: Just Wonderful! [*pause*] I can't find any other
words! Wonderful!

THE MAN: Well—well, then—

CARD PLAYER: Shall we?

THE MAN: Aha. Let's do that. Shall we!

    [*They seat themselves with a minimum of ceremony*]

THE MAN [*as CARD PLAYER is about to dish it out*]: Look at it—
Just Look At It—[*CARD PLAYER, happily, dishes it out now*]
Look At It!

CARD PLAYER: Beautiful, isn't it?

THE MAN: Perfect! Just Perfection! And look at the amount in
there! Look at that rice!

CARD PLAYER: Aha, here we go—

THE MAN: Thank you! [*Watching it heaping his plate*] Ah—
Aha—Ah—AHA—[*deep breath*] Smell it!

CARD PLAYER: Aroma it—

THE MAN: Help yourself—

CARD PLAYER: Don't worry—

THE MAN: Look at that salad!

CARD PLAYER: It's got everything in it—

THE MAN: You're telling me!

CARD PLAYER: Cucumbers, radishes, lettuce, carrots, celery—

THE MAN: This is fabulous! [*He has tasted the Curry. He is going to work on it*]

CARD PLAYER: It's that Webbs Wonder, you know—

THE MAN: Is it? [*Putting away the curry*] Oh God—God! Fabulous!

CARD PLAYER: That's what they call it—wonderful stuff, you know.

THE MAN: Taste it!

CARD PLAYER: Note the tomatoes—

THE MAN: Aha!

CARD PLAYER: Here we go—[*he has filled his plate with Curry, now he is dishing out the salad to both of them*]

THE MAN: Thank you—So Much—

CARD PLAYER: Look at it—

THE MAN: I'm in Heaven!

CARD PLAYER: Ha Ha—

THE MAN: They can Increase, and Increase my Workload! [*pause, wolfing it down*] I LOVE Increased Workloads!

CARD PLAYER: Wine?

THE MAN: Yes, Please!

CARD PLAYER: Try this—*try this*, now—[*he pours it out*]

THE MAN: Bouquet—

CARD PLAYER: Wait—

THE MAN: Burgundy?

CARD PLAYER: Beaujolais. [*pause*] '58!

THE MAN: Really? [*pause*] I—Oh—Really?

CARD PLAYER: There's the label—

THE MAN: That's what it does say—

CARD PLAYER: Try it—

THE MAN [*sipping it*]: Magnificent! Better than its bouquet!

CARD PLAYER: Is that possible?

THE MAN: Try it! [*Returns to his Curry, now wolfs salad down as well*]

CARD PLAYER [*does so*]: You're right. [*pause*] Cheers!

THE MAN: Cheers, Cheers, Dear Chap! [*He guzzles it*]

CARD PLAYER: Cheers! [*He guzzles his, after clinking glasses. Then, refills both. The meal proceeds. They eat with great relish, they polish off the bottle of wine very quickly*] [*Amid great exclamations of delight, especially from* THE MAN]

THE MAN: Enormous amount in that bowl— [*pause*] Isn't

there?

CARD PLAYER: Very generous—

THE MAN: Intensification Efforts rewarded! [*They laugh heartily, happily*]

THE MAN: Cheers!

CARD PLAYER: Cheers! [*They put another one away.* CARD PLAYER *opens a second bottle*]

THE MAN: '58?

CARD PLAYER: That's it!

THE MAN: Nature's Treasures!

CARD PLAYER: Pleasures!

THE MAN: The rice alone— [*Pours out the wine*] [*guzzling*] The quality of the Rice Alone—

CARD PLAYER: Staggering—

THE MAN: That's it! The word for it! [*pause, eats*] Staggering! Dear Fellow!

CARD PLAYER: Partner!

THE MAN [*shooting his hand out, shaking* CARD PLAYER'S]: Partners!

CARD PLAYER: Equal shares—

THE MAN: Equal everything—

CARD PLAYER: Partners! [*pause*] I say!
[*They pump hands, they laugh, they are happy*]

CARD PLAYER: Here, let me give you more salad—

THE MAN: That's good of you—

CARD PLAYER: My, my—you really are hungry—

THE MAN: Starved! That's the word for it. [*pause*] And what a supper! What a magnificent surprise of a supper!

CARD PLAYER: Enjoy it.

THE MAN: Are you enjoying it?

CARD PLAYER: I should say! [*pause*] Help yourself. There's plenty!

THE MAN: I don't want to stuff myself— [*pause*] That's the secret. [*pause*] Isn't it? [*pause*] How to get—just enough—no more—[*pause*] That point— [*pause*] One can reach it—one just has to—regulate oneself— [*pause*] Eh? Regulate. The balance. There's a certain point, after all, aha, where the balance is reached. It requires a certain sophistication of approach to perceive it. [*pause*] Become—*aware* of it—

[*pause*] Otherwise— [*pause*] the balance is tipped! [*pause*] Disastrously! Isn't it? That's about what it amounts to— Disaster!

CARD PLAYER: Ha Ha! [*More wine. They continue feasting*] When did you first taste Curry?

THE MAN: Why—in the East!

CARD PLAYER: You told me!

THE MAN: Of course—some time ago—

CARD PLAYER: Forgive me—

THE MAN: Just before the War. I was in the East. I told you. [*pause*] It seems to me, I told you— [*pause*] Didn't I tell you?

THE CARD PLAYER: You did.

THE MAN: I was in Rubber.

CARD PLAYER: Yes.

THE MAN: I definitely told you—

CARD PLAYER: As I recall—

THE MAN: That's so!

CARD PLAYER: More wine?

THE MAN: Thank you.

CARD PLAYER: You did tell me.

[*They clink glasses, drink.* THE MAN *smacks his lips*]

THE MAN: For years! [*pause*] In Rubber for years, you know! I was at the apex of my career, don't you know, when you met me—

CARD PLAYER: Partner!

THE MAN: We retire early in the East—

CARD PLAYER: My partner!

THE MAN: I would have retired by now— You Know? [*Pause. Looks at* CARD PLAYER. *Silence. In the night, far off, the bell tolls*]

THE MAN [*suddenly*]: *Who are you?*

[*A silence. They stare at one another.*]

THE MAN [*quietly, strangely*]: I was sitting near the window, you see. [*pause*] *Not here.* [*pause*] Another room. I was at a desk. The window was to my left. [*pause*] I was working, something crossed my field of vision, just the corner of it, outside the window. I looked. [*pause*] I saw a thick rope dangling. It swayed, slowly, back, and forth, very slowly.

[*pause*] Something was tied to the end of it. Far, far below, it seemed . . . [*He is silent*]

    [CARD PLAYER, *after a few moments of this silence, breaks it by giving* THE MAN *a comradely slap on the upper arm*]

CARD PLAYER: Ha Ha! [*pause*] Ha Ha Ha! [*He continues this laughter until, gradually,* THE MAN *joins in, at first very stiffly, reluctantly*]

CARD PLAYER [*after the laughter has subsided*]: Leave a little room for dessert— [*pause*] Won't you?

    [*They resume eating*]

THE MAN: I will. Don't worry.

CARD PLAYER: I've peeked!

THE MAN: Have you?

CARD PLAYER: It's Trifle!

THE MAN: Really?

CARD PLAYER: Sherry Trifle!

THE MAN: With cream on top?

CARD PLAYER: Yes!

THE MAN: Marvellous!

    [*They finish eating the main dish and salad*]

CARD PLAYER: Ready?

THE MAN: Quite!

CARD PLAYER: Just look— [*He lifts the lid off another silver bowl*]

THE MAN: I say!

CARD PLAYER: Will you have some?

THE MAN: Help yourself—

CARD PLAYER: You first—

THE MAN: Thank you—

CARD PLAYER [*heartily, scooping it out for him*]: There—There you are— [*pause*] How are you? [*pause*] More? [*pause*] Bit more now?

THE MAN: No, that's fine—just fine—thank you!

    [CARD PLAYER *dishes out to himself*]

CARD PLAYER: You know— [*pause, taking spoonful*] I'm glad we don't eat like this three times a day!

THE MAN: Heaven help us!

CARD PLAYER: Picture the size of us!

THE MAN: Some people do—

CARD PLAYER: They do, they do, you know—

THE MAN: Madness!

CARD PLAYER: Absolutely! [*pause*] It's all greed— [*pause, putting it away*] Sheer, infantile greed— [*pause*] You know.

THE MAN: Madness!

CARD PLAYER: One meal like this a day— [*pause*] Plenty! [*pause*] Unless you're engaged in—very hard manual labor—

THE MAN: Quite. Quite right. I agree, you know.

CARD PLAYER: Obesity has become a *Serious* problem.

THE MAN: It definitely has, you know.

CARD PLAYER: I know, I know.

THE MAN: This is fabulous!

CARD PLAYER: Wasn't it all—

THE MAN: I'm all set to go! [*pause*] Not right away, mind you!

CARD PLAYER: Ha Ha Ha— Of course not.

THE MAN: I'll definitely need some little rest—you know—

CARD PLAYER: Christmas—

THE MAN: What?

CARD PLAYER: Do you remember Christmas—

THE MAN: Do I!

CARD PLAYER: Ha Ha!

THE MAN: What's the matter?

CARD PLAYER: I do enjoy watching you. It's sheer joy—watching you!

THE MAN: You don't do badly!

CARD PLAYER: Quite right! I know that!

THE MAN: Ha Ha!

CARD PLAYER: Ha Ha Ha!

[*They polish off the dessert. They take second helpings*]
[CARD PLAYER *now pours coffee out for them*]

THE MAN: Aha—

CARD PLAYER: Enjoy yourself—

THE MAN: I do, you know. It's one of the rare, real pleasures of life. Perhaps the *one* real pleasure—

CARD PLAYER: Quite right!

THE MAN: I've always enjoyed my food!

CARD PLAYER: Quite, Quite Right!

THE MAN: Life— [*pause*] it's so brief—

CARD PLAYER: Isn't it—

THE MAN: Who knows? At any time—any moment—

CARD PLAYER: We're flesh and blood—

THE MAN: That's *all we are*!

CARD PLAYER: We never know—any of us—from moment to moment—

THE MAN: That's it. The moment comes—and when it comes—however it comes— [*pause*] we don't know about it! There we are, out of this life, this world [*pause*] The darkness! The long, long Darkness—

CARD PLAYER: Eternal—

THE MAN: That's it!

CARD PLAYER: All over—

THE MAN: A terrible moment— the most vicious, cruel moment—

CARD PLAYER: It's in us—

THE MAN: Quite right! That's the most terrible thing! In us you know!

[*A silence. They are looking at one another*]

THE MAN [*at last, quietly*]: The most—vicious—moment. [*pause*] You know?—

[*They are very quiet. Finally, they turn away from one another. Very quietly, they sip coffee*]

CARD PLAYER [*finally*]: By the way—

THE MAN: What?

CARD PLAYER: Have you got it?

[*A silence*]

[THE MAN *peers over his coffee cup. He puts it down, finally*]

THE MAN: No.

CARD PLAYER: You haven't got it?

THE MAN [*after a pause*]: I disposed of it.

CARD PLAYER: Did you? [*a pause*] How did you?

THE MAN [*after a pause*]: It wasn't difficult. [*pause.* CARD PLAYER *waits*] I thought it would be—*quite* difficult.

[*A pause. More coffee*]

CARD PLAYER: How did you?

THE MAN: The truth is, it turned out to be very simple. [*pause*] The perfect truth is—it practically disposed of itself. [*pause*]

213

Yes. [*pause*] That's the truth—[*pause*] You know.

    [CARD PLAYER *waits, patiently*]

THE MAN [*finally*]: You see, I was more or less just turning the corner— [*pause*] You know the corner— [*pause*] I was just coming around the *other side* of the corner— [*pause*] [*sips coffee*] When I saw him.

CARD PLAYER [*after a pause*]: Who?

THE MAN: I don't know! [*pause*] I'd never laid eyes on him before!

CARD PLAYER [*finally*]: Describe him.

THE MAN: Why— [*pause*] quite—unremarkable, really. [*pause*] Black suit, white shirt, striped tie— [*pause*] Sort of a—pear-shaped faced— [*pause*] Bowler hat—

CARD PLAYER: An umbrella?

THE MAN: What?

CARD PLAYER: Did he have an umbrella?

THE MAN [*after a pause*]: Yes! [*another pause*] Do you know him?

CARD PLAYER: I've never seen him?

THE MAN: Nor I! I assure you!

    [*A silence*]

CARD PLAYER: What happened?

THE MAN: Horn-rimmed glasses.

CARD PLAYER: What?

THE MAN: He had black, horn-rimmed glasses.

    [*A pause*]

CARD PLAYER: I see.

THE MAN: A moustache.

CARD PLAYER: Did he?

THE MAN: Not a—big moustache. Not one of those. [*pause*] Just a little one. A crisp, neat little strip, above the lip— [*pause*]

CARD PLAYER: Yes?

THE MAN: Quite tall.

CARD PLAYER: Oh?

THE MAN: Yes, an inch or two, not any more, shorter than I— [*a pause*] Blue eyes— [*a longer pause*] He had a wart on his cheek—yes—high up, on the cheekbone— [*pause*] Not a big wart.

CARD PLAYER [*after a pause*] : A wart—

THE MAN: Yes.

[*Silence*]

CARD PLAYER: What happened?

THE MAN: He carried a light brown briefcase.

[*Silence*]

THE MAN: It had *no* initials on it.

[*Silence*]

THE MAN: I had just turned the corner—

CARD PLAYER: Yes?

THE MAN: I saw him. [*pause*] He was standing at the bus stop.

[*A silence*]

CARD PLAYER: *What* bus stop?

THE MAN: The bus stop. [*pause*] You know the bus stop!

CARD PLAYER [*after a pause*] : *No*. [*pause*] No, I don't know the bus stop.

THE MAN [*after a pause*] : You don't?

CARD PLAYER: No.

[*A silence.* THE MAN *is staring at him*]

THE MAN [*finally*] : *The* bus stop. [*pause*] It's been there all the time! [*pause*] All the time, you know!

CARD PLAYER [*finally*] : Has it?

THE MAN: Of course! [*pause*] I'm sure you know!

[*A silence*]

CARD PLAYER: What happened?

THE MAN [*uneasy, but plunging on*] : He was the only one at the bus stop. [*pause. Watches* CARD PLAYER] You know— when you come to think of it—that certainly is a very strange place for a bus stop.

CARD PLAYER [*after a pause*] : Is it?

THE MAN: Yes! I've never seen a bus come along there, you know! Never! Not once! [*pause*] I've never— [*pause*] I've never seen *anything* come along there— [*pause*] You know?

[*A silence*]

CARD PLAYER [*finally*] : Anyhow—

THE MAN: There he was.

CARD PLAYER: At the bus stop.

THE MAN: Quite right. The bus stop.

[*Pause*]

CARD PLAYER: What happened?

THE MAN [*in stride again*]: Well, you see, it was simple. Extraordinarily simple! I walked over to him, after observing him, from a discreet distance, for five minutes or so—

CARD PLAYER: How—discreet was the distance?

THE MAN: Oh—well— *Well,* ten, fifteen yards—no more— [*pause*] Rest assured! I'm always discreet! You know! [*pause*]

CARD PLAYER: Well?

THE MAN: Well, I reached him. I halted before him. He turned his gaze on me. I decided to get straight to the point, after all, in matters like this, it's best to come straight to the point. [*pause*] Isn't it? [*pause*] I had no time to waste! [*pause*] I said to him, 'Would you like it?'
[*Pause*]

CARD PLAYER: I see.

THE MAN: Yes.
[*Pause*]

CARD PLAYER: That's what you said to him.

THE MAN: That's right, yes, that's what I said to him.
[*Pause*]

CARD PLAYER: And he?

THE MAN: Oh, well, he said, 'What?'
[*Pause*]

THE MAN: He had a—deep voice. [*pause*] A rather deep voice, you know.
[*Pause*]

CARD PLAYER: Go on.

THE MAN: Well, then I took it out of my pocket. I had made a sort of a packet of it, I had it wrapped in a very nice cloth. A nice piece of cloth. [*pause*] Colorful. [*pause*] I said to him, 'This'. [*longer pause*] He stared at the packet. I think he was really quite impressed by the packet. [*pause*] The cloth.

CARD PLAYER: I see.

THE MAN: Yes.
[*A silence*] [THE MAN *sips coffee*]

CARD PLAYER: Then?

THE MAN: Well, as I say, he stared at it—possibly—oh—possibly

216

for two minutes. [*pause*] I felt uneasy. Yes, there, for a moment, I felt distinctly uneasy. [*pause*] I thought he might be a policeman. [*pause*] Well, you never know, Do You? [*pause*] Then, he lifted his eyes, slowly, very slowly. He looked at me. [*pause*] They were brown. [*pause*] I saw the wart. [*pause*]

CARD PLAYER: He said—?

THE MAN: 'Yes!'

    [*Pause*]

CARD PLAYER: 'Yes'?

THE MAN: That's right! One word, that was all— 'Yes!'

    [*Pause*]

CARD PLAYER: So you handed it to him.

THE MAN: Yes! And I was off, immediately, like a shot! Why should I linger? The transaction was concluded. I had business to attend to, I had no further words to exchange with him. Did I? [*pause*] It was over, our little transaction— Over. [*pause*] You see what I mean? [*pause*] I'm sure you appreciate what I mean! [*pause*] Quite simple! The whole affair—extraordinarily simple! [*pause*] Eh? [*A long pause*] I wonder—if his bus came? Or whatever—he was waiting for there— [*pause*] I wonder— [*longer pause*] On my way back, he was no longer there.

    [*A long silence.* CARD PLAYER *looks at him.* THE MAN, *a coffee cup raised to his lips, looks back at him. He holds the coffee cup a long time, looking at him*]

CARD PLAYER [*finally, affably, breaking the moment*]: Well, you certainly disposed of it!

THE MAN [*Also smiling, lowering the coffee cup*]: It was simple! Ridiculously simple!

CARD PLAYER: I'm very, very happy for you.

THE MAN: Thank you!

CARD PLAYER: That's just how it is sometimes, isn't it? Perhaps a good deal of the time! Something which seemed so insuperable—so absolutely—*immovable*— [*pause*] Suddenly, things fall into place, almost on their own, the thing is done! Eh? [*pause*] Marvellous!

THE MAN: True, true.

CARD PLAYER: It's just one of the mysteries of life. We take it too much for granted, this mysterious thing, Life!

THE MAN: Very true.

CARD PLAYER: Origins, origins, a question of origins! If only one could get down to Origins! [*pause*] And, of course, Relationships. The incredibly complex, interwoven, interdependent relationships— [*pause, leaning forward*] of these Origins— [*pause*]

THE MAN: Yes. [*somewhat weakly*]

[*A pause*]

CARD PLAYER: More coffee?

THE MAN: Yes, thank you!

CARD PLAYER: First rate—isn't it?

THE MAN: As always!

CARD PLAYER: It's a blend. The secret is in the blend, you know.

THE MAN: I've grown extremely fond of coffee. You know, I never used to Look at coffee!

CARD PLAYER: Ha Ha! Expresso, you know—

THE MAN: Quite! I know!

CARD PLAYER: The country's full of Expresso Bars!

THE MAN: I—

[*He is cut off by a knock on the door. Two knocks, in succession, slow, clear, deliberate.* THE MAN *is frozen.* CARD PLAYER *does not appear to have heard it*]

CARD PLAYER: What?

[*The knock comes again, somewhat louder. This time,* CARD PLAYER *hears it. He puts down his coffee cup, slowly*]

THE MAN [*low voice*] What was that?

CARD PLAYER: A knock.

THE MAN: *At the door?*

[*Pause. It comes again*]

CARD PLAYER: Yes. [*pause*] There's someone at the door.

THE MAN: *Our* door?

[*The knock comes again*]

CARD PLAYER: Yes. Our door.

THE MAN: *How?*

CARD PLAYER [*after a pause. More knocks*]: I don't know. [*pause*] There it is, though.

THE MAN: A visit? [*pauses, listens*] Is it a visit? [*pause*] What do you think, are we—*actually having a visit?*

CARD PLAYER: I don't know.

[*A silence. Again, the knock*]

THE MAN: What shall we do?

[*Pause*]

CARD PLAYER: Answer it.

THE MAN: *What?*

CARD PLAYER: We could answer it.

[*Pause*]

THE MAN: *Why?*

CARD PLAYER: It may not stop. [*pause*] It may not, you know.

THE MAN [*finally*]: You have a point there. [*pause*] Definitely. [*pause*] Yes. [*pause*] It might go on—and on—

CARD PLAYER: All night!

[*Pause. The knocking continues, the same, steady pattern*]

THE MAN: We'd better answer it.

CARD PLAYER: I think so.

THE MAN: We *might as well* answer it.

CARD PLAYER: Definitely. [*pause*] Let's go.

[*Cautiously, they get up and go towards the door. The knocking ceases*]

THE MAN [*low voice*]: Do you think he's gone?

CARD PLAYER: No. He's out there.

[*Pause. Again, after a few moments, the knocking is heard*]
[*Then, again, it ceases*]

THE MAN: How shall we do this ?

CARD PLAYER [*thinking a moment*]: Look—pull open the door, very quickly. That will expose him at once, completely. Stand aside. Here, by my side. [*pause*] That's it. Side by side. [*pause. They get into position, beside the door,* THE MAN *nearest it. They brace themselves. Then,* CARD PLAYER *signals*] Now!

[THE MAN *pulls open the door, and as soon as he does so, a powerful burst of music fills the room; it is 'National Emblem' [Bagley] or one of the stirring Sousa marches, played very well, a rousing, first-class rendering. It is coming apparently from a transistor radio which the man now confronting us, in the doorway, wears dangling at his side from around his neck. He is quite tall, almost as tall as* THE MAN. *He is, one soon recognizes, much like the description* THE

MAN *gave of the individual he encountered at the bus stop. With one exception—his clothes are quite shabby, the bowler hat, in particular, is a sad relic. He is not dirty. It is his clothes. They are extremely shabby. The briefcase, the umbrella are old, beaten, worn. The only item which is not in this state, in fact, which is in a very bright and new state, is the transistor radio. The march bursts forth a few moments longer, as he looks from* THE MAN *to the* CARD PLAYER *and back again—who stand there, stiffly, dumbfounded—then he lifts a hand and very deftly, but carefully, turns off the set. We hear the click and then, silence. The three of them stand there*]

THE MAN [*finally*] [*sharply*]: Yes?

THIRD MAN: Excuse me. [*pause*]: I'm sorry to bother you.

THE MAN: What do you want? Who are you?

THIRD MAN: Well you see— [*pause.* THE MAN *looks at him closely, looks at* CARD PLAYER, *then back again*] I'm the gentleman from the bus stop! You gave me a package. Don't you recall?

[THE MAN *looks again from him to* CARD PLAYER *and back again*]

THE MAN [*slowly*]: Oh—yes—I recall—

THIRD MAN: Well, you see— [*pause*] The point is— [*pause*] The fact of the matter is— [*longer pause*] Would you mind if I came in?

[THE MAN *looks at* CARD PLAYER *again*]

THE MAN: Not at all—come in, come in.

[*He enters.* THE MAN *shuts the door. They stand there*]

THIRD MAN: Thank you. [*pause*] Yes, thank you. [*He stares at* CARD PLAYER]

THE MAN: This is my associate—[*pause*] My partner—

THIRD MAN [*nodding*]: How do you do—

CARD PLAYER: How are you—

[THIRD MAN *turns to* THE MAN *again*]

THIRD MAN: Well, you see—

THE MAN: Are you hungry?

THIRD MAN: Pardon?

THE MAN: Have you eaten?

THIRD MAN: Well—in point of fact—

THE MAN: Look here—we're just finishing our dinner—there's plenty left though— Plenty! Would you like to join us?

THIRD MAN: Well—

CARD PLAYER: Do join us—

THIRD MAN [*thinking it over*]: Alright. [*pause*] Alright, then [*pause*] Thank you. Yes. Thank you very much. [*pause*] Thank you.

[*They move over to the table, ushering him to it*]

THE MAN: Here—hang your hat up somewhere—let me take it— And your—other things—

THIRD MAN [*Handing him hat, umbrella, briefcase*]: That's very kind of you. Thank you.

THE MAN [*pointing to transistor set*]: And—that?

THIRD MAN [*smiling*]: Oh, no, thank you. I'll just keep that with me, if you don't mind. [*pause*] You don't mind?

THE MAN: No— [*unconvincingly*] Not at all!

THIRD MAN: Oh, thank you.

THE MAN: Not at all.

THIRD MAN: May I just— May I just say, though—

THE MAN: Yes?

THIRD MAN: The fact is—the whole point is— [*pause*] I'm in coffee.

THE MAN [*putting things down, glancing at* CARD PLAYER]: Oh?

THIRD MAN: Yes. [*pause*] Yes, you see— [*pause*] [*seats himself, as* CARD PLAYER *waits on him*] I'm in the City. [*pause*] Thank you. Thank you so much. [*pause*] I was just on my way to the City today when you saw me.

THE MAN [*crossing*]: Were you?

THIRD MAN: Yes, indeed, I was—

THE MAN: You mean you were waiting for a bus there to take you into the City?

THIRD MAN: Yes [*pause*] Every day, you know. [*pause*] I'm there every day, rain or shine— [*pause*] Haven't you seen me?

THE MAN [*exchanging a glance with* CARD PLAYER]: Go on—

THIRD MAN [*to* CARD PLAYER]: So good of you, thank you— [*to* THE MAN *now*] Well, you see, the point is—

THE MAN: Yes?

THIRD MAN [*reluctantly*]: It's—about that package you gave me—

THE MAN: Yes—

THIRD MAN: Well—you see—it was good of you—awfully good of you—I must say—let me state that emphatically—straight away— [*pause*] I recognized and appreciated your act for what it was, for it's not something you see much of these days— Yes, an act of generosity, motivated by a real desire to share with others—I understand that, fully, completely—I appreciate that, as only a man of my generation can appreciate that—

THE MAN [*after a pause*]: Yes—

THIRD MAN: Well—you see— [*pauses, embarrassed*] The point is, you see— [*pauses, struggles*] I'm terribly afraid— [*pause*] I'm terribly, terribly sorry to tell you— [*pause*] I can't keep it. [*Halts*] [*A silence*] No. You see, shortly after you presented it to me, as a matter of fact, just after you had turned and were walking away from me, I opened it. [*Another silence*] Well, you see, it's very nice, very, very nice, oh yes—I examined it and I was aware of that—in perfect order, very nice, indeed— [*pause*] A lovely thing! [*Pulls the pistol out of his coat pocket, holds it out flat in his hand*] Really! [*pause*] But I really can't keep it. [THE MAN *and* CARD PLAYER *stare at the pistol*] The fact is, I called on you tonight specifically for the purpose of returning it.

THE MAN [*finally*]: Did you?

THIRD MAN: Yes. [*Silence*] I—wanted to return it earlier, as a matter of fact—the moment I saw it. [*pause*] You hadn't yet gone out of sight, so— [*pause*] I followed you. [*Silence*] Oh, I followed and followed you! [*pause*] Didn't you go a long way! [*pause*] You certainly walked a long way—I thought you would walk to Manchester!

THE MAN: Manchester?

THIRD MAN: Yes! [*pause*] That's the old Manchester line— [*pause*] Didn't you know that?

THE MAN [*after a pause*]: No.

THIRD MAN: Oh, yes! [*pause*] Never mind. Just never mind. It's not important! [*pause*] Of no importance! [*pause*] At first, I was hoping to catch up with you, and return it to you on the spot, so to speak, you see. Then, I decided it would be more prudent to follow you, at a discreet distance, to your home and effect the transfer or return, whichever you prefer, there. [*pause*] In the privacy of your own home, you see. [*pause*] I mean, you know how things are these days, you never know, do you—It's not like it used to be! You never really know—*who's looking.* [*pause*] So you see, here I am. And if you don't mind, I'd like to return it.

THE MAN [*finally*]: You followed me—all the way?

THIRD MAN: Oh, yes, all the way up the line! [*pause*] You certainly went a long way! [*pause*] Didn't you?

THE MAN [*casting a glance at* CARD PLAYER]: Go on—

THIRD MAN: Well, you see—I'm here! [*pause*] I came to return it. [*Silence. They stand there, he with his arm still extended*] Well, you see, that is to say— [*pause*] It's awfully nice—I wish. I do wish— [*pause*] But, it's really—awkward, yes, that's the word, awkward for me—in the City each day—this in my pocket—or in my desk—the same as my pocket— [*pause*] Well, it—it wouldn't do, would it? It just—some-how— [*He fumbles for words*]

CARD PLAYER [*finally*]: How long have you been—in coffee?

THIRD MAN: All my life! The whole of my life, you know!

THE MAN [*finally*]: We have—very good coffee—

CARD PLAYER: Sit down, have a bite—come—there's plenty here—

THE MAN: It's beef curry! [*pause*] What do you think of that? Eh? [THIRD MAN *seems pleased, actually*]

CARD PLAYER: Do you want to wash up a bit? Look here, you can do that—just behind there—

THE MAN: Not to worry, this will keep nice and warm, we have those clever little warmers, you know—
    [*Pause*]

CARD PLAYER: Do that—freshen yourself up—
    [*Pause*]

THIRD MAN: Well— [*pause*] Well, that's—awfully good of you—

CARD PLAYER: Quite alright! [*pause*] Just over there—

THIRD MAN: Thank you— [*pause*] Yes—thank you— [*pause*]

Smells *awfully* good! [*pause*] I've worked up quite an appetite you know! [*pause*] Yes, come to think of it— [*pause. He still holds the pistol. He looks at it*] What shall I do with this?

CARD PLAYER [*casually*]: Oh, lay it down. Anywhere.

THIRD MAN: This desk alright?

CARD PLAYER: Yes, fine.

[*He gingerly places the pistol on a corner of* CARD PLAYER'S *desk*]

[*They all look at it. Silence.* THIRD MAN *smiles, ill at ease*]

THIRD MAN [*finally, moving*]: I won't be a minute. [*pause*] I'm sorry I had to return it! [*pause*] I hope you understand. [*Near the screen*] Behind here?

CARD PLAYER: Yes. There.

[*He disappears behind the screen. We hear water running, splashing*]

[CARD PLAYER *and* THE MAN *stand there, looking after him*]

THE MAN [*finally, low voiced*]: What do you think of that?

CARD PLAYER: I don't like it.

THE MAN: It's quite amazing.

CARD PLAYER: He followed you all the way.

THE MAN: I know. It's amazing.

CARD PLAYER: Your Report's going to have quite some novel entry, isn't it?

THE MAN: Indeed! [*pause*] Extraordinary. [*pause*] All the way! [*pause*] He certainly *must* have kept a discreet distance —[*pause*] Or is he a phantom? [*pause*] I never saw him! I never once was aware of him! [*pause*] You know how careful I am— [*pause*] The *extreme care* I *always* take—

[*Silence*]

CARD PLAYER: I don't like it.

THE MAN: Nor I! I must admit. [*pause*] There's something— something quite— [*pause*] *chilling* about it— [*pause*] That cock and bull story— 'the City' —Ha! [*pause*] Who does he take us for?

CARD PLAYER: I don't like it—

THE MAN: And the bus stop! Claiming he's out there each day, at the bus stop! [*pause*] I've never seen him there! [*pause*]

And what a time to be going into the City! Fishy. Very fishy!
[*Sounds of splashing and running water continue—then
stop, finally*]

CARD PLAYER [*cautioning him*]: Here he comes—

THE MAN [*very low voice*]: I've never seen him—
[THIRD MAN *emerges from behind the screen. He is nicely
scrubbed and combed*]

CARD PLAYER: Well—how are we? Ha Ha—Eh? All set for a
good meal?

THIRD MAN: Yes, thank you!

CARD PLAYER: Sit down, dear chap, make yourself at home—
that's it! There's plenty here—a very nice meal indeed for
you! [*The genial host, he seats* THIRD MAN *and starts dishing
out food for him*] How about it? How's that for you?
[*Pours wine*] Bit of wine for you?

THIRD MAN: Thank you! [*pause*] I'm overwhelmed—really!

CARD PLAYER: Tuck in—Don't be bashful!

THIRD MAN: I believe I will! Thank you! [*He does so. They
watch him. He obviously is famished. He is greatly enjoying
the meal*]

THIRD MAN: I say—I do say! You know—

CARD PLAYER: We liked it—

THIRD MAN: Splendid, you know! [*pauses, lifts glass*] Cheers!
All the very best! [*pause, sips*] Ah—the best—yes— [*pause,
sips*] That is a glass of wine, isn't it? I say! [*pause*] The
very best to you! [*pause*] Thank you!

CARD PLAYER: Enjoy it. We're only too glad to provide it. Life
is so short. What is it without a glass of wine once in a
while?

THIRD MAN: What indeed, Eh? What Is It? [*continues eating,
with great relish*] What is it? [CARD PLAYER *turns now,
slowly, goes to his desk. He glances at the pistol. He does not
touch it. He studies his cards. He picks up the deck, deals
himself a hand. He plays.* THE MAN *stands near the dinner
table. He watches* THIRD MAN *eat. From time to time he casts
a glance at* CARD PLAYER. *finally, he goes to his desk, pulls out
a Form, looks, thinks, then begins to write.* THIRD MAN *continues his feast. He smacks his lips*] Splendid!

THE MAN [*looking up, nodding, faintly smiling*]: Enjoy it.

FADEOUT, SLOW

SCENE: *The same. About half an hour later.* THIRD MAN *is through eating. He is sitting back, sipping coffee, smoking a cigar. He blows huge clouds of smoke.* THE MAN *is checking over his completed Report.* CARD PLAYER *is concentrating on his game. The pistol is still on his desk.*

THIRD MAN: Ahhhh—

THE MAN [*Rising, glancing at him, crossing the room towards the* CARD PLAYER]: Feeling better now?

THIRD MAN: Oh, indeed; Indeed. Streaks better now.

[THE MAN *has placed his Report before the* CARD PLAYER, *who immediately takes out his big rubber stamp and with his customary vigor stamps it*]

THE MAN [*watching this*]: I thought you would.

THIRD MAN: I feel wonderful!

CARD PLAYER: *Right!*

THE MAN [*Taking the Report from him, he walks over to the new cupboard, opens it, finds the proper place for it, and places it there*]: I really thought you would. [*pause*] A meal like that really puts a man on top. [*pause*] Doesn't it?

THIRD MAN: Do let me pour you chaps some coffee!

CARD PLAYER: I've had plenty, thanks.

THIRD MAN: What about you? [*to* THE MAN]

THE MAN [*closing the cupboard*]: Thank you. I'd like that.

THIRD MAN [*pouring cup for him*]: There you are. [*pause*] There now.

THE MAN [*accepting the cup, sitting at the dining table*]: Thank you very much. [*sips*] [*Eyes* THIRD MAN]

THIRD MAN [*sipping*]: Excellent quality, you know. [*pause*] I must say. Take it from one who knows!

THE MAN: Well, I don't suppose it's really much to a chap like you—

THIRD MAN: Wrong, there! I tell you, I'm quite impressed.

THE MAN: There's coffee—and coffee— [*pause*] Isn't there? [*sips*]

THIRD MAN: How right!

THE MAN: Like everything else— [*pause*] Everything else in life— Right?

THIRD MAN: Right!

[*A silence*] [*They look at one another.* CARD PLAYER *carries on with his game, uninvolved*]

THIRD MAN [*finally*]: I've been in coffee for years. [*pause*] Years, you know.

[*A silence*]

THIRD MAN: And that's a strange thing, in a way— [*pause*] I started in Tin! [*pause*] I soon got out of it. [*pause*] Coffee gripped me—it really got hold of me— Hypnotically, almost.

[*A silence*]

THE MAN [*quietly*]: How are things?

THIRD MAN: Splendid!

[*pause*]

THE MAN [*quietly*]: As good as they used to be?

THIRD MAN: My dear chap—Better Than Ever!

[*pause*]

THE MAN: Really?

THIRD MAN: Expanding! You've hit the nail right on the head, my chap!

[*A silence*]

THE MAN [*finally*]: I thought I had.

THIRD MAN: Why, I daresay, the demand in the past fifty years— [*He halts.* THE MAN *is staring at him*]

THIRD MAN [*finally*]: Increased tenfold! Yes! Why, it's one of those situations where those of us in the field have to run— yes, Run—to stand still! [*pause*]

THE MAN: I see.

THIRD MAN: I'm sure you see! A man of your obvious, quick perspicacity can't fail but see!

THE MAN [*finally*]: Thank you.

THIRD MAN: Not at all. [*pause*]

THE MAN: I do thank you.

[*A silence*]

THIRD MAN [*leaning forward*]: Do you know, you and I hit it off splendidly.

[*Silence*]

THE MAN [*finally*]: Don't we?

THIRD MAN: A—a meeting of minds! I daresay. It isn't every day, to put it mildly, that actually happens. How many

times do you find yourself at absolute loggerheads with someone you may be talking with? Absolute! No—no contact
whatever! It's horrible. A horrible feeling, Eh? You feel like
you're talking to lead, just a horrible lump of lead. [*pause*]
Don't you? [*pause*] But us, here, we two—why—I sense the
contact—it's a pleasure! *Contact!* I mean it in the real sense
of the word. Not *connivance*. You understand me. *Not that,*
you know. You get plenty of that nowadays! Oh, plenty and
Plenty of *that*, these days! [*pause*] in fact—in point of fact
—there's hardly anything else today!

[*They stare at one another.* CARD PLAYER *throws down a
hand. The sound is quite audible*]

THIRD MAN [*looking over at him*]: Good game?

CARD PLAYER: Fair. [*pauses, studies cards, marks score*] Fair,
thank you.

THIRD MAN: Play often?

CARD PLAYER: Oh—now and again.

[*pause*]

THIRD MAN: I'm a chess man myself. [*pause*] Bit of a chess man,
you know. [*pause*] Have to watch myself. I can go on for
days, once started. [*pause*] Days. [*pause*] That's the way
chess is, it can get hold of you— [*pause*] Chess Fever. Yes.
Quite real, you know. [*pause*] Oh, I don't get that bad, no,
I keep a pretty close watch on myself. [*pause*] Can happen—
I've seen it happen, in actual fact. You know.

[*A silence.* CARD PLAYER *is nodding his head*]

THIRD MAN: You can get quite *carried away* in it!

CARD PLAYER [*finally*]: I know.

[*Silence. For some reason,* THIRD MAN *stares at the cupboards now*]

THE MAN: More coffee?

THIRD MAN: Thanks. [*pause, turning slowly away from the
cupboards*] Thanks very much.

THE MAN: Not at all.

THIRD MAN: Are you a chess man?

THE MAN: No, I don't go in much for games, I'm afraid.

THIRD MAN: It's just as well. [*pause*] Just As Well. [*pause*]
Time won't stand still for chess. [*pause*] It rushes by, it completely disregards it. Doesn't pay the slightest attention to it!

228

[*pause*] It's true. [*pause*] That's why I gave it up.

THE MAN: Chess?

THIRD MAN: Yes.

[*pause*]

THE MAN: I'm sorry to hear that.

THIRD MAN: Are you?

THE MAN: Yes. [*pause*] It seems such a—noble game. [*pause*] Noble, civilized game.

THIRD MAN: Yes—I suppose—well, you are right. [*pause*] Thing is— [*pause*] The thing is— It gets hold of you. [*pause*] It can get quite a diabolical hold on you. [*pause*] And time—as I say— [*pause*] doesn't give a damn for it!

THE MAN: I see.

THIRD MAN: I'm sure you see. [*pause, sips coffee*] It's a question of *time*, after all, isn't it? [*pause*] An infant, a child, thinks he has the whole of it, All of it, forever, and ever. Doesn't he? Timelessness! In the nursery, All is Timelessness! And vengeance. That's it, isn't it? Yes. Vengeance! [*pause*] *Justice!* [*pause*] Its cry comes down from the nursery, through the ages, touching all of us, keeping us all in line, nicely, neatly— [*pause*] Doesn't it? [*pause*] Look around! [*pause*] *Doesn't it?* [*pause*] It stalks our life, encloses us, Haunts Us! [*A long pause.* CARD PLAYER, THE MAN *stare at him*] But the point, for our purposes—Time! Making the most of what little bit is available to us! For we soon find out, don't we, once out of childhood, once in the world, How Little is really available to us! [*pause*] Precious, minute bit available to us . . . [*pause*] No game, I'm afraid, can stop it. [*pause*] It can't be stopped! It moves—relentlessly! [*pause*] Need I tell you? [*pause*] [*quietly, wistfully*] Only the infant commands it . . . [*A silence*]

THE MAN [*finally*]: I'm in Rubber.

THIRD MAN [*looking up, smiling*]: Are you?

THE MAN: I meant— [*pause*] I *was* in Rubber. [*pause*] I meant to say.

THIRD MAN: Were you? Is that a fact?

THE MAN: Oh, yes. [*pause*] It was interesting.

THIRD MAN: In the City?

THE MAN: No, no. [*pause*] The East. All over the East. [*pause*]

That end of it—you know.

THIRD MAN: How interesting!

THE MAN: Yes. All over the East. [*pause*] I spent a good chunk of my life there— [*pause*] the East.

THIRD MAN: Calcutta?

THE MAN: What?

THIRD MAN: Do you know Calcutta?

THE MAN: I only got there once, twice— [*pause*] briefly. [*pause*] I don't know it.

THIRD MAN: Beautiful! [*pause*] In a way. [*pause*] But, depressing. Yes, quite depressing. [*pause*] That—stark poverty, you know! [*pause*] Unless one shuts one's eyes—why—yes, that's what it takes, living out there—doesn't it? [*pause*] The ability to shut one's eyes! [*pause*] Terrible, terrible problem. [*pause*] How can they surmount it? Do you have any idea? Can they?

THE MAN: Well—of course—the population—

THIRD MAN: Exactly! That's it! You're right on it! It's all a question of population—isn't it? That is the fundamental problem, and they must come to terms, face to face, with it.
[*Silence*]

THE MAN: I was for the most part in Burma.

THIRD MAN: Oh, yes. [*pause*] I spent some time in South America, of course. Fascinating, really. [*pause*] Of course, there's a certain amount of eye-shutting to be done there as well. But at least, the problems seem—manageable. It does seem to have about it some possibility of *solution*. [*pause*] I get there once in a great while now. Not very often! I'm not what I used to be! [*pause*] Yes, I'm just most of the time in the City now, there, my desk, working away, my little office there—
[*A silence*] [THE MAN *stares at him*]

THE MAN [*finally*]: We retire early in the East, you know.

THIRD MAN [*after a pause*]: My oldest boy is at University. I have two daughters. Both at school. [*pause*] I would have retired long ago. Yes, I'm sure. [*pause*] But—an expensive family, you see.

THE MAN: Where's your home?

THIRD MAN: Leatherhead. [*pause*] Just outside Leatherhead.

[*pause*] Very nice there, actually.

THE MAN: Is it—on its own? [*pause*] There in the country?

THIRD MAN: Oh—more or less, yes, pretty much on its own, I would say.

THE MAN: Garden?

THIRD MAN: Rather!

THE MAN: Keeps you—busy, does it?

THIRD MAN: Ho, does it! My dear wife, bless her! She *does* keep me on it! Yes, all the hard digging, weeding, spraying, all that, and so on—you know— [*pause*] She does the rest. [*pause*] The picking—

THE MAN: Spinach?

THIRD MAN: Yes!

THE MAN: You grow spinach? [*pause*] *Spinach?*

THIRD MAN: Superb spinach! My dear chap! [*pause*] Like it, do you?

THE MAN: Only fresh, you know.

THIRD MAN: Why of course!

THE MAN: It's got nothing, nothing at all otherwise—has it?

THIRD MAN: Indeed not!

THE MAN: Freshly picked, cooked—a bit of butter—

THIRD MAN: Lovely!

THE MAN: Try the same thing—frozen! You know—out of one of those—packets—

THIRD MAN: Dreadful!

THE MAN: Shocking, Terrible stuff—isn't it?

THIRD MAN: Just Dreadful; Imagine a generation growing up, possibly never knowing the taste of it save from a packet!

THE MAN: Appalling—isn't it?

THIRD MAN: Why, that's mild! That's putting it pretty mildly, dear fellow!

THE MAN: Those Americans, you know—

THIRD MAN: I know—

THE MAN: They've introduced all this junk into our markets— They're the ones, you know!

THIRD MAN: It ought to be banned! Banned, you know!

THE MAN: Ban *all* Americans!

[*A silence. They are looking at one another*]

THIRD MAN [*finally*]: You and I certainly see eye to eye.

[*Silence*]

THIRD MAN [*turning away finally, looking about, fixing on the cupboards again*]: Those are certainly handsome cupboards, you know.

THE MAN: Yes. Rather nice, aren't they?

[*pause*]

THIRD MAN: I see you keep a padlock on one of them.

THE MAN: You're right. [*pause*] I don't know why, really.

THIRD MAN: Ah, well, it's just as well. [*pause*] After all, there are only two of you here.

THE MAN [*after a pause*]: Quite.

THIRD MAN: One should be—more than sufficient. [*pause*] Would you say?

THE MAN: Absolutely. [*pause*]

THIRD MAN [*turning, leaning forward, facing him*]: What does your friend do?

THE MAN: Why— [*pause*] he's my associate— [*pause*] my partner. [*pause*] Didn't I tell you?

THIRD MAN: Well, yes—in a way— [*pause*] What I meant was —what I'm trying to say—

THE MAN: I don't know. [*pause*] I think he might be a lawyer, though. [*pauses*] Fundamentally, I must say, I do believe the position is— [*pause*] He's a lawyer, you know. [*pause*] I'd almost be prepared to state that as an out and out fact, yes, I would, you know.

THIRD MAN: Should I ask him?

THE MAN: No, I wouldn't do that. It's pointless. You'll find— I'm sure you'll find—he won't answer your query. [*pause*] He'll ignore it—completely! [*pause*] He turns to stone. He'll give you a long, stony stare. And say nothing. Absolutely, nothing! [*pause*] Then, in a minute, he'll return to his game.

THIRD MAN: I see.

[*A silence*]

THIRD MAN [*finally*]: Well—Well, thank you—thank you both very much! A marvellous meal!

CARD PLAYER: That's alright.

THE MAN: Pleasure, I'm sure!

THIRD MAN: Yes— [*gives a yawn*]

THE MAN: Sleepy?

THIRD MAN: Yes. As a matter of fact— [*pause*] I shall have to be going—

THE MAN: Going?

THIRD MAN: Yes. [*pause*] I have to get back, you know?

THE MAN: Oh?

THIRD MAN: I'll just pop out to the bus stop.
[*A silence*]

THE MAN: Is there anything—running at this hour? [*pause*] Do you think?
[*Pause*]

THIRD MAN: Shouldn't there be?

THE MAN: I don't know. [*pause*] There may not be.
[*Silence*] [THIRD MAN *looks worried*]

CARD PLAYER: Don't worry about it, though. [*pause*] You can spend the night here.
[*Silence*. THE MAN *looks at him*]

CARD PLAYER: We've plenty of room!

THIRD MAN: Well—

CARD PLAYER: I doubt very much you'll find anything running now— [*pause*] Not this hour!
[*Silence*]

THIRD MAN: I— [*pause*] It's no trouble to you?

CARD PLAYER: Of course not!

THIRD MAN: Well— [*pause*] That's very good of you— [*pause*] Yes, very good indeed of you!

CARD PLAYER: A pleasure!
[*Silence*. THIRD MAN *looks around. His eyes fall on the two bunks*]

CARD PLAYER: We've got a spare bed. Quite comfy. Just like ours. We'll set it up for you.

THIRD MAN: Why—thank you. [*pause*] I'm much obliged. [*Looks all around*] Are you sure though there is nothing running?

CARD PLAYER: Not at this hour. I assure you. [*pause*] I'm quite prepared to assure you.
[*Silence*]

THIRD MAN: Well. [*pause*] Alright, then! [*pause*] I'm much obliged to you. [*A long silence*]

THIRD MAN: That's very, very nice of you.

FADEOUT

SCENE: *The same. About an hour later.* CARD PLAYER *and* THE MAN *are up, but* THIRD MAN *is now in a bunk at one end of the room, asleep. The dining table and all signs of dinner are gone. Except for coffee.* THE MAN, *at the moment, is pouring himself another cup of coffee.* CARD PLAYER *is seated at his desk, at his game.*

CARD PLAYER: Is he asleep?

THE MAN: Yes.

    [*A silence*]

CARD PLAYER [*finally*]: We'll have to keep him.

THE MAN: *What?*

CARD PLAYER: Keep him.

THE MAN: *Just because he followed me?*

CARD PLAYER [*nodding in the direction of the pistol, still on his desk*]: What are you going to do with it?

THE MAN: I don't know.

CARD PLAYER: You'd better take charge of it.

THE MAN: I don't want it, you know.

CARD PLAYER: It just can't be left laying about, you know.

    [*Silence.* THE MAN, *reluctantly, rises, crosses, pockets the pistol*]

CARD PLAYER: What are you going to do with it?

THE MAN [*after a pause*]: I'll try again. [*pause*] I'll try to dispose of it.

CARD PLAYER: Try to be—more careful, this time.

    [*Silence.* THE MAN, *rather sullenly, sits down again*]

THE MAN: What about Leatherhead! [*pause*] They'll be looking for him, down in Leatherhead. [*pause*] Won't they? [*pause*] That could lead to—quite a complicated situation, you know.

CARD PLAYER [*chuckling, mocking him*]: Leatherhead. [*pause*] Does he look like anybody from Leatherhead?

THE MAN: Well—you never know! [*pause*] It's one of those things. You just can't know—Can You?

CARD PLAYER: We'll have to keep him. [*pauses*] He's seen

everything. [*pause*] We'll just have to keep him.

THE MAN: Suppose—he won't stay? [*pause*] Suppose he doesn't want to stay? [*pause*] Eh?

CARD PLAYER: He'll stay.

THE MAN: How do you know?

CARD PLAYER: It's my job. [*pause*] It's my job to know.

[*A silence*]

THE MAN [*finally*]: I don't think he'll stay. [*pause*] I think, first thing tomorrow, soon as he's ready, first thing—he'll be out at that—bus stop. [*pause*] Wait and see!

CARD PLAYER: So? [*pause*] You told me yourself— No bus runs along there.

THE MAN: I've never *seen* a bus along there.

CARD PLAYER: I'm sure there isn't one.

THE MAN [*later*]: You never know. These buses run everywhere. It's amazing, really. If you only knew! They get everywhere— [*pause*] *I know.*

CARD PLAYER: Not there. I can guarantee that. I can give an iron-clad guarantee on that.

[*Silence*]

THE MAN: What's the stop there for?

CARD PLAYER: I don't know. [*pause*] I just wouldn't know. [*pause*] It may be an old bus stop. Perhaps there actually was a route along there—once. [*pause*] Long ago.

THE MAN: Actually, it's quite a new stop. [*pause*] Quite modern fresh, well-attended to. [*pause*] Oh yes. No doubt about that, you know. [*pause*] A nice, fresh, well-kept, modern bus stop—that.

[*Silence*]

CARD PLAYER: Of no importance. [*pause*] There are all kinds of possibilities. All kinds. We can't bother ourselves about them! What's it to do with us? [*pause*] What's a bus stop, a bus route got to with us, anyway?

THE MAN: It's—funny though. Isn't it?

CARD PLAYER [*after a pause*]: The only point is—we've got to keep him.

[*Pause*]

THE MAN: And—the City?

CARD PLAYER: Forget it.

THE MAN: Leatherhead, the City—

CARD PLAYER: All of it! [*pause*] It's irrelevant, of absolutely no concern to us. Don't you see?

THE MAN [*after a pause*]: That—radio thing—

CARD PLAYER: He's very considerate with it, hasn't played it once, I doubt he'll ever bother us with it!

THE MAN: You think so—?

CARD PLAYER: Definitely.

[*A silence*]

THE MAN [*finally, jerking his head toward the cupboard*]: Did you notice—two and a half page Report today!

CARD PLAYER: I noticed.

THE MAN: You've never seen a Report that long—have you?

CARD PLAYER: No.

THE MAN: I thought you would read it. [*pause*] I thought surely, this one you would read! [*pause*] You didn't!

[*Silence*]

CARD PLAYER: He saw—everything.

THE MAN: What's the difference? [*pause*] What is there to see? What *is* the difference?

CARD PLAYER [*looking at him*]: Aren't you tired?

THE MAN: No.

CARD PLAYER: You ought to get some sleep. You have a hard day ahead of you! [*pause*] A very *heavy* day ahead of you. When did you last sleep?

THE MAN: You know that as well as I do. You're always around.

CARD PLAYER: There you are! [*pause*] You need sleep! You can't go on pushing yourself like this. You definitely can't, you must have sleep, you know.

THE MAN: I'm not sleepy.

CARD PLAYER: Well, lie down then, rest, get yourself off your feet. [*pause*] My God, man, you can't go on pushing yourself like this!

THE MAN: I'm alright.

CARD PLAYER: You need sleep.

THE MAN: Don't tell me what I need!

CARD PLAYER: You're my responsibility! What do you mean?

THE MAN: My foot! We're partners! Equal in every way. Why should you tell me what I need?

[*Silence. He faces* CARD PLAYER]

THE MAN: *Why should you?*

[*A silence. They stare at one another. Finally,* CARD PLAYER *resumes his game*]

THE MAN [*finally, waving a hand towards* THIRD MAN]: Look at him! Just look at him!

CARD PLAYER: He's wise. He knows when to sleep.

THE MAN: Wise! He's just loaded up, overcome by all that wine, food. [*pause*] It's probably the first meal he's had in days! [*pause*] Days, you know!

CARD PLAYER: I wouldn't know.

THE MAN: *I'd* know!

CARD PLAYER: Don't be so sure.

THE MAN: I'm perfectly sure! [*pauses, looks around, crosses toward* THIRD MAN, *notes his briefcase on a chair near his bunk*] Look here! His briefcase—

CARD PLAYER [*turning, glancing*]: Say, that's private property—

THE MAN: Private property! [*pause*] The man comes in, sponges off us, sleeps in our bed—Indeed! Private Property!

CARD PLAYER: It's *private property.*

THE MAN: Well, I'm going to look into this 'private property'— I'm going to show you— I'll prove to you what the man is! Ha! A fraud! A mad little fraud! Sponger! That's what he is! [*He opens the briefcase and starts pulling items out*] Ha Ha—yes—you'll see—wait—look here—aha—you'll see— quite a little collection I'll bet—you'll see! [CARD PLAYER *looks on, disapprovingly, but makes no attempt to halt him*] [*The items he pulls out appear to be papers, journals, etc*] What's this? [*pause*] What's all this?

CARD PLAYER: Bring it over here.

THE MAN [*obviously disappointed, and doing so, looking over the papers, incredulously now*]: 'Financial Times'—'The Economist'—'Coffee Journal'—'Coffee Man's World'— [*trails off into a mumble, places the items on* CARD PLAYER's *desk*]

CARD PLAYER [*Examining them*]: Quotations—orders—Letters of transactions— Board of Trade information— telegrams— cables—Orders— More Orders— Memoranda— Personal Memoranda— A letter in—Chinese, it looks like— More letters— [*pause*] A shoe horn— [*pauses*] A packet marked

'J.E.—Confidential'— [*pause*] Another 'T.E.—Highly Confidential'— [*pause*] and one more— 'Absolutely Confidential'—

[*He looks up from this considerable pile of items at* THE MAN, *who is standing there, gaping, yet not totally defeated*]

THE MAN [*at last*] : That's—the lot, is it?

CARD PLAYER [*indicating the empty briefcase*] : See for yourself.
[THE MAN *peers into it*]

THE MAN [*finally*] : The shoehorn—

CARD PLAYER : What?

THE MAN : *What About The Shoehorn?*

CARD PLAYER : Good God! A man's entitled to own a shoehorn! Carry it around, take it to bed, if he likes! [*pause*] A shoehorn!

THE MAN : Have you seen his shoes?

CARD PLAYER : Come on— Come on, now!

THE MAN : Look at those shoes! [*pause*] Ridiculous shoes!

CARD PLAYER : My God you're petty. Sometimes, Impossibly Petty!

THE MAN : Well, man, let's face it! Look here—would an apparently prosperous, thriving coffee man run around in shoes like that? [CARD PLAYER *does not answer. He only starts to put everything back into the briefcase, carefully.* THE MAN *grows more irritated*] *I Ask You!*

CARD PLAYER [*finally*] : *Very* petty. You have a very petty streak in you. [*pause*] It's your background. I'm sure. [*pause*] I'm quite appalled by it! Have I ever told you? [*pause*] You're a snob, a bit of a snob, you know.

THE MAN : I'm not! I'm certainly not a Snob at all, not a bit of it, not by any stretch of the imagination, rest assured! I won't have these—gross accusations—slanders—flung about at me— No— I won't have it, you know!

CARD PLAYER : Then why all the business about his shoes? Eh? What have they do with what the man is? Eh? His shoes! [*pause*] How do you know—why—why he may be the *Head of the Coffee World!* Yes! *Top Man!* Would You Know? You were in *Rubber!* What Would You Know? And a long time ago at that, too! Would You Know? It might surprise

you. Wouldn't it give you a little surprise, though! I suppose
—yes—I can just imagine it— That would Floor you!

[*A silence.* THE MAN *glares at him*]

THE MAN [*finally, beginning quietly, then gradually louder*]:
You're a frustrating fellow to live with, you know. [*pause*]
What were you telling me, just a while ago? Remember?
Leatherhead? You mocked Leatherhead! The very IDEA of
Leatherhead! Didn't you? [*pause*] Sometimes, sometimes I
find myself wishing—thinking— Yes—it might be best—
[*pause*] It might just possibly be best—*if our partnership
were dissolved!* Completely, Totally Dissolved! [*pause*] *You
Know?*

CARD PLAYER [*quietly*]: You're free to do that. You're completely at liberty, anytime, as you *know*—to do that. [*pause*]
You know.

[*Silence.* CARD PLAYER *goes on with his game.* THE MAN
*glares at him a while longer. Then, vanquished, he walks
toward the chair with the briefcase, lays it down. He turns,
stares at the soundly sleeping* THIRD MAN. *He touches the
pocket in which the pistol lays*]

CARD PLAYER [*without turning, quietly*]: What are you doing
there?

[THE MAN *goes through a struggle. His hand glides into his
pocket. The struggle reaches its climax. The hand emerges,
empty. He turns, at last, and shuffles slowly, suddenly very
tired, across the room, toward his bunk*]

THE MAN: I'm going to bed.

CARD PLAYER: Good. That's a good idea, you know.

THE MAN: I don't know. [*pause*] I'm tired. [*pause*] That I
know.

CARD PLAYER: A good sleep—you'll see—you'll be up bright—
early—on top of the world! [*pause*] A new man, tomorrow!

THE MAN [*very sleepily, desperately*]: Tomorrow—

CARD PLAYER: What?

THE MAN [*starting to peel his clothes off*]: Aren't you—tired?

CARD PLAYER: Tired? [*pause*] I'm here all the time, what do I
do? Why should I be tired? [*pause*] Oh, I'll get some rest,
later on. [*pause*] Don't you worry! [*He chalks up his latest
score on his pad*]

[THE MAN *drapes his clothes over a chair. He is in his long-johns. He takes the pistol out of his coat pocket. He puts it under his pillow.* CARD PLAYER *sees this*]

CARD PLAYER: Could it—go off?

THE MAN: What?

CARD PLAYER: Is there any chance of it going off—during the night—under there?

THE MAN: No. [*pause*] Don't be silly—

CARD PLAYER: It must get quite warm under there. [*pause*] Are you sure? [*pause*] Quite sure of that?

THE MAN: Not a chance! [*He falls into bed, crawls under the covers*] Good night.

CARD PLAYER [*somewhat worried*]: Good night. [*pause*] [*more cheerily now*] Sleep tight!

[*Silence*]

CARD PLAYER: Comfy? [*pause*] How are you? [*pause*] Alright? [*pause*] Everything alright—there?

THE MAN [*mumbling*]: Alright. Fine. [*pause*] Thank you . . . No dreams . . . I hope . . . for once . . .

CARD PLAYER: I'm glad!

THE MAN [*still mumbling, half asleep*]: I'm going out—

CARD PLAYER: What?

THE MAN: To my office. Old office. In the street. Waiting for streetcar. [*pause*] There's quite large queue, as usual, streetcar. Men, women, all well-dressed, proper, waiting. Streetcar . . . [*pause*] I have only an undershirt on. [*pause*] Nothing else. Absolutely nothing—else. [*pause*] Understand me. [*pause*] T-Shirt. [*pause*] Yankee type T-Shirt, *nothing more.* [*pause*] No shoes. Not even shoes . . . slippers . . . [*pause*] Understand . . . me?

[*Silence*]

[CARD PLAYER *listens to him*]

THE MAN: Humiliated . . . completely . . . Where are my clothes? Pants, trousers . . . Where? [*pause*] I wish I could find them. I want to leave the queue, return home, Find Them . . .

[*Silence*]

CARD PLAYER [*finally*]: Do you?

THE MAN: No. [*pause*] Street car comes. I get on it. *As I am.*

[*pause*] Briefcase. I carry a briefcase. [*pause*] *I go to the office* . . .

    [*Silence*]

CARD PLAYER: Good night!

THE MAN: I have it often . . .

    [*A silence*]

CARD PLAYER [*finally*]: Asleep?

THE MAN: No . . .

    [*Silence*]

CARD PLAYER: Take him with you.

THE MAN [*drowsily*]: What?

CARD PLAYER: I forgot. I should have told you. [*pause*] When you go out—he'll have to go with you.

THE MAN: What?

CARD PLAYER: He'll have to go. Can't have him hanging about here all the time! [*pause*] Sorry, can't be helped, you know!

THE MAN: The dream—

CARD PLAYER: Can you hear me?

THE MAN: I hear you—

CARD PLAYER: Just can't be helped. I'm terribly sorry I hadn't told you. Very sorry, you know—

THE MAN [*trailing off fast*]: Oh?

CARD PLAYER: He'll be no bother! I'm sure he won't play that thing, not if you don't want him to, I'm sure, you know!

THE MAN: No . . .

    [*He falls asleep*]

CARD PLAYER [*finally*]: Good night!

    [*He goes on playing. All is quiet. Then, after a while, the phone rings. It does not disturb the sleeping men. The* CARD PLAYER, *after a while, rises, crosses to it, answers it. As usual, he simply picks it up, holds it to his ear, and listens*]

CARD PLAYER [*finally, definitively*]: Certainly.

    [*He hangs up, returns to his desk, resumes his card game*]

FADEOUT

SCENE: *The same. Several hours later.* CARD PLAYER *is still at it. The other men are sleeping. But, presently,* THIRD MAN *stirs. He stretches, yawns.*

THIRD MAN [*yawning*]: Was that the alarm?

CARD PLAYER [*chuckling, turning to him*]: Hello, Hello! No, my dear chap, not at all! There's no alarm!

THIRD MAN [*waking fully*]: How are you?

CARD PLAYER: First rate, thanks. And you?

THIRD MAN: Top of the form! [*pause*] Yes. [*pause*] I think. [*pause*] Where am I? [*pause*] By the way.

CARD PLAYER: Why, you're here! [*pause*] [*grinning*] The bus stop! [*pause*] Present—return of present— [*pause*] Beef Curry! [*pause*] You don't remember?

THIRD MAN: And wine! Yes, I remember! Of course, ha ha, splendid, I do remember! [*pause*] What time is it?

CARD PLAYER: It's quite early. [*pause*] Much before the time you usually rise—I imagine!

THIRD MAN: Oh no, not at all. I'm up very early. Up and about, yes, an hour or so work in the garden before breakfast, oh yes. My good wife sees to that! She keeps me on my toes, you know! [*pause*] An alarm wakes me. The dear sets it each evening for me! It goes off—right in my ear! [*pause*] That's probably why I thought I heard an alarm just now, no doubt. Yes—no doubt, you know.

CARD PLAYER: Ah, well, if you're accustomed to rising early—

THIRD MAN: I can assure you quite early!

CARD PLAYER: It's not really—too, *too* early—

THIRD MAN: Isn't it?

CARD PLAYER: No, not really.

THIRD MAN: I catch the train.

CARD PLAYER: What?

THIRD MAN: After breakfast! I'm driven to the station, I catch the train.

CARD PLAYER: I see.

THIRD MAN: It's not a long journey.

CARD PLAYER: To the station?

THIRD MAN: From.

[*A silence*]

THIRD MAN: Still, you'd be surprised. I get quite a lot of work done. [*pause*] On the train.

CARD PLAYER: Good line, is it?

THIRD MAN: Splendid! My dear chap—Just Splendid!
  [*Pause*]

CARD PLAYER: Not too crowded?

THIRD MAN: No, not when I catch it. Oh, later on, along the route—

CARD PLAYER: Yes.

THIRD MAN: But I don't mind! After all—my fellow men!
  [*pause*] And I'm comfy. Nice and comfy. [*pause*] Yes.
  [*He sits up somewhat, looks about*]

CARD PLAYER: Sleep well?

THIRD MAN: Very well! Thank you. [*pause*] I usually don't, in a strange bed. Amazing, really! This little thing doesn't look like much, but it certainly is comfy. [*pause*] I can well understand why you chose them! Surprisingly comfy!

CARD PLAYER: We like them.

THIRD MAN: It's very important, a very important thing, isn't it, to rest well—

CARD PLAYER: It is indeed.

THIRD MAN: The day's tasks, the hard world's tasks, problems— some of them very sticky problems—are confronted, engaged with *verve*, confidence—

CARD PLAYER: *Right*.

  [*A silence.* THIRD MAN *looks at him, sits up all the way now. He pulls aside the covers, eases his legs over the side of the bed. He sits on the edge of the bed. He is fully clothed. He stares at* CARD PLAYER]

THIRD MAN: Well— [*pause*] I'd better be going—

CARD PLAYER: What?

THIRD MAN: I'd better be going now.

CARD PLAYER: Oh, no, not just now! Why—what kind of host do you take me for? [*pause*] You haven't washed—or had breakfast—why—you can do both here, you know. I wouldn't dream of letting you go without either, nor would my associate, I'm sure, you know!

THIRD MAN: Well—

CARD PLAYER: You must stay, we certainly can't send you off just like that, you know!

THIRD MAN [*after a pause*]: Well—thank you— [*pause*] That's very decent of you.

CARD PLAYER: Not at all! Why, it's only decent, Christian behavior, you know. Civilized! [*pause*] Isn't that so?

THIRD MAN [*after a pause, smiling*]: Yes. That's so. [*pause*] That's exactly so. [*pause*] But—do you mind— Can we wait a bit? I'm not terribly hungry, just yet.

CARD PLAYER: Why, anytime you like, anytime—at your convenience, dear fellow—

[*A silence.* THIRD MAN *looks around. He lingers for a few moments on* THE MAN, *soundly asleep in his bunk*]

THIRD MAN: When does he breakfast—generally?

CARD PLAYER: Anytime. [*pause*] He has no regular time.

THIRD MAN: And you?

CARD PLAYER: Oh, anytime. It doesn't matter!

THIRD MAN: I see.

CARD PLAYER: Yes— [*pause*] I don't usually have very much. [*pause*] Dinner is my meal! Now, I wouldn't skimp dinner for anything, you know.

THIRD MAN: Well—we can all breakfast together— [*pause*] In that case— Can't we?

CARD PLAYER: Excellent idea! Yes, indeed! [*pause*] Only thing—

THIRD MAN: Yes?

CARD PLAYER: You see—it's really difficult to know when He'll get up—

THIRD MAN: I see.

CARD PLAYER: Yes, so—please—don't stand on ceremony. If you get hungry—just let me know.

THIRD MAN: Thank you.

CARD PLAYER: Not at all.

[THIRD MAN *stretches, looks around, finds his shoes. He puts on his shoes. Then, he looks around again, he finds his transistor set. It was under the covers. He holds it, and is about to switch it on. He has second thoughts, looking up, seeing* CARD PLAYER. *He puts the set down—on the chair near his bed, which holds the briefcase*]

THIRD MAN: I should have phoned.

CARD PLAYER: What?

THIRD MAN: I should have phoned Leatherhead.

[*Pause*]

THIRD MAN: They will have missed me. I should have phoned to let them know. Not very considerate of me. [*pause*] They certainly will have missed me, you know.

[*A silence*]

THIRD MAN: I wonder why I didn't phone to let them know?

[*Another silence. He looks around, he sees the phone finally*]

THIRD MAN: I say— [*pause*] would you mind— [*pause*] Do you think I can phone them from here?

CARD PLAYER: Well, you know, I'd be only too happy. Yes, that's so. But, and I'm very embarrassed to tell you this, really—I—ah—I can barely bring myself to tell you this— [*pause*] I'm really very sorry—but the phone's out of order. [*pause*] Yes. [*pause*] You see—

[*He halts. There is a silence*]

THIRD MAN [*finally*]: Oh, well. Never mind. I shall phone them first thing from the office.

CARD PLAYER: I *am* sorry.

THIRD MAN: Never mind, never mind—dear chap!

[*Rises, looks around*]

CARD PLAYER: Want to wash up? All that?

THIRD MAN: If you don't mind—

CARD PLAYER: Not at all! I think you'll find everything you need there. [*pause*] There's a spare razor somewhere, there.

THIRD MAN: Thank you. [*pause*] Indeed—

CARD PLAYER: A pleasure!

[*Silence.* THIRD MAN *is looking at his desk, at the spot where he had laid the pistol*]

THIRD MAN [*chuckling*]: It's gone, I see.

CARD PLAYER: What? [*pauses, begins to chuckle too*] Oh, yes, it is gone, you know. [*pause*] He took re-possession of it just before retiring.

THIRD MAN: I'm terribly sorry about it all—

CARD PLAYER: That's alright!

THIRD MAN: I hope I haven't caused any inconvenience. May I assure you, that wasn't my intention at all!

CARD PLAYER: I know it wasn't! Why, that thought never entered my mind—I assure you!

[*A silence*]

THIRD MAN: Well— [*starts to walk toward the screen*]

CARD PLAYER: You'll find everything there—

THIRD MAN: Thank you!

[*He disappears behind the screen.* CARD PLAYER *returns to his game. Water running, splashing, behind the screen*]

THIRD MAN: I've found the razor!

CARD PLAYER: Oh fine. [*pause*] I'm glad.

THIRD MAN: Jolly good razor—

CARD PLAYER: Yes, I think so—

THIRD MAN: Nothing worse than trying to shave with an inferior razor!

CARD PLAYER: Quite right! I should say!

[*Silence*]

CARD PLAYER: By the way—

THIRD MAN: Yes?

CARD PLAYER: I've been meaning to ask you—please don't feel you have to answer this—

THIRD MAN: What is it, chap?

CARD PLAYER: Oh, it's just something—something I've been trying to ask you—I don't know why, really—

THIRD MAN: Yes—?

CARD PLAYER [*after a pause*]: Are you happy in your work?

[*A silence. Sounds behind the screen cease*]

THIRD MAN [*finally*]: No. [*Silence. Then, he emerges slowly from behind the screen. He has lather on his face. He holds a razor. He stands near the screen*] Not—entirely. [*pause*] No.

CARD PLAYER [*looking at him*]: You don't think me rude, asking that—

THIRD MAN: Certainly not.

[*Silence*]

CARD PLAYER: Because you see—as a mater of fact— [*pause*] It just seemed the kind of question I should ask you— [*pause*] Almost—almost as if—you wanted me to ask you—

THIRD MAN [*after pause*]: Is that so?

CARD PLAYER: I must say, Yes—Quite so.

THIRD MAN [*after a pause*]: As a matter of fact—

CARD PLAYER: Yes?

THIRD MAN: To put it plainly— [*pause*] I'm glad you did!

[*pause, walks towards him*] Yes. Very glad. Because—it seems —why, it almost seems—all these years—so many years— [*pause*] it seems I've just been waiting for someone to ask me that! [*pause*] Yes! [*pause*] You probably know how it is— day in—day out—year after year— [*pause*] Monotonous years!

CARD PLAYER: I know.

THIRD MAN: There you are.

    [*A silence*] [*Halts now, about half way to* CARD PLAYER. *Stands there*]

CARD PLAYER: Well—

THIRD MAN: Yes?

CARD PLAYER: Have you ever considered changing your work?

    [*Silence*] [THIRD MAN *stares at him*]

CARD PLAYER: I mean, if the opportunity came along, *presented itself*—and you happened to like the opportunity presenting itself— [*pause*] Would you, in fact—

    [*A silence*]

THIRD MAN [*finally*]: I—don't know. [*pause*] I just don't know. [*pause*] It's a big thing, quite a Step, you know. [*pause*] You know how it is. Years and years—routine—a certain— stability, security based on this routine— [*pause*] It's quite a thought! Quite a—grave thought, really—

CARD PLAYER: Yes.

    [*Silence*]

THIRD MAN: Why do you—ask?

CARD PLAYER: Well, yes, you see, I'll be blunt, perfectly blunt with you—if you don't mind— [*pause*] I have *an opening* here.

    [*A silence*]

THIRD MAN: You do?

CARD PLAYER: Yes, I do.

    [*Pause*]

THIRD MAN: What—sort of opening— May I ask?

CARD PLAYER: You certainly may ask! [*pause*] Oh, I don't suppose it's anything like what you're accustomed to—I mean, the caliber of work you have been engaged in. I'm trying to say, it doesn't engage the *intellect*, no, probably not in the same way. [*pause*] I daresay.

[*A silence*]

THIRD MAN: What is it?

CARD PLAYER: It engages, as you would soon see, something else, yes, some other quality, some other very specific quality is involved. [*pause*] You see— [*pauses, lowers his voice*] My associate, my partner, if you like, is overworked. [*pause*] He's very, very good; but—overworked. [*pause*] I'm afraid so. [*pause*] This is because our workload has recently been *doubled*, more or less. [*pause*] He's very, very competent, understand. The point is—he is not getting younger, and with this new workload—this very nearly doubled workload— [*pause*] I'm afraid— Yes— [*pause*] Too much overworked.

THIRD MAN [*after a pause*]: I see.

CARD PLAYER: What I'm getting at— What I'm trying to say to you— [*pause*] is this: I would like to extend a share in our enterprise—a working partnership to be precise—to you.

[*A silence*]

THIRD MAN: I see.

CARD PLAYER: Yes. You would, in effect, be an equal partner. Equal in every way. With every privilege.

THIRD MAN: I see.

CARD PLAYER: And you would be working specifically—beside him. [*indicating* THE MAN] Yes, right alongside him.

THIRD MAN: I see.

CARD PLAYER: I daresay, yes, if I may say so—you would find him most congenial. A most congenial person indeed to work with. [*pause*] Of course—of course, you know—as I mentioned— [*pause*] he's not getting any younger! And I would certainly appreciate it, yes, it would be in all our interests, really, including his, if you would— [*pause*] keep an eye on him. [*pause*] Yes, sort of—keep a very friendly eye on him. [*pause*] You see what I mean. [*pause*] You would see, very quickly, I'm sure. [*pause*] He's very good, as I mentioned, but he does get rather tired these days and has a tendency to—digress, shall we say. [*pause*] Get himself involved in—oh—odd little quirks, situations, that's what I mean to say. [*pause*] That—aha—that package, for instance. You know. [*pause*] That sort of thing does require a little watching over— [*pause*] a friendly kind of—scrutiny, shall we say. [*pause*] That's all. He's perfect otherwise. [*pause*] He handles his job beautifully— [*pause*] just perfectly—you know.

[*A silence.* THIRD MAN *stares at him*]

THIRD MAN [*finally*] : I see.

CARD PLAYER : Good.

THIRD MAN : And you would require me to—

CARD PLAYER : I would *like* you to—

THIRD MAN : Yes—

CARD PLAYER : Work alongside him, share the workload—yes— perform the same job exactly as he— [*pause*] Exactly.

[*Pause*]

THIRD MAN [*finally*] : What does he do?

[*Silence.* CARD PLAYER *stares at him*]

CARD PLAYER [*finally*] : You've seen him! [*pause*] Why—you followed him yesterday— All the way!

[*Pause*]

THIRD MAN : I see.

CARD PLAYER : Certainly.

[*Silence*]

CARD PLAYER [*finally*] : Except the Reports.

THIRD MAN : What?

CARD PLAYER : You wouldn't have to touch the Reports. [*pause*] No, he would continue taking care of those, yes, exclusively. That is to say, it would be his task, exclusively. [*pause*] Follow me? [*pause*] It would be most unwise, I should say, attempting to *redistribute* that part of the workload. [*pause*] It's a *thing*—a—genuine speciality with him; one can't touch it. [*pause*] It would be—disaster, I'm sure— [*pause*] touching it.

[*Pause*]

THIRD MAN : I see.

CARD PLAYER : I'm glad. [*pause*] I *am* glad.

[*Silence*] [*They remain there,* THIRD MAN *staring*]

CARD PLAYER [*finally*] : Well—what do you think of it?

THIRD MAN : Well, of course it's a very big step—

CARD PLAYER : Of course it is!

THIRD MAN : It requires—some thinking—

CARD PLAYER: Quite!

THIRD MAN: It's the kind of thing one really—wants to give a *good think* to—

CARD PLAYER: That goes without saying! Without a doubt! Of course!

[*A silence*]

THIRD MAN: May I think about it?

CARD PLAYER: Do! By all means! Please do!

THIRD MAN: Thank you.

CARD PLAYER: Not at all.

THIRD MAN: It's really—a most generous offer. [*pause*] Thank you. [*pause*] Thank you so much.

CARD PLAYER: Pleasure!

[*They remain there. Then, slowly,* THIRD MAN *turns and heads for the screen. He disappears behind it. Soon, we hear water running, etc.* CARD PLAYER, *smiling, returns to his game. Soon, he starts to whistle a tune. It is, 'Together'. He whistles it very softly, and keeps time beautifully. He caresses the air with his whistle. Some time passes.* THE MAN *starts to stir in his bunk, apparently disturbed by the whistling. He wakes, slowly, and sits up on his elbows, staring at* CARD PLAYER, *who continues whistling, concentrating on his game*]

THE MAN [*finally*]: What are you doing?

CARD PLAYER [*looking up, after a brief pause*]: Whistling.

[*Silence*]

THE MAN: I've never heard you whistling.

CARD PLAYER: Oh, yes, I whistle.

[*Silence*]

THE MAN: What were you whistling?

CARD PLAYER: Why—I don't know. [*pause*] Some old tune.

THE MAN: From a movie?

CARD PLAYER: What?

THE MAN: Is it from an old movie?

CARD PLAYER [*quietly, staring at him*]: I don't know.

THE MAN: What are you looking at? [*pause*] I went to movies. Once. Quite a few movies! [*pause*] Yes. [*pause*] You might like to know.

CARD PLAYER: I know.

[*A silence*]

CARD PLAYER: Did I wake you?

THE MAN: I don't know. [*pause*] Is it time to get up?

CARD PLAYER: Not—exactly.

THE MAN: I think I'll get up.

CARD PLAYER: That's alright. Do get up.

THE MAN: How long have you been up?

CARD PLAYER: Why—

THE MAN: *What?* Not again!

CARD PLAYER: Not to worry—I'll make it up. [*pause*] I got a bit involved. [*pause*] I just couldn't leave it.

THE MAN: That—little pastime— [*pause*] That *vocation* of yours—it's going to get the best of you one day! Mark my word! I know!

CARD PLAYER: I'll get plenty of sleep while you're out.

[THE MAN *sits up. He feels under his pillow. He is reassured. He looks around. His eyes fall on the empty bunk, across the way*]

THE MAN: Is he gone?

[*At that moment, sounds of splashing. He has his answer*]

THE MAN: He's not gone? [*pause*] What's he still doing here? [*pause*] He should be gone!

CARD PLAYER: Don't you remember?

THE MAN: What?

CARD PLAYER: Try to remember— [*pauses, leans forward, very low voice*] He knows everything. We can't let him go. We've got to keep him. [*pause*] I've worked something out so that we can keep him.

THE MAN: *Here?*

CARD PLAYER: Yes, of course. [*pause*] Here.

[*A silence*]

THE MAN: I remember.

CARD PLAYER: Good. Oh, good. I'm glad you remember.

THE MAN: I don't like it. [*pause*] But I do remember.

CARD PLAYER: It's not a question of *liking* it, is it?

THE MAN: I don't know. [*pause*] I don't see much sense in it.

CARD PLAYER: *What?*

[*And the* THIRD MAN *walks out from behind the screen, nicely washed, spruced up, shaved. He is just brushing his battered bowler hat off. They stare at him*]

CARD PLAYER [*all bonhomie*]: Well—Well, Well! Feel better? I say, you look better!

THIRD MAN: I must say, I feel tons better!

CARD PLAYER: Ha Ha!

THIRD MAN: Ha Ha Ha!

[*They have a good laugh.* THE MAN *looks on*]

THIRD MAN [*noticing him, finally*]: Hello there! [*pause*] How are you?

THE MAN [*sullenly*]: Alright.

THIRD MAN: I didn't wake you? I must have made quite a row back there. Did I wake you?

[*Pause*]

THE MAN [*flatly*]: No.

[*Silence*]

CARD PLAYER: Well! Aha, Well! We can have a little breakfast now! [*pause*] How about that?

THIRD MAN: Jolly good!

CARD PLAYER: Hungry?

THIRD MAN: Jolly hungry!

CARD PLAYER: Good! Worked up a little appetite, did you?

THIRD MAN: I should say.

CARD PLAYER: Good! I don't know what there is today—what do you fancy?

THIRD MAN: Oh—whatever you have—I'm not fussy!

CARD PLAYER: It will be nice, I assure you. [*pause. Looks at* THE MAN] Hungry?

THE MAN: No.

CARD PLAYER: Oh, well, have a *little* bite with us, eh?

THE MAN: I suppose.

CARD PLAYER: That's fine! Well it must be getting near the time— [*pauses, looks at* THE MAN]

CARD PLAYER [*to* THE MAN]: Get it, will you?

[THE MAN *moves, rises, reluctantly. He is in his longjohns. He walks toward the door.* THIRD MAN *stares at him. He opens the door. He pulls in a large trolley loaded with covered silver dishes, glasses, other breakfast accoutrements*]

[THIRD MAN *rushes forward to help*]

THE MAN [*resentfully*]: That's alright. I can manage. [*He pulls the trolley in*] I can manage— [*He stops in the center of the room. The sides of the trolley open and form a table. He lays the places*]

CARD PLAYER: There! There you are! I'll wager it's a nice breakfast. Eh? What will you wager? [*pause. Rises*] Come on then—pull up a chair! [THIRD MAN *moves eagerly to the table.* THE MAN *goes to his bunk, starts pulling on his trousers*]

CARD PLAYER [*pulling cover off largest tray*]: Here—look at this! Look, will you?

[THIRD MAN *gazes with rapture at the breakfast.* THE MAN *comes near soon, glances at it in an aloof manner*]

THIRD MAN: I say!

CARD PLAYER: Not bad, eh?

THIRD MAN: First rate— First rate, you know!

CARD PLAYER: Smell the coffee?

THIRD MAN: Um Hmmmm! Just smell that coffee!

CARD PLAYER: Ha Ha! What do you think, eh? Glad you stayed?

THIRD MAN: Indeed! Why, this is excellent!

[*Further remarks of this nature are exchanged between them.* THE MAN, *meantime, looks on, glumly, quite resentful of* THIRD MAN's *presence*]

CARD PLAYER [*finally*]: Right! Tuck in, eh?

THIRD MAN: After you—

CARD PLAYER: Ha Ha! Oh no, after *you*—

THIRD MAN: You first!

[THE MAN, *meantime, starts serving himself. They look on lovingly as he fills his plate. It is a hearty breakfast—bacon and eggs, sausages, etc.*]

THIRD MAN: Aha—

CARD PLAYER: Lovely—

THIRD MAN: You next—

CARD PLAYER: I wouldn't dream of it—

THIRD MAN: Please—

CARD PLAYER: I insist—

[*Finally,* THIRD MAN *gives in, fills his plate.* THE MAN *is pouring himself coffee. He has already started his breakfast. Then,* CARD PLAYER *fills his plate. They are all eating*]

253

THIRD MAN: First rate!

CARD PLAYER: A good breakfast—that's what a man needs!

THIRD MAN: Correct! A good send-off—it's just the ticket—it's *what's required*!

CARD PLAYER: A man needs it!

THIRD MAN: You're right!

CARD PLAYER: Like it?

THIRD MAN: Perfect! Done to perfection. [*enjoying it*] Wait till I get home—I'm going to tell the wife!
   [*A silence*]

THIRD MAN: I must say, you certainly do enjoy fine fare. A fine fare!

CARD PLAYER: We manage.

THIRD MAN: Are these two meals I've had the pleasure of taking with you fairly representative samples, would you say?

CARD PLAYER: Well—I— Personally, I think so. [*pause*] Yes, I would say so. [*turns to* THE MAN] Would you say?

THE MAN [*as before*]: I would say.

CARD PLAYER: You see? We both say!

THIRD MAN: Splendid! Splendid! [*pause*] I must say.

CARD PLAYER: We like to eat. It's a pleasure. One of life's *true* pleasures.

THIRD MAN: Quite, oh, yes—I agree.

CARD PLAYER: It would hardly be worth living—one is tempted to say—without it— [*pause*] Would it?

THIRD MAN: It's a thought. Indeed, a thought. [*pauses, takes second helpings*] I must say, you do have fine fare! [*pauses, puts it away*] Each night I go home, and I hope to find, all the way there, in fact, I'm hoping to find—I'm hoping I'll find some exquisite, exotic Oriental fare! You know, tasty, out of this world—yes [*pauses. Sips coffee*]

CARD PLAYER: Is that so?

THIRD MAN: That's so.

CARD PLAYER: And you find?

THIRD MAN: I'm afraid—

CARD PLAYER: Yes?

THIRD MAN: It—all depends—

CARD PLAYER: Oh?

THIRD MAN: Yes—

CARD PLAYER: Well—

THIRD MAN: Oh—it's solid food. [*pause*] You know.

CARD PLAYER: I see.

THIRD MAN: Not Oriental fare, I'm afraid! No, just—wholesome—solid food— [*pause*] You know?

THE MAN: Do you like it?

THIRD MAN: I must confess to you—to you both— [*pause*] No.

CARD PLAYER: Well, there you are. There you are! Eh?

THIRD MAN: Yes.

CARD PLAYER: We have tremendous variety here. Yes, from day to day, meal to meal—we never know what will be next— Why, we've seen the most exotic dishes!

THIRD MAN: How exciting!

CARD PLAYER: I find it so. I know *he* finds it so. Why, sometimes, yes, it's all we talk about! For days on end! [*turns to* THE MAN] Isn't that so?

THE MAN: Yes. [*Finishing his breakfast, swallowing more coffee*] [*He rises, goes to his bunk. Takes a towel, crosses the room*]

CARD PLAYER: Had enough? Sure?

THE MAN: Yes. [*He disappears behind the screen*] [*We see the towel draped over the screen*]

CARD PLAYER [*in low voice*]: You see?

THIRD MAN: Yes—I observed that—indeed—

CARD PLAYER: All those years—out there— [*pause*] The East! [*pause*] Vast, endless estates— Those Rubber estates— You know—

THIRD MAN: Hmm. Yes. Could be. Quite. A possibility, you know.

CARD PLAYER: Well! [*They finish breakfast*] Never mind. [*pause*] Enjoy it? [*pours more coffee*]

THIRD MAN: *Adored* it!

CARD PLAYER: Ha Ha. That's the style.

THIRD MAN: Ha Ha Ha. [*pause*] Ha!

CARD PLAYER [*As they sip coffee*]: Well— [*pause*] Well—what do you think? [*pause*] Have you been able to give things a think?

THIRD MAN: Well—you know—

CARD PLAYER: There's no hurry. There's all the time in the world. *Don't worry.*

THIRD MAN: Well—as a matter of fact—

CARD PLAYER: Yes?

THIRD MAN: In point of fact— [*pause*] I have been thinking—

CARD PLAYER: Yes?

THIRD MAN: And I'm inclined to say—in all fairness, yes, I'm almost *bound* to say—

[*Silence.* CARD PLAYER *waits, expectantly*]

THIRD MAN: Is the offer still open?

[*Pause*]

CARD PLAYER: My dear chap! *Open!* Just for you—of course— Quite Open!

THIRD MAN: Well, then, if you don't mind—that is to say, if you're willing—

CARD PLAYER: You'll *accept?*

[*Pause*]

THIRD MAN: Yes.

CARD PLAYER [*overjoyed*]: Marvellous! First class! Splendid! My Chap! [*grabs him by the hand*] Welcome! Welcome aboard! Splendid!

[*At this point,* THE MAN *emerges from behind the screen. He is dressed. He looks upon the scene with disgust*]

THE MAN [*finally*]: I'm going.

CARD PLAYER [*turning to him*]: Oh—you're ready—

THE MAN: Yes.

CARD PLAYER: Had enough breakfast?

THE MAN: Yes.

CARD PLAYER: Sure?

THE MAN: Quite sure.

CARD PLAYER: Well, I can see your point! A nice, early start— yes—might as well be going. [*pause.* THE MAN *starts to move off*] Oh—I have some news for you— [*pauses.* THE MAN *halts*] I have what I think will be a very welcome piece of news for you.

THE MAN [*finally*]: What?

CARD PLAYER: I'll come straight to the point. [*turns to* THIRD MAN] As you'll see, I'm that kind of chap, I don't meander, I come straight to the point. I'm a great believer in coming

Straight to The Point! Always! You'll see! [*to* THE MAN *now*] The fact is, I believe I've solved this little increased workload problem. Yes, I believe I can safely say it's been nicely resolved. [*pause*] The fact is, the very *wonderful* fact is— [*pauses, lays a hand on* THIRD MAN's *shoulder*] He's joining us!

THE MAN [*after a pause*]: Is he?

CARD PLAYER: Indeed! Our very dear friend here has very kindly offered to join us. [*pause*] Enter our partnership! Yes, do what he can to—push forward our enterprise! [*pause*] Isn't that marvellous?

THE MAN [*after a pause*] [*flatly*]: Marvellous. [*pause*] Just marvellous.

CARD PLAYER [*to* THIRD MAN]: Welcome aboard! [*They shake hands*] Here [*to* THE MAN *now*] Join us—place your hand on ours— [THE MAN *stands there*] All three of us—hand on hand — [THE MAN *moves now, slowly*]: That's it—come on now— [*He reaches them, places his hand on theirs, reluctantly, listlessly*] Partners! [*pause*] That's it—just it— The three of us— [*pauses*] Here's to us! Best of luck, all the best— [*pause*] To Us!

    [*He laughs heartily, and so does* THIRD MAN. THE MAN *gives a grunt, a wry sort of smile*]

CARD PLAYER [*breaking up the handclasps, finally*]: Well! [*pauses*] [*Rises*] Well now! [*pauses*] Work now! Eh? Yes, all of us, a full day's work in hand—before us— [*pause*] We face it with confidence! Vigor! [*pause*] Renewed vigor! [*pauses, turns to* THIRD MAN] Thanks to you! Aha! Yes! You're a life-saver— No doubt about it!

THIRD MAN [*modestly*]: Ah, well, I'm glad to do my bit—

CARD PLAYER: That's it—we do our bit—

    [*Pause*]

THE MAN: I'm going. [*Starts to go*]

THIRD MAN: And I! Just a minute—let me get my coat—a few odds and ends—eh? Will you? I'll be right with you! There's a good chap! I'm coming— [*he addresses* CARD PLAYER, *while moving*] Thank you—thank you so much for the breakfast— that Lovely breakfast— [*He runs about, picking up things, he disappears behind the screen to get some of them*]

THE MAN [*staring at* CARD PLAYER]: I don't like it.

CARD PLAYER [*in low tones*]: What can we do? There's nothing else we can do. We're keeping him. Be thankful. At least we've succeeded in that!

THE MAN: I don't at all like it.

CARD PLAYER: He won't touch the Reports. He won't have a thing to do with Reports. They're your province, entirely. That's the crux of our enterprise, the Key to everything! You're solely in charge of them! Absolutely. [*pause*] Try to understand. [*pause*] We've got to keep him. [*pause*] Keep your eyes on him—

[*Pause*]

CARD PLAYER [*very quietly*]: Have you got it?

THE MAN [*tapping bulge in his pocket*]: I've got it.

CARD PLAYER: It's yours, entirely. [*pause*] No licence, but certainly—*yours*, entirely. [*pause*] Far be it from me to suggest anything. Even hint at anything. [*pause*] We're in a very difficult situation. [*pause*] There it is, you've got it. [*pause*] *Do what you like with it!*

[*Pause. They look long at one another*]

THE MAN: I've got it.

[THIRD MAN *emerges, he is fully prepared now, the transistor set in place as well*]

THIRD MAN: Here we are!

CARD PLAYER: Splendid!

THIRD MAN: Shall we?

[THE MAN *glares at him. Then, he starts for the door*]

THIRD MAN [*following him, waving to* CARD PLAYER]: Cheerio, then!

CARD PLAYER: Take care!

[*They leave, as* THIRD MAN *gives him a knowing nod*]

[CARD PLAYER *looks after them a moment or two, then heads for his desk. As he nears it, the phone rings, in the normal way. He halts in his tracks, heads for it. He picks it up, listens, says nothing*]

CARD PLAYER [*finally*]: Right! [*pause*] Thank you.

[*He hangs up. He goes to his table. He starts to play his game. He whistles. It is 'Put Your Little Foot Right Out' He studies the cards*]

FADEOUT

SCENE: *The same. Some time later. The trolley is gone. The* CARD PLAYER *is still at it. At the moment, he is totalling up his score. He enters the score on the pad. He is satisfied. He yawns, he stretches. He sits there. He shuffles the deck. He deals himself another hand . . . Presently the door opens, slowly.* CARD PLAYER *looks up.* THIRD MAN *enters. The door closes.* THIRD MAN *stands near the door, his back against it. He looks unhappy. He stands there.*

CARD PLAYER [*finally*]: Hello.

    [*Pause*]

THIRD MAN: How are you—

    [*A silence*]

CARD PLAYER: You're—alone?

THIRD MAN: Yes.

    [*A silence*]

THIRD MAN [*finally*]: A very—strange thing happened. [*pause*] I'd like to tell you about it.

CARD PLAYER: Please do.

THIRD MAN [*trying*]: You see—

CARD PLAYER: Yes?

    [*Pause*]

THIRD MAN: We got there without incident. [*pause*] We walked up the line, [*pause*] The old Manchester line—

    [*Pause*]

CARD PLAYER: Yes?

THIRD MAN: Quite a distance. You know the distance—

CARD PLAYER: Yes—

THIRD MAN: *Miles*—up the line—

    [*pause*] [*He moves, slowly, he walks toward* CARD PLAYER]
    [*They stare at one another*]

THIRD MAN [*finally*]: When we got there—

CARD PLAYER: The right?

THIRD MAN: What?

CARD PLAYER: Did he walk to the right?

    [*pause*]

THIRD MAN: Yes—

CARD PLAYER [*urgently*] : Twenty-five feet? Twenty-five to the right?

THIRD MAN: Yes—

CARD PLAYER: And left?

THIRD MAN: Yes.

CARD PLAYER: Ten feet? Exactly ten feet? *Left?*

THIRD MAN: Yes!

[*A silence. They are immobile*]

CARD PLAYER [*finally*] : Well?

THIRD MAN: Nothing!

CARD PLAYER: *Nothing?*

THIRD MAN: Absolutely. Nothing!

[*A silence.* CARD PLAYER *sits back in his chair, disappointed*]

THIRD MAN [*advancing a little closer*]: But here— look here now—what I wanted to tell you— [*pause.* CARD PLAYER *gazes on him, unhappily*]

CARD PLAYER [*rather listlessly*] : Yes?

THIRD MAN: Just as he—finished— [*pause*] I happened to turn away, to look up the line. Yes, I looked up the line. [*pause*] Because, I thought I had heard—of all the astonishing things—

CARD PLAYER: Yes?

THIRD MAN: A train.

CARD PLAYER [*perking up now*]: Yes?

THIRD MAN: Yes. Distinctly. Coming toward us. Far away. Down that line. [*pause*] *That* line. [*pause*] A train—

CARD PLAYER: Are you sure?

THIRD MAN: Yes! When I turned, I no longer *thought*—I was *sure!* A train!

CARD PLAYER: What happened?

THIRD MAN: Well, you see—before long, it appeared. Roaring, plunging over that dip, you know it, straight out of the horizon. [*pause*] I stood there, petrified, I can't describe my amazement! It came on. It roared at a fantastic speed, nearer and nearer. Suddenly, somehow, I whirled about. I wanted to see him, call out to him, warn him and share my astonishment with him. [*pause*] I saw him. [*pause*] He was standing directly in front of me. Not more than eight or ten feet from me. [*pause*] He had— [*pauses*] [*pulls the pistol out of his pocket] This* in his hand. He was pointing it at me, he was *taking aim*, pointing it straight at me! [*pauses, he raises his arm, the pistol in his hand, demonstrating. He is in fact about eight feet from* CARD PLAYER] I saw his eyes. That was very strange, at that moment, wasn't it . . . [*pause*] There was a very—hurt look in his eyes—and then—coldness— [*pause*] yes, suddenly, a very—*frightening coldness*— [*pause*] and fear. [*pause*] Yes. Fear . . .

CARD PLAYER: Then?

THIRD MAN: There was a roar, a most fantastic, deafening roar —from behind me— [*pause*] I forgot everything, I whirled about— [*pause*] I saw the train, not more than a hundred yards from us. It was hurtling toward us— There was a burst of steam, smoke— It enveloped me, everything— I couldn't see anything! I heard, though, I heard the train— roaring by! It was quite a long train, I suppose, but in little more than a flash it was by— [*pause*] Slowly, the black cloud lifted. I could see. I looked down the line. There was nothing. The train had gone! I was amazed at its speed . . . that's all, for the moment, I could think of! Then, I suddenly realized, *he* was gone! Yes—*Gone!* [*pause*] I looked all around, up, down, to the sides, I searched the line—every- where— [*pause*] Not a sign! *Nowhere!* [*pause. He lowers the pistol. He holds it flat in his hand, extending it forward, staring at it*] This was all I found. [*pause*] It was the only thing I found.

[*A silence*]

CARD PLAYER [*calmly*]: May I have it?

THIRD MAN: Why—yes— [*pause*] *Certainly.*

[*He offers it to* CARD PLAYER, *who nods his head, indicat- ing the pistol should be placed on his desk*] [THIRD MAN *does so*]

[*A silence*]

CARD PLAYER [*finally*]: Well! [*pause*] Quite a Report! [*pause*] I've never—heard such a Report! [*pause*] Amazing— [*pause*] Really. [*pause*] And on your first day! [*pause*] You must be —quite shaken— [*pause*] Yes— [*pause*] I'm sure— [*pause*] I'm certainly sure! That's sure!

THIRD MAN: I wanted to look more, but it was getting late, I thought I should come back and let you know—

CARD PLAYER: Quite! I understand! [*pause*] This is—quite a blow— [*pause*] Why— we've been partners for years! Years, you know! [*pause*] Indeed. Quite a blow—

[*Silence*]

CARD PLAYER [*finally*]: If he's—gone— [*pause*] If he doesn't turn up— [*pause*] You and I will be on our own! [*pause*] Here, you and I—on our own!

THIRD MAN: I'll go back now, I'll look some more—

CARD PLAYER [*rising, slowly, coming around his desk, toward* THIRD MAN]: Of course, and let us hope—he turns up— [*pause*] However faint the prospect, at the moment, let us hope— [*pause*] Indeed—

THIRD MAN: I'll go back now—

CARD PLAYER: Of course!

THIRD MAN: I'll return when I can—I'm going to look *thoroughly*.

CARD PLAYER: Please do! I hope he turns up! [*He crosses slowly toward* THE MAN's *desk. He pulls open a drawer, takes out a Form*] [THIRD MAN *stares at it*] Yes, I certainly hope he does— [*pauses*] This is our Form— [*pause*] what we use to make up our Report— [*pause*] When you come back—if he hasn't turned up— [*pause*] Do you think— [*pause*] Would you mind— [*pause*] Could I show you how it's made up?

[THIRD MAN *keeps staring at it*]

CARD PLAYER: I hope you don't think me crass, bringing this up now— [*pause*] I'm not, you know. [*pause*] You'll find out, you'll see—I'm not at all, you know. [*pause*] It's just— the circumstances—the possibly—very sad circumstances— [*pause*] the need to prepare, to push on with our enterprise— [*pause*] Whatever the—circumstances—

THIRD MAN [*after a pause*]: I understand.

CARD PLAYER: I'm glad you do.

[*Silence*]

THIRD MAN: I'm going, now.

CARD PLAYER: Take all the time you want, search carefully— [*pause*] We've plenty of time now— [*pause*] That's something else I wanted to tell you— [*pause.* THIRD MAN *listens*] Yes, while you were out, I received fresh instructions—

[*pause*. THIRD MAN *listens*] The Workload has been restored to Normal! [*pause*] Well, practically Normal! Intensification Efforts are to be reduced to such a bare minimum that one can indeed say—*Normal!* [*pause*] A pity he's not here to know. [*pause*] He would have appreciated that. [*pause*] I know. [*pause*] Knowing it.

THIRD MAN [*after a pause*]: I'm going— [*He starts for the door. He halts. He looks back*] It's all very strange— [*pause*] Whatever—what in the world— [*pause*] What was a train doing on *that* line? [*pause*] That—*ancient*—*decrepit* line?

CARD PLAYER [*after a while*]: I don't know.

[THIRD MAN *stands there, stares at him*]

THIRD MAN [*finally*]: I'm going.

CARD PLAYER: Good luck! Take all the time! [*pause*] Dinner will be ready, not to worry, anytime— [*pause*] There's no hurry. [*pause*] Anytime . . .

[THIRD MAN, *after a moment longer, opens the door, and departs*]

[CARD PLAYER, *after a while, turns to the table, picks up the pistol examines it. Then, he walks toward the bunks. He glides his hand along the wall behind the bunks. He moves, touches something. The wall slides open, and out, so that it is now seen to form a storage unit, its door the part of the wall opening out. Inside are rows and rows of pistols. They are on display, as it were, each hung very neatly.* CARD PLAYER *muses over them, then searches. He finds a space. He cleans the pistol off, he fastens it in the space. He lingers over the collection, admiringly. Then, he closes the wall. It slides shut. It is as before. Nothing noticeable. He walks away, slowly, heading for his desk. The phone rings. He halts, stiffens. It only rings two or three times, then stops. He stands a moment longer, then, obviously relieved, continues toward his desk. He sits down. In the distance, far off, the bell we have heard before tolls. A number of times. He studies his cards. He picks them up. He starts to whistle, slowly, lovingly, 'Blowing Bubbles'. About half way through, he stops, looks up, looks around, mainly at the bunks and surrounding area. He looks, he listens, it seems, for some little while. There is a*] *slightly worried expression on his face. At last, he lowers his head, returns to his game. The whistling resumes, very slowly, quietly—*

FADEOUT—CURTAIN